A GUIDE TO STATISTICS OF SOCIAL WELFARE IN NEW YORK CITY

A GUIDE TO STATISTICS OF SOCIAL WELFARE IN NEW YORK CITY

DUBOIS

WELFARE COUNCIL OF NEW YORK CITY

ARTES
VERITAS
SCIENTIA
LIBRARY OF THE
UNIVERSITY OF MICHIGAN
TUEBOR

IMPORTANT

For "Directions for Using the Guide," see p. 1.

A GUIDE TO STATISTICS OF SOCIAL WELFARE IN NEW YORK CITY

By

FLORENCE DUBOIS

❦

Study 3 of the Research Bureau of the Welfare Council

❦

Published by the

WELFARE COUNCIL OF NEW YORK CITY

1930

W. C. 30

THE WELFARE COUNCIL OF NEW YORK CITY

Officers

President
....

Chairman, Executive Committee
HOMER FOLKS

Vice-Presidents
MRS. NICHOLAS F. BRADY
DWIGHT W. MORROW
HERBERT H. LEHMAN
JAMES H. POST
FREDERIC B. PRATT
FELIX M. WARBURG

Chairman, Finance Committee
JAMES H. POST

Secretary
GEORGE J. HECHT

Treasurer
WINTHROP W. ALDRICH

Executive Director
WILLIAM HODSON

Research Bureau

NEVA R. DEARDORFF, *Director*

Research Committee, 1927–1930

PORTER R. LEE, *Chairman*

BAILEY B. BURRITT
ROBERT E. CHADDOCK
F. STUART CHAPIN
STANLEY P. DAVIES
GODIAS J. DROLET
LOUIS I. DUBLIN
HAVEN EMERSON, M.D.
HOMER FOLKS
C. LUTHER FRY
SAMUEL A. GOLDSMITH
RALPH G. HURLIN
F. ERNEST JOHNSON
WILLFORD I. KING
PHILIP KLEIN
REV. BRYAN J. MCENTEGART
E. B. PATTON
STUART A. RICE
ARTHUR L. SWIFT, JR.
EDGAR SYDENSTRICKER

Subcommittee of Research Committee on Statistical Guide

ROBERT E. CHADDOCK, *Chairman*

GODIAS J. DROLET
SAMUEL A. GOLDSMITH
RALPH G. HURLIN
PHILIP KLEIN

FOREWORD

THE Guide to Statistics of Social Welfare in New York City is intended to serve three purposes: first, to put into the hands of students of social welfare and of administration of social agencies a subject index of the items of statistical information now in existence which relate to the welfare of the people of New York City; second, to promote the use of such authentic material as now exists; and third, to indicate the extent of the statistical information on each aspect of social welfare.

The growth of governmental and other great administrative organizations has increased many fold within the last few years the output of statistical material on the conditions and the transactions of society. The invention of machinery has enabled statistical services to record and tabulate many more items of information than were possible under the old hand methods and to analyse their data in elaborate ways. These forces have created scores, if not hundreds, of sources of information and thousands of items and combinations. As community-wide programs for social welfare develop, it becomes increasingly necessary to gather up all the available information, to use it in the formulation and criticism of proposed measures, and to develop it in an orderly fashion.

It was out of this general situation that the decision to construct and publish this Guide to the welfare statistics of New York came. Moreover, an acceptable model in the Guide to the Current Official Statistics of the United Kingdom was at hand. Obviously, the imitation of the British Guide could not be slavishly executed, however, and the needs of the New York situation modified the plan for the construction of the New York Guide. The following policies have been adopted in the selection of material to be indexed:

1. In general no statistical material collected prior to 1920 is included. Exceptions to this are references to earlier

statistical information used for comparative purposes and the Census of Manufactures taken in 1919 by the United States Bureau of the Census.

2. All statistics bearing upon the size and characteristics of the population of New York City and its subdivisions have been included.
3. All statistics on the factors bearing on social welfare of the city as a whole and of boroughs, have been included. This kind of material comes from two main sources.
   a. All statistics relating to governmental activities to enhance the welfare of the whole population or of any group have been included.
   b. Wherever private or voluntary effort has been sufficiently coordinated to construct statistical pictures of the whole effort for a borough or for the city, such statistics have been included. No effort has been made, however, to bring together references to fragmentary information in the hope thereby of affording a complete picture. Wherever the technical problem of putting together information from scattered sources has been solved, a reference is made to the consolidated statement. When sample studies have been found, however, which are so large or so significant that they have been considered indicative of conditions in one or more boroughs, they have been included. Also, studies of special districts, which are comprehensive of those districts and which have been considered as of special interest and value, have been indexed.
4. In general, only the statistical items appearing in primary sources of information have been included. In some cases, however, in which items from various primary sources have been gathered together in a form particularly convenient for reference, those secondary sources have been indexed.
5. References to comparative statistics for other communities have not been included, although such data are sometimes given in the publications covered by the Guide.

Although, as Professor Bowley points out,[1] almost all effort in the field of social statistics has had its origin in some form of administrative purpose, it is possible to make a distinction between statistics descriptive of the population and conditions in society and statistical facts collected and tabulated primarily for administrative purposes, i.e., records of processes undertaken within a single organization and results of those processes. In general, administrative statistics thus narrowly limited have been excluded, but in a few instances where they afforded or supplemented important information about a condition of the population, they have been included.

The work of indexing this statistical information was an integral part of the establishment of the Research Bureau of the Welfare Council. The preparation of the index for printing and distribution was a special project which seemed warranted in view of the need throughout the community for such a means of referring quickly and accurately to the sources of this rapidly expanding body of authoritative information.

NEVA R. DEARDORFF
Director, Research Bureau

[1] Bowley, A. L. Nature and purpose of the measurement of social phenomena. 2nd ed. London, King & Son, 1923. p. 5 (Introduction).

PREFACE

THE Guide to Statistics of Social Welfare in New York City, constructed in accordance with the policies stated in the Foreword, contains statistical references indexed under a series of topics, as shown in the table of contents. In the selection of those topics, a logical outline of the field has not been attempted, nor has there been an effort to classify the data under topics which are equal, even approximately, in interest and importance. The intention, in preparing the Guide, has been simply to note the material under those headings which might most readily come to the mind of the reader of the Guide.

As a convenience to the reader, numerous other topics not shown in the table of contents, have been inserted to direct attention to those topics under which items appear. These supplementary topics are of two kinds, according to the purpose of the reference which appears under them:

1. A topic which shows merely that different wording has been chosen, e.g., **MATERNITY CLINICS.** See: *Clinics, Prenatal.*

2. A topic which refers to specific items found under other topics, e.g., **ANNULMENT OF MARRIAGE.** See: *Divorce* 1, 4, 6, 7, 10.

For the convenience of the reader, cross references have been inserted under the topics under which material is indexed. These cross references are of two kinds, as follows:

1. "See also" references, pointing to specific items which contain additional information regarding the topic in hand.

2. "Other allied topics," which refer to topics having some general bearing on the subject, but which do not give additional information regarding that topic precisely.

Dates which appear in the items under "Statistical References," pages 3–272, indicate that the statistics referred to have been collected as of those dates. Dates which appear in entries in the "List of Sources of Information," pages 273–301, are dates of publication.

The Guide contains references to statistics available October 1, 1929. The latest issues of annual reports which had appeared up to that time have been included. Reports which have been issued since that date and prior to June 1, 1930, are indicated by an asterisk in the "List of Sources of Information," pages 273–301. Special studies for the years 1920–1928 have been inspected and in addition those special studies which were available at the office of the Welfare Council during the period Jan.–Sept., 1929. The work with periodicals has included the years 1920–1928. Besides the inspection of material in libraries, a list was compiled of all organizations from which it seemed probable that additional material suitable for the Guide might be obtained. Letters of inquiry were sent to the organizations, and calls were made upon those at which data suitable for indexing were found. Information is requested regarding any special studies and regarding any material in periodicals which may have been overlooked in the preparation of the Guide and which should be included in the material indexed.

Because of the voluminous detail in tracing and indexing all changes in series of data in annual reports from the year 1920 to October 1, 1929, the procedure has been adopted of indexing only the latest report available. Accordingly, special studies published in annual reports are found in the Guide only if published in the latest report available. Hence, it is requested that information regarding significant material from these studies be forwarded to the Research Bureau of the Welfare Council, in order that such data may be noted for current reference and may be included with the material to be presented in subsequent editions of the Guide. If readers are interested in learning that additional data, if any, regarding a given topic, have come to hand since October 1, 1929, they may obtain the desired information by addressing the Research Bureau of the Welfare Council.

Throughout the work of preparing the Guide, valuable assistance was given by Mrs. Mary Chantler Hubbard, who also prepared the "List of Sources of Information." Part of the visiting of private organizations in order to index data available was done by Miss Blanche Allen.

The Guide has been prepared, in large part, from the resources available in the three libraries at which material was inspected, namely, the Russell Sage Foundation Library, the New York Public Library, and the Municipal Reference Library. Grateful acknowledgment is made to the several librarians from whom aid has been received, and especially to those of the Russell Sage Foundation Library who advised regarding specific problems. Special acknowledgment is made also to Dr. C. C. Williamson, Director of Libraries and Dean of the Library School, Columbia University, who arranged that the Guide should be tested by experimental use before publication.

FLORENCE DUBOIS

CONTENTS

DIRECTIONS FOR USING THE GUIDE

1. In the table of contents find the topic under which it seems probable that the data desired may have been indexed, and turn to the page indicated

or

2. Without consulting the table of contents, turn to the topics in the body of the Guide, which are arranged alphabetically, and inspect the topic under which it seems probable that the data desired may have been indexed.

3. In addition to the references shown under the topics inspected, read all items to which cross references are made, in order to obtain additional information on the given topic.

4. For each item containing the information desired, note the source number given at the right of the item and turn to the corresponding number in the "List of Sources of Information," pages 273–301.

STATISTICAL REFERENCES

*** A later report has been issued, prior to June 1, 1930.**

ABORTION, CRIMINAL

Source Number

See: *Accidents* 1
Arrests and summonses 1
Correction 20

ACCIDENTS

1. Deaths from accidents and negligence, by specific cause, under the following main headings: fractures and contusions; falls; street vehicles; railroads; burns and scalds; wounds; drowning; poison. Each borough. 1927, 1928. p. 138. **131**

2. Deaths from accidents, by kind of accident, age (under 5; 5–14; 15–24; 25–44; 45–64; 65 and over), and sex; death rates by kind of accident and age. 1919, 1920, 1921. p. 276–277. **136 Sept. 2, 1922**

3. Miscellaneous casualties by kind of accident (collapse of building; fist fight; etc.). Each borough. 1928. p. 8–9. **114**

4. Deaths of children under 15 years of age from accidents, by type of accident (accidents, motor vehicle; burns; drowning; falls; other) and age (under 5; 5–9; 10–14). 1927. **105**

See also: *Accidents, Elevator* (entire)
Accidents, Highway (entire)
Accidents, Motor vehicle (entire)
Accidents, Railroad (entire)
Accidents, Street railway (entire)
Asphyxiation 2–4
Bellevue-Yorkville district 9, 10
Bronx, Borough of 1
Burns (entire)

ACCIDENTS *(continued)*

Source Number

See also: *(continued)*
Courts 55–57
Deaths and death rate 38–41, 44–46, 52, 54, 60–63, 65
Drowning 1
East Harlem 6–8, 10
Falls (entire)
Homicide 2, 5, 6
Poison (entire)
Workmen's compensation (entire)

ACCIDENTS, AUTOMOBILE

See: *Accidents, Motor vehicle*

ACCIDENTS, ELEVATED TRAIN

See: *Accidents, Street railway*

ACCIDENTS, ELEVATOR

1. Deaths from elevator accidents, by type of accident. Each borough. 1928. p. 9. **114**
2. Elevator accidents which were investigated by the Bureau of Buildings: (a) by location (factory; hotel; etc.); (b) by cause; (c) persons killed and persons injured, by type of elevator (passenger; freight; sidewalk). Manhattan. 1928. p. 117–118. **111**

See also: *Accidents* 1

ACCIDENTS, HIGHWAY

1. Persons killed and persons injured in vehicular highway accidents: (a) by age (16 and under; over 16) and cause; (b) by age and time of day; (c) by law which was violated. Current month. **147**
2. Deaths from street accidents by sex. Each county. Period Jan.–June, each year, 1928, 1929. p. 44–49. **146**
3. Persons killed and persons injured in street accidents, by age (16 and under; over 16). Each month, Jan.–June, each year, 1928, 1929. p. 75. **146**

ACCIDENTS, HIGHWAY *(continued)*

Source Number

4. Persons killed and persons injured in vehicular highway accidents: (a) by age (under 16; 16 and over), 1927, 1928; (b) by cause of accident, 1928. p. 30–33. ***144**

5. Deaths caused by highway accidents, by type of accident: automobile; horse-drawn vehicle; etc. Each borough. 1928. p. 6. **114**

6. Deaths from highway accidents by age (5-year periods) and sex. Each borough. 1928. p. 6. **114**

7. Deaths and death rate from street accidents by type of accident: horse vehicle; street car; automobile. Each year, 1898–1927. p. 507. ***244**

8. Children (16 years and under) killed and children injured in vehicular highway accidents: (a) by cause (roller skating in roadway; running off sidewalk; etc.); (b) by location (avenues; side streets; streets with traffic lights); (c) by time of day; (d) by age of children (under 7; 7–10; 11–16). Each public school district and each parochial school. Current month. **147**

9. Deaths of children under 15 years of age from street accidents, by type of accident (wagon; automobile; etc.), age, and sex. 1925, 1926. p. 66. **136** Apr. 23, 1927

10. Accidents on all transportation lines under the jurisdiction of the New York State Transit Commission, by type of transportation (surface car; subway and elevated; bus; etc.): (a) nature of accident (car collision; boarding car; etc.); (b) injuries received. 1927, 1928. p. 59–60. ***212**

11. Accidents on all transportation lines under the jurisdiction of the New York State Transit Commission: (a) nature of accident (collision; electric shock; etc.); (b) persons injured (passengers; employees; others); (c) serious accidents by degree of injury (death; amputated limbs; etc.). Each type of transportation: surface lines; subway and elevated lines; etc. 1927. p. 24. ***211**

ACCIDENTS, HIGHWAY *(continued)*

Source Number

12. Persons killed and persons injured in grade crossing accidents. Each railroad. Each year, 1914–1923. p. 58. **260**

See also: *Accidents* 1
Accidents, Motor vehicle (entire)
Accidents, Street railway (entire)
Bellevue–Yorkville district 20
Deaths and death rate 45, 61

ACCIDENTS, MOTOR VEHICLE

1. Deaths from automobile accidents, current four weeks, combined, and corresponding weeks of preceding year; deaths and death rate for year ending on last day of current four weeks and for corresponding preceding year. **291**

2. Deaths from automobile accidents (pleasure cars and commercial trucks, combined) by 5-year age groups and sex. Each borough. 1928. p. 7. **114**

3. Deaths and death rate from automobile accidents: (a) total deaths; (b) deaths due to accidents in the city. 1926, 1927. p. 268. **317** Feb. 3, 1928

4. Deaths from automobile accidents: (a) total deaths in the city, and death rate, each year, 1923–1927; (b) deaths of city residents due to accidents outside the city, 1926, 1927. Each borough. p. 3427–3428. **317** Dec. 28, 1928

5. Deaths due to automobile accidents: (a) by sex, each borough, each year, 1923–1927; (b) by age groups and sex, period 1923–1927. p. 30–31. **136** June 2, 1928

6. Deaths from automobile accidents compared with automobile registrations. Each year, 1917–1926. p. 54. **260**

7. Deaths and death rate from automobile accidents. Each borough. Each year, 1922–1926. p. 3138. **317** Dec. 23, 1927

8. Deaths from automobile accidents by type: (a) primary; (b) in collision (with railroad trains; with street cars). Each borough. 1925. p. 149. ***292**

ACCIDENTS, MOTOR VEHICLE *(continued)* Source Number

9. Automobile fatalities in New York City. Each year, 1900–1924. p. 55. Chart only. **260**

10. Automobile accidents reported to the Police Department: number of accidents; persons injured; persons killed. 1922, 1923. **265**

See also: *Accidents* 1, 2, 4
Accidents, Highway 5, 7, 9–11
Courts 55–57
Deaths and death rate 38–44, 60–62, 72, 73, 75
Homicide 2

ACCIDENTS, RAILROAD

See: *Accidents* 1
Accidents, Highway 5, 9–11
Deaths and death rate 38, 60–62, 72, 74

ACCIDENTS, STREET CAR

See: *Accidents, Street railway*

ACCIDENTS, STREET RAILWAY

1. Accidents on street railway lines: (a) deaths by type of person (passengers; employees; others); (b) serious injuries by type of person; (c) serious injuries by nature of injury (fractured skull; broken limb; etc.). Each line. 1927. p. 214–215. ***211**

2. Street railway accidents (total; fatal): (a) surface railways (Manhattan; Bronx; B.M.T.); (b) rapid transit railways (I.R.T.; B.M.T.). Each year, 1908–1927. p. 128–129. ***211**

3. Persons killed in street railway accidents: (a) passengers; (b) employees; (c) others. Each year, 1908–1927. p. 129. ***211**

4. Accidents involving surface cars: number of (a) vehicles, and (b) persons, struck by surface cars. Each month, 1914–1923. p. 56. **260**

ACCIDENTS, STREET RAILWAY *(continued)*

Source Number

See also: *Accidents* 1, 2
Accidents, Highway 5, 10, 11
Deaths and death rate 61, 72, 74
Street railways 5

ACCIDENTS, SUBWAY

See: *Accidents, Street railway*

ACCIDENTS, VEHICULAR

See: *Accidents, Highway*

ADOLESCENT OFFENDERS

1. Adolescent offenders in Manhattan in the Court of General Sessions, Court of Special Sessions, Men's Night Court, Fifth District Court, and Women's Court: (a) by age (each year, 16–20); (b) by disposition of first offenders; (c) by previous court record and age, for Court of General Sessions, Court of Special Sessions, and Women's Court. Each court. Specified month, 1921. **43**

See also: *Correction* 3, 8, 18, 19, 26, 31, 32, 38, 58, 61, 67, 69, 73, 75
Courts 7–9, 24, 25, 127, 129
Truants 1

Other allied topics: *Delinquents, Juvenile*
Wayward minors

AGED DEPENDENTS

See: *Dependents, Aged*

AGED PERSONS

See: *Age of population*
Dependents, Aged

AGE OF POPULATION

Source Number

1. Estimated mid-year population by age: under 1; 1; 2; 3; 4; 5-year groups to 85 and over. 1928. p. 3. **135**

2. Total persons by age (under one year; under 5; 5–9; 10–14; etc. . . . 100 and over; age unknown; single years of age, 1–24), sex, and color (white; Negro; other), each borough, 1920; by age only, each borough, 1910. p. 295–299. **285**

3. Total persons by age (under one year; 1–4; 5; 6; 7–9; 10–13; 14; 15; 16–19; 20; 21–44; 45 and over; age unknown), sex, and color (white; Negro; other). Each tabulation tract (one or more sanitary districts having a combined population of 1000 or more). 1920. p. 2–819. **51**

4. Persons by age (under 5; 5–14; 15–24; 25–44; 45–64; 65 and over), for total, for white, and for Negro. Each borough. 1920. p. 367. **285**

5. Persons by age: under 7; 7–13; 14–15; 16–17; 18–20; 10 and over; 21 and over by sex; 18–44 by sex. Each assembly district and each borough. 1920. p. 63–68. **288**

6. White persons by age (under one year; under 5; 5-year periods to 100 and over; age unknown; single years of age, 1–24), sex, nativity, and parentage. Each borough. 1920. p. 295–299. **285**

7. White persons by age (under one year; 1–4; 5; 6; 7–9; 10–13; 14; 15; 16–19; 20; 21–44; 45 and over; age unknown), sex, nativity, and parentage. Each tabulation tract (one or more sanitary districts having a total population of 1000 or more). 1920. p. 2–819. **51**

8. White persons by age (under 5; 5–14; 15–24; 25–44; 45–64; 65 and over), nativity, and parentage. Each borough. 1920. p. 367. **285**

9. Children 5 to 15 years of age in Manhattan and number and per cent of these living in the lower East Side. 1920. p. 136. **270**

AGE OF POPULATION *(continued)*

Source Number

See also: *Bellevue-Yorkville district* 2
Boy population (entire)
Bronx, Borough of 3
Citizenship of population 3, 5–7
Color of population 4, 5
East Harlem 2, 3
Education 1–5
Illiteracy (entire)
Language 1, 2
Marital condition of population (entire)
Nativity of population 5, 6
Occupations, Children engaged in (entire)
Occupations, Persons engaged in 2–10
Population estimates, 1930 and later 4
Recreation 6, 8
Religion of population 3
Richmond, Borough of 3–5, 8–10

AGRICULTURE

1. Farms: (a) number, 1910, 1920; (b) number by size, 1925. Each county. Part I, p. 190–197. **296**

2. Land in farms: (a) number of acres, 1910, 1920, 1925; (b) number of acres by type of land (crop land; pasture land; etc.), 1925; (c) crop land harvested, 1924. Each county. Part I, p. 190–197. **296**

3. Acreage in farms: (a) total, classified according to number of acres per farm, 1925; (b) crop land harvested, classified according to number of acres per farm, 1924. Each county. Part I, p. 237–241. **296**

4. Farmers: (a) number by tenure (full owners; part owners; etc.); (b) per cent of tenants (cash; other) who were relatives of landlord. Each county. 1925. Part I, p. 190–197. **296**

5. Farm population: (a) by age (under 10 years; 10 years and over), color (white; colored), and tenure (owned farms; managed farms; tenant farms); (b) by sex, **296**

AGRICULTURE *(continued)*

Source Number

5. *(continued)*
color, and tenure. Each county. 1925. Part I, p. 224–229.

See also: *Occupations, Persons engaged in* 3
Workmen's compensation (entire)

ALCOHOLISM

1. Deaths from alcoholism. Each borough. Each year, 1898–1927. p. 509. ***244**
2. Cases of alcoholism discharged and total discharges from hospitals of the New York City Department of Public Welfare; from Bellevue and Allied Hospitals. Each year, 1914–1927. p. 509. ***244**
3. Alcoholics received at the New York County Penitentiary and recommended for segregation, by type: habitual drinkers; periodical drinkers; convivial drinkers; occasional drinkers; dipsomaniacs. 1928. p. 79. **121**

See also: *Correction* 51
Deaths and death rate 38, 52, 60–62, 65

Other allied topics: *Drunkenness*
Saloons

ALIMONY

See: *Divorce*

AMBULANCES

1. Ambulance calls of hospitals under the jurisdiction of the Board of Ambulance Service: number of calls by disposition of case (died on arrival; treated and not removed; etc.), each hospital. Manhattan and Bronx; Brooklyn; Queens; Richmond. 1926. p. 14–15. **108**
2. Ambulance calls of hospitals under the jurisdiction of the Board of Ambulance Service, by nativity of patient. 1926. p. 12. **108**

AMBULANCES (*continued*)

Source Number

3. Ambulance calls of hospitals under the jurisdiction of the Board of Ambulance Service, by injury or disease of patient. 1926. p. 13. **108**
4. Conditions for which ambulances under the jurisdiction of the Board of Ambulance Service were called, each injury or disease. 1920, 1921, 1922. p. 50. **216**
5. Number of ambulance calls to hospitals (public; private) under jurisdiction of the Board of Ambulance Service, per day, per week, per month, and total for year. 1926. p. 10. **108**
6. Number of ambulances maintained and operated by hospitals (public; private) under jurisdiction of the Board of Ambulance Service. 1926. p. 10. **108**

See also: *Hospitals* 6

AMERICANIZATION

1. Americanization classes under the supervision of the Division of Extension Activities of the public schools, by type of center at which held (school; factory; neighborhood or church house; library): (a) classes; (b) sessions; (c) aggregate attendance by sex; (d) average attendance. 1926/27 and 1927/28. p. 721. **124**

See also: *Education* 68
Naturalization (entire)

ANNULMENT OF MARRIAGE

See: *Divorce* 1, 4, 6, 7, 10

ANTHRAX

1. Cases and deaths. 1928. p. 53. **131**
2. Cases and deaths. 1927. p. 4. **317 Supp. # 70**
3. Cases, each month, 1919–1923; cases and deaths by sex and age, each year, 1919–1923. p. 145–146. **133 July, 1924**

ANTHRAX *(continued)*

Source Number

4. Persons suffering from anthrax: by occupation; by source of infection; by recovery; by treatment given; by outcome of case classified by place of treatment. Period 1919–1923. p. 147–153. **133 July, 1924**

See also: *Deaths and death rate* 38, 60, 61
Diseases, Occupational 1, 2
Diseases, Transmissible 2, 3, 7, 9

APARTMENTS

1. Apartments (old-law; new-law); vacant apartments (old-law; new-law). Each borough. Specified month, 1909–1929. p. 66–67. **186**

2. Number of apartments and number of vacant apartments in tenements (old-law; new-law). Each borough. Specified month, 1909, 1916, 1917, 1919, 1920, 1921, and each year, 1923–1928. p. 20. **185**

3. Per cent of vacancies in apartments. Specified month, 1909–1925. p. 13. **180**

4. Per cent distribution of vacancies in tenements, by size of apartment. Each borough. Jan. 1, 1928. p. 28. **185**

5. Tenements (old-law; new-law): (a) number of apartments; (b) number of deaths. Each borough. Each year, 1917–1925. p. 18. **276 Apr., 1926**

6. Tenements; apartments (occupied; vacant); extent of occupancy of tenements; distribution of apartments (total; vacant; occupied) by rent per room per month. Manhattan by district (18 districts). Dec., 1928. p. 82–96. **186**

7. Vacancies in tenements (old-law; new-law) by rent per room per month. Manhattan; Bronx; Brooklyn; Queens. Early part of each year, 1927, 1928, 1929. p. 72–75. **186**

8. Vacant apartments in tenements (old-law; new-law) by rent per room per month. Jan., 1928. p. 45. **185**

APARTMENTS *(continued)*

Source Number

9. Vacancies in tenements (old-law; new-law) by rent per room per month. Manhattan; Bronx. 1927, 1928. Queens; Richmond; Brooklyn. 1928. p. 47–48, 51–53. **185**
10. Vacancies in tenements (old-law; new-law) by rent asked per room. Five specified areas in Manhattan. Jan., 1927. p. 30–31. **184**
11. Tenement vacancies (old-law; new-law) by apartment rent per month. Each borough. Jan., 1928, Dec., 1928. p. 68. **186**
12. Vacancies in tenements (old-law; new-law) by apartment rent per month. Each borough. Jan., 1927, 1928. p. 31. **185**
13. Vacant apartments by rent ($50 or under; over $50). Each borough. 1925, 1927, 1928. p. 32. **185**
14. Vacant apartments in New York City, by monthly rental (below $25; $25–50; over $50). Each borough. Jan., 1924. p. 5. **138**
15. Apartments in new-law tenements distributed according to monthly room rents. Manhattan. 1924, 1925, 1926. p. 19. **184**
16. Rate of evacuation of old-law tenements: (a) number of apartments abandoned; (b) per cent abandoned of total which were occupied in Apr., 1920. Manhattan; Brooklyn; Bronx, Queens, and Richmond. Each year, 1920–1928. p. 60. **186**

See also: *Housing* 1, 3, 5–10, 13–15, 17
Housing construction 4
Housing surveys 1, 3–7
Rent 2, 4, 6–9
Tenements (entire)

AREA OF CITY

1. Square miles. Each county. 1920. p. 119–120. **284**
2. Square miles. By district, each borough. Separate sheet for each district. **241**

AREA OF CITY *(continued)*

Source Number

3. Acres. Each ward. [1920]. p. 283. **133 Dec., 1924**

4. Acres. Each borough. 1910, 1920. p. XXI. **51**

5. Acres. Each borough section, each borough. 1910, 1920. p. XXXI–XXXIII. **51**

6. Acres. Each tabulation tract (one or more sanitary districts having a total population of 1000 or more), each borough. 1920. p. 834–837. **51**

7. Acres. Each sanitary district having a density of 16 or more persons per acre in 1920, and for districts, combined, which had a population of fewer than 16 persons per acre. Each borough. 1920. p. XIV–XIX. **51**

8. Acres. Each sanitary district which was without population, each borough. 1920. p. 834–837. **51**

9. Square miles, acres, and available acres. Each borough. [1928]. p. 2. **42**

See also: *Bronx, Borough of* 4
Density of population 4–7
Parks 1

ARRESTS AND SUMMONSES

1. Arrests and summonses by disposition of cases (discharged; convicted [reprimanded; sentence suspended; etc.]; delivered to other authorities; died awaiting trial; failed to answer summons), and sex, each offense: offenses grouped as against the person; against chastity; against family and children; against public health, etc.; against administration of government; against property rights; general criminality; juvenile delinquency; witnesses, lunatics, etc. 1927, 1928. p. 60–99. ***144**

2. Arrests and summonses. Each specified precinct. For a specified period during 1928. p. 149–174. **162**

3. Arrests: (a) total and for intoxication, each year, 1900–1927; (b) arrests, each year, 1900–1927, and cases ***244**

ARRESTS AND SUMMONSES *(continued)*

Source Number

3. *(continued)*
reported, each year, 1915–1927, each selected offense. p. 510.
4. Arrests and summonses and rate per 10,000 population, for all causes, combined, and for each specified cause. Each year, 1910–1926, and annual average, 1910–1918 and 1920–1926. **94**

See also: *Arson* (entire)
Assault and robbery (entire)
Delinquents, Juvenile 9
Drug laws, Violation of 2, 3
Drunkenness (entire)
Felonies 2, 5, 6, 11, 12, 19
Food inspection 4
Mendicants (entire)
Misdemeanors 2
Prostitution 1
Recreation 6, 8
Traffic regulation, Violation of 1
Violence, Crimes of 1
Women's Bureau, Police Department (entire)

ARSON

1. Arrests for arson by disposition of cases: convicted of arson and sentenced; convicted of juvenile delinqency; etc. Manhattan, Bronx and Richmond, combined; Brooklyn and Queens, combined. 1928. p. 46–47, 58. **130**

See also: *Arrests and summonses* 1
Correction 20
Courts 56, 57
Felonies 2, 3

ASPHYXIATION

1. Deaths from asphyxiation, by type of asphyxiation. Each borough. 1928. p. 9. **114**
2. Asphyxiations by illuminant gas: accidental; suicidal. Each borough. Each year, 1918–1923. p. 1. **199** July, 1925

ASPHYXIATION *(continued)*

Source Number

3. Accidental asphyxiations by illuminant gas: (a) by place where accident occurred (tenement house; store; etc.); (b) by cause of escape of gas (open jet on cooking stove; defect in stove; etc.). Each borough. 1923. p. 1. **199** **July, 1925**

4. Accidental asphyxiations, by cause of escaping gas (defective gas stove; leak in meter; etc.) and result (died; recovered). 1922. p. 112. **133** **May, 1923**

See also: *Accidents* 1, 2
Deaths and death rate 38, 60, 61
Homicide 5, 6
Suicide 1–3

ASSAULT

See: *Arrests and summonses* 1, 3, 4
Correction 21, 50, 54, 83, 84
Courts 12, 13, 15, 18, 21–23, 38, 55–57, 91–93, 96, 97, 100, 105, 108, 110, 115, 122
Delinquents, Juvenile 3, 5
Felonies 1, 5, 7, 10, 12, 13, 15, 18, 19
Homicide 5, 6
Negroes 7
Violence, Crimes of 1, 2

ASSAULT AND ROBBERY

1. Cases reported to the Police Department, by classification (store or shop; residence; etc.): (a) cases reported; (b) cases in which arrests were made. Period Jan.–June, each year, 1928, 1929. p. 42. **146**

2. Cases reported to the Police Department, by classification (store or shop; residence; etc.): (a) cases reported; (b) cases in which arrests were made. 1927, 1928. p. 42. ***144**

3. Cases reported to the Police Department, by amount of loss (more than $10,000; more than $1,000 but not more than $10,000): number of cases; estimated ***144**

ASSAULT AND ROBBERY *(continued)*

Source Number

3. *(continued)*
total loss; number of cases in which arrests were made; number of cases in which property was partly or fully recovered. 1927, and each quarter, 1928. p. 42, 44, 49.

See also: *Arrests and summonses* 1, 3
Correction 20
Felonies 1
Violence, Crimes of 1, 2

AUTOMOBILES

See: *Motor vehicles*

BABY HEALTH STATIONS

1. Work done at 95 baby health stations in New York City for (a) babies under two years, (b) others: cases on hand at beginning of year; cases received during year by source; cases dropped during year by cause; deaths during year by principal cause (diarrhea; congenital debility; respiratory diseases; contagious diseases; other causes). Each operating organization: New York City Department of Health; New York Diet Kitchen; etc. 1928. ***47**

2. Baby health stations of the New York City Department of Health: total babies registered during year by age on admission (under 1 month; between 1 and 2 months; 2–3 months; 3–6 months; 6–9 months; 9–12 months; 1–2 years); number of babies on register at end of year, by age at end of year (under 1 year; between 1 and 2 years); character of feeding (breast fed exclusively; bottle fed exclusively; breast and bottle fed). 1928. p. 37. **131**

3. Registration, age on admission, and character of feeding (as in 2), of babies at the baby health stations operated by the New York City Department of Health. 1924. p. 118. Same, each borough, 1922, in December, 1923, issue. p. 123. **133 Oct., 1925**

BABY HEALTH STATIONS *(continued)*

Source Number

4. Infants admitted to baby health stations of the New York City Department of Health, by age (age-groups under 1 year). Per cents. Each year, 1915–1920. p. 249. **133 Oct., 1921**

5. Number of baby health stations operated by the New York City Department of Health, and enrollment by age (under 1 year; 1–2 years; under 2 years). Each year, 1911–1920. p. 249. **133 Oct., 1921**

6. Infants admitted to baby health stations operated by the New York City Department of Health, by character of feeding (as in 2). Per cents. Each year, 1913–1920. p. 248. **133 Oct., 1921**

7. Babies visited by the nurses of the baby health stations of the New York City Department of Health; new babies enrolled; total under supervision; sick babies; deaths. Summer, 1924. p. 119. Same, each borough, summer, 1922, in June, 1923, issue. p. 126. **133 Oct., 1925**

8. Summer attendance at baby health stations of the New York City Department of Health. Queens. 1923, 1924. p. 252. **133 Nov., 1924**

See also: *Clinics* 1, 12, Note
Health service (entire)
Nurses 3
Nursing service 3
Physical examinations 10

BANKS

See: *Business* 1
Savings banks (entire)

BATHING ESTABLISHMENTS

1. Establishments under permit from the New York City Department of Health. Each borough. 1928. p. 108–109. **131**

See also: *Licenses* (entire)

BATHS, PUBLIC

Source Number

1. Patrons of the interior public baths by sex, each bath. Manhattan. Each month, 1928. p. 88–89. **111**

2. Number of patrons of free public floating baths by sex. Manhattan. Season of 1928. p. 86. **111**

3. Reported attendance at the interior public bath by sex. Bronx. Each month, 1928. p. 28. **109**

4. Patrons of the public baths (including the Municipal Bath, Coney Island). Brooklyn. 1928. p. 36. **110**

5. Patrons of the interior public bath by sex. Queens. Each month, 1927. p. 79. ***112**

See also: *Community centers* 1
Recreation 10

BEACHES, BATHING

1. Miles of waterfront available for public bathing. [1928]. p. 114. **262**

2. Lifeguards; rescues; deaths; bodies recovered. Coney Island, Brooklyn. 1928. p. 36. **110**

See also: *Parks* 8
Recreation 3
Waterfront (entire)

BEGGARS

See: *Mendicants*

BELLEVUE-YORKVILLE DISTRICT

1. Population of the Bellevue-Yorkville District. Each sanitary area. Federal census, 1920; State census, 1925; and estimated population, each year, 1922–1927. p. 5. **12**

2. Estimated population by age (under 1; 1–4; 5–14; 15–19; 20–44; 45 and over) and sex. Each year, 1922–1927. p. 5. **12**

BELLEVUE-YORKVILLE DISTRICT *(continued)*

Source Number

3. Births and birth rate among residents. Each sanitary area. 1925, 1926, and period 1922–1926. p. 7–8. **12**

4. Stillbirths and stillbirth rate among residents. Each sanitary area. 1925, 1926, and period 1922–1926. p. 31. **12**

5. Stillbirths by cause, and per cent of total births. 1926. p. 78–80. **99**

6. Deaths and death rate by leading causes: typhoid and paratyphoid fever; measles; scarlet fever; whooping-cough; diphtheria; tuberculosis; cancer; organic heart disease; bronchopneumonia and pneumonia; diarrhea and enteritis; chronic nephritis; cerebral hemorrhage, apoplexy, and diseases of the arteries; puerperal diseases and conditions; congenital debility and malformations; violent deaths (suicide, homicide, and infanticide excepted). Each sanitary area. 1925, 1926, and period 1922–1926. p. 12–21. **12**

7. Deaths from leading causes (as in 6), by age (under 1; 1–4; 5–14; 15–19; 20–24; 25–44; 45–59; 60 and over) and sex. 1925, 1926. p. 22. **12**

8. Deaths among total population, among residents, and among non-residents, from leading causes, arranged according to frequency among total population: organic heart disease; bronchopneumonia and pneumonia; tuberculosis; cancer; violent deaths (suicide, homicide, infanticide excepted); cerebral hemorrhage, apoplexy, and diseases of the arteries; congenital debility and malformations; chronic nephritis; diarrhea and enteritis; measles; diphtheria; puerperal diseases and conditions; whooping-cough; typhoid and paratyphoid fever; scarlet fever. Each year, 1922–1926. p. 44. **12**

9. Deaths and death rate from selected causes: organic heart disease; pneumonia (all forms); tuberculosis (pulmonary; other); accidents by kind and age. Each sanitary **12**

BELLEVUE-YORKVILLE DISTRICT *(continued)*

Source Number

9. *(continued)*
area. 1925, 1926, and for period 1922–1926 or shorter period. p. 33–41.

10. Death rate from leading causes (heart disease; pneumonia; tuberculosis; cancer; accidents; debility and malformation; cerebral hemorrhage; Bright's disease; diarrhea and enteritis; measles; diphtheria; puerperal diseases; scarlet fever; whooping-cough; typhoid fever; other causes), for (a) New York City, (b) Bellevue-Yorkville district. 1922. p. 5. **230 Mar.-Apr., 1925**

11. Deaths by age (under 1; 1–4; 5–14; 15–19; 20–44; 45 and over): total number; annual average number; annual average death rate. Each sanitary area. Period 1922–1926. p. 11. **12**

12. Deaths of (a) residents, (b) out-of-town transients. Each sanitary area. 1925, 1926, and period 1922–1926. p. 9–10. **12**

13. Deaths and death rate of residents. Each sanitary area. 1922. p. 9. **230 Mar.-Apr., 1925**

14. Deaths and death rate from organic heart disease of residents of Bellevue-Yorkville district. Each sanitary area. Period 1922–1924. **237**

15. Infant deaths among residents, (a) total deaths, (b) by leading causes: measles; scarlet fever; whooping-cough; diphtheria; influenza; erysipelas; meningococcus meningitis; tuberculosis of the respiratory system; tuberculosis of the meninges and central nervous system; other forms of tuberculosis; syphilis; rickets; meningitis; diseases of the ear and of the mastoid process; bronchitis; bronchopneumonia; pneumonia; diarrhea and enteritis (under 2 years); congenital malformations; congenital debility; premature birth (not stillborn); injury at birth (not stillborn); other diseases peculiar to early infancy. Each sanitary area. 1925, 1926. p. 23–27. **12**

16. Infant deaths among residents, by age and leading causes: measles, scarlet fever, whooping-cough, diphtheria, and **12**

BELLEVUE-YORKVILLE DISTRICT *(continued)*

Source Number

16. *(continued)*
influenza; tuberculosis; syphilis; diseases of the ear and of the mastoid process; bronchitis, bronchopneumonia, and pneumonia; diarrhea and enteritis (under 2 years); congenital debility and malformations; premature birth (not stillborn); injury at birth (not stillborn); other diseases peculiar to early infancy. 1925, 1926. p. 30.

17. Infant deaths among residents, by age, each sanitary area, 1925, 1926, and period 1923–1926; by age and sex, 1925, 1926. p. 28–29. **12**

18. Maternal deaths among residents, subdivided as (a) puerperal septicemia and (b) other puerperal conditions. Each sanitary area. 1925, 1926, and period 1922–1926. p. 32. **12**

19. Morbidity among residents in the Bellevue-Yorkville district, by age, for (a) diphtheria and (b) scarlet fever. Each sanitary area. 1925. p. 42. **12**

20. Street accidents in the Bellevue-Yorkville district: number of accidents; age and sex of (a) persons injured and (b) persons killed; causes of accidents to (a) children and (b) adults; time of day of occurrence of accidents for (a) children and (b) adults; map showing location of street accidents. Period Jan.–June, 1927. **11**

21. Physical defects among third-grade school children in the Bellevue-Yorkville district: average defects per child; defects found by age groups; by sex; etc. 1925/26. **10**

22. Schools (public; Catholic): (a) number by type (elementary; high; vocational); (b) registration by type. Each year, 1925–1927. p. 6. **12**

See also: *Tuberculosis* 9

BIRTHPLACE OF POPULATION

1. Native population by place of birth: each State; continental United States, State not reported; each outlying possession; born at sea under United States flag; **285**

BIRTHPLACE OF POPULATION (*continued*)

Source Number

1. (*continued*)
American citizens born abroad. Each borough. 1920. p. 670, 676, 679.

2. Persons born in New York State, persons born in other States, and persons born in foreign countries, for total, for white, and for negro, 1920; per cent of total population and per cent of native population, born in New York State, born in other States, and born in foreign countries, for total, for white, and for Negro, 1910. Each borough. p. 663. **285**

3. Foreign-born persons by continental groups. Each borough. 1900, 1910, 1920. p. 735. **285**

4. Foreign-born persons by country of birth. Each borough. 1920. p. 729-731. **285**

5. Foreign-born persons by sex and principal countries of birth, 1920; for sexes combined, 1900, 1910. In order of rank as of 1920. Each borough. p. 747. **285**

6. Foreign-born persons by country of birth. 1910, 1920. (Data according to pre-war map). p. XXVII. **51**

7. Foreign-born white persons by continental groups. 1920. p. 21. **206**

8. Foreign-born white persons by country of birth. Each county. 1920. p. 18–19. **206**

9. Foreign-born white persons by country of birth. Each assembly district and each borough. 1920. p. 63–68. **288**

10. Foreign-born white persons by country of birth. Each borough section, each borough. 1910, 1920. p. XXXI–XXXIII. **51**

11. Foreign-born white persons by country of birth. Each sanitary district having 300 or more persons per acre. 1920. p. XIII. **51**

12. Foreign-born white persons by sex and country of birth. Each tabulation district (one or more sanitary districts having a total population of 1000 or more). 1920. p. 2–819. **51**

BIRTHPLACE OF POPULATION *(continued)*

Source Number

13. Foreign-born white persons by country of birth. 1920. Gain or loss, 1910–1920. (Data according to pre-war map). p. XXIII. **51**

See also: *Citizenship of population* 4, 5
Density of population 8
Language 5, 6
Richmond, Borough of 5–7, 11

BIRTHS AND BIRTH RATE

1. Births and birth rate; stillbirths. Current month. **179**

2. Births and birth rate: (a) each year, 1898–1928; (b) each borough, 1928; (c) corrected for residence of mother, each borough, 1928. p. 133–134, 167. **131**

3. Births and birth rate. Each borough. Current monthly through Dec., 1927. **133**

4. Birth rate per 1000 population; stillbirth rate per 1000 live births. Annual average, period 1921–1925, and each year, 1925, 1926. p. XII, XV. ***176**

5. Births: (a) by sex and color (white; Negro; Chinese; Japanese); (b) by sex and parentage; (c) by method of attendance (physician; midwife; other). Each month, 1928. p. 155. **131**

6. Births: (a) by country of birth of both parents; (b) for mixed parentage, by country of birth of mother. Selected countries. 1928. p. 141, 156. **131**

7. Births: (a) by sex and color (white; Negro; other); by sex and "nativity of parents" (parentage). 1927. p. 134. **136 Sept. 1, 1928**

8. Births by sex. Each month, 1926. p. 80. ***279**

9. Births and stillbirths, by color (white; Negro; other). 1925. p. 110. **136 July 10, 1926**

10. Primiparous births and total births: by color (white; Negro; Chinese; Japanese); by nativity of parents; by **136 June 26, 1926**

BIRTHS AND BIRTH RATE *(continued)*

Source Number

10. *(continued)* attendance at birth (physician; midwife); by legitimacy; by place of birth (dwelling; institution; hotel; other). 1925. p. 102.

11. Births by (a) legitimacy, (b) attendant at birth, (c) month of birth. 1926. p. 46–47. ***176**

12. Plural births per 1000 total births. Each year, 1916–1926. p. XIII. ***176**

13. Plural births (twins; triplets). Each month, 1928. p. 155. **131**

14. Per cent of births attended by (a) physicians, (b) midwives. 1921. p. 89. **297**

See also: *Bellevue-Yorkville district* 3
Bronx, Borough of 1, 3
East Harlem 5–7, 13
Illegitimacy 1, 2
Infant deaths 4
Midwives (entire)
Sanitary district 2
Vital statistics (entire)

BLIND PERSONS

1. Number of blind persons and number of these blind persons in institutions, as registered with the New York State Commission for the Blind. June 30, 1928. p. 8. ***156**

2. Number of adult blind, not inmates of public or private institutions, who receive money from the City; amount of money distributed. 1926. p. 26. **148**

3. Public school classes for the blind, combined, and other schools for the blind in New York City, each school: (a) instructors by sex; (b) pupils enrolled by sex and grade; (c) pupils graduated at end of year; (d) pupils in special departments. 1926/27. p. 4–5. **303**

4. Jewish blind in Brooklyn: estimated number of Jewish blind in Brooklyn compared with non-Jewish blind; **24**

BLIND PERSONS *(continued)*

Source Number

4. *(continued)*
age, sex, and marital condition; contacts with agencies; per cent native-born; sources of application for aid, by sex; time known to agency, by sex; nativity by sex; citizenship by agency contacted; causes of blindness, each cause; vocational training by occupation; vocational training by schooling; sex, age, and marital condition; age when became blind, by sex; occupation, by sex; ability to read script, by sex. [1928].

See also: *Education, Public* 15, 16
Family service 2

BOARDING HOMES FOR BUSINESS WOMEN

1. Organized homes for employed women: (a) classification by general occupation groups or by source of information (room registries; questionnaires; etc.) of number of women reporting, cost of rooms, salaries, present housing, preferred housing, location of housing, dependents; (c) analysis of differences in room rents, wages, occupations, etc., of girls registering at Y.W.C.A., Y.W.H.A., and Y.W.C.A., colored branch. Manhattan. Data obtained between Jan., 1920, and Apr., 1921. **38**

2. Roman Catholic boarding homes for business girls: capacity; rates; age limits. Each home in Manhattan and Bronx. 1928. p. 91. ***40**

BOARDING HOMES FOR CHILDREN

1. Foster homes for children under the supervision of the Bureau of Child Hygiene of the New York City Department of Health, classified by number of children allowed by each permit: (a) permits granted; (b) inactive permits; (c) children actually boarded. 1928. p. 35. **131**

2. Permits issued for boarding children; children allowed on permits; children actually boarded. 1920. p. 178. **136** June 4, 1921

3. Jewish children receiving foster home care: (a) children by sex and by agency placing them; (b) per cent of **27**

BOARDING HOMES FOR CHILDREN (*continued*)

Source Number

3. (*continued*) total dependent children that were placed in foster homes; (c) children by age; (d) source of commitment; (e) number of children placed in family providing foster home care; (f) types of care received prior to admission to placing-out organization; (g) parental condition; (h) hereditary defects of parents; (i) occupation of parent; (j) length of stay of child; (k) problem children by type of problem presented; (l) mentality of children; (m) motives of foster mothers in accepting children for care; (n) economic status of foster homes. May 1, 1926.

See also: *Children, Dependent or neglected* 1, 3, 4

BOY POPULATION

1. New York City boys 9–18 years old: age (single years); nativity; size of family; religion; school registration; occupation; Sunday school registration. Each borough. 1926. **88**

See also: *Education* 6
Movement of population 1

BRIDGES

1. Bridge traffic count for 24 hours in both directions: cars; total vehicles; number of passengers in cars, in all vehicles; number of pedestrians. Each bridge. Oct., 1927, 1928. p. 7. ***210**

2. Vehicular traffic over city bridges for 24 hours: motor; horse. Each bridge. 1927. p. 190. **20**

BRONX, BOROUGH OF

1. Population (total; under 5 years); marriages and marriage rate; births and birth rate (live; still); deaths and death rate (a) by age (all ages; under 1 year; under 5 years) and (b) by cause (heart diseases; Bright's disease and nephritis; diseases of the arteries; cerebral hemorrhage and apoplexy; diabetes; **234**

BRONX, BOROUGH OF *(continued)*

Source Number

1. *(continued)*
pneumonias; cancer; tuberculosis; accidents; suicide; homicide; appendicitis; influenza; hernia; puerperal state; typhoid fever; congenital debility and malformations; diarrhea and enteritis; diphtheria and croup; measles; whooping-cough; scarlet fever). Each year, 1913–1923. p. 30–31.

2. Deaths of Bronx residents by age (under 1; 1–4; then 5-year periods to 80 and over) and sex. Each year, 1920–1928. p. 32. **234**

3. Estimated population, each year, 1910–1927; school registration (elementary; high), each year (Sept.), 1920–1927; building construction and number of families, each year, 1920–1927; age and sex composition of population, July 1, 1927; births (local; corrected), 1925, 1926; incidence of leading communicable diseases (measles; scarlet fever; pneumonia; tuberculosis; influenza; diphtheria; venereal diseases; chicken pox; whooping-cough; mumps; others). Period 1921–1925. p. 5–11. **234**

4. Total land area and park area; number of schools, colleges, etc., by kind of school; money spent in building operations and number of residence buildings by type of building (one-family; two-family; etc.); total miles of transportation lines; estimated population. Published annually. **14**

NOTE: See all items in the Guide which are given for each borough.

BUILDING

1. Number of buildings by classification of building (10 classes). Each borough by section or ward. Year ending Mar. 31, 1928. p. 18, 39, 43, 48, 51, 55. ***150**

2. Permits for new buildings and estimated cost, by type of building: dwelling; church; etc. Each borough. 1926, 1927, and period Jan.–June, 1928. p. 178–180. ***252**

BUILDING *(continued)* Source Number

3. Building permits issued: number and estimated cost of (a) residential buildings, (b) industrial and commercial buildings, (c) public buildings, (d) all other new construction, (e) alteration and repairs. Each borough. First nine months of 1927 and 1928. p. 416. Published monthly (varies) prior to Oct., 1928. **188 Oct., 1928**

4. Permits for new construction issued: number of buildings and cost, by intended use of building, (a) housekeeping (one-family; two-family; etc.), (b) non-housekeeping (hotel; lodging house; etc.), (c) non-residential (amusement; church; factory; etc.). Each borough. Period Jan.–June, 1927, 1928. p. 120, 124, 129, 134. Published annually in October. **314**

5. Total and per capita expenditures for (a) new buildings, (b) repairs, (c) new housekeeping dwellings; number of families provided for and ratio per 10,000 of population. 1928. p. 154–155. Published annually in May. **314**

6. New buildings for which permits were issued, by intended use of building (one-family dwelling; church; etc.) and cost. Each borough. 1926, 1927. p. 40–41, 57, 71, 84. **312**

7. Population and volume of construction, shown by index numbers. Each year, 1922–1926, and average, 1914–1926. p. 74. **314 June, 1927**

8. Buildings by type (dwelling; tenement; hotel, etc.): (a) applied for; (b) completed; (c) buildings demolished. Manhattan. Each year, 1918–1928. p. 104. **111**

9. New building by type (dwellings by cost; churches; etc.): (a) number of plans; (b) number of buildings; (c) estimated cost. Manhattan. Each year, 1923–1928. p. 102–103. **111**

10. Applications and plans for new buildings, classified by type (tenement; church; etc.). Bronx. 1928. p. 24. **109**

11. New buildings by classification (tenement; school; etc.): applications; buildings; families; estimated cost. Brooklyn. 1928 p. 27–28. **110**

BUILDING *(continued)*

Source Number

12. Number of new buildings; estimated cost. Brooklyn. Each month, 1927, 1928. p. 29. **110**

13. New building: (a) commenced; (b) completed, by type of building; (c) estimated cost. Each ward, Brooklyn. 1928. p. 30–31. **110**

14. Number and cost of buildings (brick; frame) completed; number of families, stores, garages, accommodated. Brooklyn. Each year, 1926–1928. p. 32. ***17**

15. New buildings (a) erected and occupied, (b) under construction, by Postoffice station districts and type of building (one-family house; two-family house; church; etc.). Brooklyn. Jan. 1 to June 1, 1926. p. 6. **16 July 3, 1926**

16. New buildings: (a) plans and applications for new buildings and estimated cost by type (frame dwelling; brick store; etc.), each year, 1923–1927; (b) number of families accommodated, 1927; (c) applications, buildings, and estimated cost, each month, 1927. Queens. p. 89–91. ***112**

17. New buildings by classification (dwelling; church; etc.): number of plans; buildings; estimated cost. Richmond. 1927. p. 108. ***113**

See also: *Bronx, Borough of* 3, 4

Other allied topics: *Apartments*
Churches
Dwellings
Education
Hospitals
Hotels
Housing
Housing construction
Housing surveys
Stores
Tenements
Theatres

BURGLARY

Source Number

1. Cases of burglary reported to the Police Department by type (residence; loft; etc.). Jan.–June, each year, 1928, 1929. p. 42. **146**
2. Cases reported to the Police Department, by type: residence (day; night); loft; etc. 1927, 1928. p. 41. ***144**

See also: *Arrests and summonses* 1, 3
Correction 20, 50, 54, 83 ,84
Courts 12, 13, 15, 16, 18, 21–23, 38, 91–93, 96, 97, 100, 105, 108, 110, 115, 122
Delinquents, Juvenile 3, 5
Felonies 1–5, 7, 10, 12, 13, 15, 18, 19
Negroes 7
Violence, Crimes of 1, 2

Other allied topics: *Larceny*
Robbery

BURNS

1. Deaths from burns, by cause of burn. Each borough. 1928. p. 10. **114**

See also: *Accidents* 1, 2, 4
Deaths and death rate 38, 60, 61

BUSINESS ESTABLISHMENTS

1. Number of business establishments, by type: hotels; firms in office buildings; firms in other than office buildings; banks and trust companies; manufacturing establishments; amusement places and theatres. By district, Manhattan. 1923. Separate sheet for each district. **241**

See also: *Building* 1–4, 6, 9–11, 13, 15–17

Other allied topics: *Manufactures*
Stores

BUSINESS SCHOOLS

See: *Education*

CAMPS

Source Number

1. Camps (108) reporting to the Children's Welfare Federation: number of camps; number of children and mothers cared for; free and paid cases; type of organization by which camps are run (settlements; churches; etc.); number of camps full to capacity. 1928. ***46**
2. Camps under auspices of Catholic Charities in Manhattan and Bronx: capacity; children in camp, by sex; age range of children; staff (religious; lay). Each camp. 1928. p. 83. ***40**

See also: *Outdoor relief* 1
Settlements 3–5

Other allied topic: *Vacation homes*

CANCER

1. Deaths. Current month. **179**
2. Death rate (refined; adjusted; crude) for cancer and other malignant tumors combined. Each borough. 1925. p. 93. ***292**
3. Death rate. Each year, 1898–1921. p. 346. **136** Nov. 4, 1922
4. Deaths classified by organs attacked and sex, for (a) all persons, (b) persons under 40 years. 1920. p. 347. **136** Nov. 4, 1922

See also: *Bellevue-Yorkville district* 6–8, 10
Bronx, Borough of 1
Clinics 1, 12, Note
Deaths and death rate 1, 3, 4–7, 38, 39, 41–48, 50, 52, 60–63, 65, 73–75
East Harlem 6–10
Hospitals 17, 20
Negroes 8
Vital statistics 6, 12

CANDY INDUSTRY

1. Women workers in 25 candy factories: number of workers; hours worked; age; salary; nationality; etc. **55**

CANDY INDUSTRY *(continued)*

Source Number

1. *(continued)*
Manhattan, Brooklyn, and Long Island City (combined). 1927.

2. Seasonal variation in employment and payroll for women candy workers in New York City. June, 1923–Dec., 1927. p. 34. Chart only. **55**

See also: *Employment* 2, 4, 7, 8
Food products industry 1
Hours of work 2
Manufactures 1, 11
Occupations, Persons engaged in 3, 10
Salaries and wages 1–4, 6, 7

CARRYING WEAPONS

See: *Arrests and summonses* 1
Correction 20, 50, 54, 83
Courts 12, 13, 18, 21, 22, 38, 55–57, 70, 77, 79, 105, 108
Felonies 2, 4, 5, 7,, 10, 12, 13, 15, 18

CATHOLIC SCHOOLS

See: *Education*

CEMETERIES

See: *Interments* (entire)
Parks 2

CHEMICAL INDUSTRY

1. The chemical industry in New York and its environs: number of plants and number of employees, by section of New York City (a) Manhattan below 59th Street, (b) Manhattan above 59th Street, Bronx, and Richmond, (c) Kings and Queens, 1900, 1912, 1917, 1922; length of occupancy of chemical plants in Manhattan, Brooklyn, Queens, Richmond, [1923]; number of acres occupied by chemical plants in Manhattan, Brooklyn, Long Island City, Richmond, 1923; number of **257**

CHEMICAL INDUSTRY *(continued)*

Source Number

1. *(continued)* employees in the chemical industry by branch of industry and sex, Manhattan south of 59th Street, 1922; number of chemical plants by number of employees and branch of industry, 1900, 1912, 1917, 1922; number of employees by branch of industry (a) Manhattan below 59th Street, (b) Manhattan above 59th Street, Bronx, and Richmond, (c) Kings and Queens, 1900, 1912, 1917, 1922. "The Chemical Industry." p. 9–49.

See also: *Manufactures* 1, 3, 4, 11
Occupations, Children engaged in (entire)
Occupations, Persons engaged in 3, 10
Salaries and wages 1–6
Workmen's compensation (entire)

CHICKEN POX

1. Cases. Current week. **317**
2. Cases; deaths; case rate; death rate; fatality rate. 1927. p. 5. **317 Supp. # 70**

See also: *Bronx, Borough of* 3
Deaths and death rate 38, 60, 61
Diseases, Transmissible 1–5, 7, 9, 11, 12

CHILD-CARING INSTITUTIONS

NOTE: Current statistical information (bed capacity; beds vacant; etc.) for Protestant institutions for children may be obtained from the office of the Federation of Agencies Caring for Protestants.

CHILDREN, DEPENDENT OR NEGLECTED

1. Institutions or homes for dependent or neglected children: children under care, Feb. 1, 1923, by sex and location (in the institution; outside, but under supervision of the institution in free family homes; outside, but under the supervision of the institution in boarding family homes); children received, by sex, **281**

CHILDREN, DEPENDENT OR NEGLECTED (*continued*)

Source Number

1. (*continued*)
and children disposed of (placed in free family homes; placed in boarding family homes; returned to parents; legally adopted; otherwise disposed of), by sex, period Feb. 1–Apr. 30, 1923. Each institution in New York City, with auspices of institution or home, year organized or incorporated, and color and age-range of children admitted. p. 98–101, 157.

2. Institutions for dependent or neglected children and for adults: inmates present (children; adults, by sex), Feb. 1, 1923; adults received, and adults left or died, period Feb. 1–Apr. 30, 1923; adults present, Apr. 30, 1923. Each institution in New York City, with auspices of institution, year organized or incorporated, and color of persons admitted. p. 240–241. **281**

3. Child-placing agencies in New York City: children disposed of (placed in free family homes; placed in boarding family homes; returned to parents; legally adopted; otherwise disposed of), by sex. Each agency, with auspices of agency and year organized or incorporated. Period Feb. 1–Apr. 30, 1923. p. 196. **281**

4. Humane and protective societies in New York City: children in shelter, by sex, Feb. 1, 1923; children given attention, by sex, and children disposed of (no ground for action; adjusted without removal from home; placed in detention home or institution; transferred to child-placing agency; placed in free family homes; placed in boarding family homes), period Feb. 1–Apr. 30, 1923. Each society. p. 205. **281**

5. Number of public charges in homes for children, classified by number of years during which such charges have been retained in institutions. Dec. 31, 1927. p. 84. **157**

6. Cases of normal children: number of (a) families and (b) children involved in investigations of the New York City Department of Public Welfare, by type of investigation. 1926. p. 21. **148**

CHILDREN, DEPENDENT OR NEGLECTED *(continued)*

Source Number

7. Children committed to the New York City Department of Public Welfare and found eligible for placement in free family homes, who were (a) referred to, and (b) placed by placing-out agencies (receiving City money; not receiving City money), each agency; children referred and children placed, by religion. 1926. p. 21–22. **148**

8. Number of (a) children and (b) families applying to the City for commitment, by religion (Catholic; Protestant; Jewish); number and per cent of children approved, by religion. 1926. p. 16. **148**

9. Number of children proposed to the City for commitment. Each year, 1912–1926. p. 16. **148**

10. Number of children committed by the New York City Department of Public Welfare by reason for approval; number of children refused by cause. 1926. p. 17. **148**

11. Country of birth of children (a) proposed to the City for commitment, (b) committed; parents of both groups by country of birth. 1926. p. 18. **148**

12. Number of children committed by the City whose discharges were applied for; number of families applying; total number of applications for discharge approved and disapproved, by reason of disapproval. 1926. p. 19. **148**

13. Number of children committed by the New York City Department of Public Welfare to child-caring institutions, by type of institution (dependents; delinquents; blind; etc.) and source of commitment (Department of Public Welfare; Children's Court; returned from trial, from hospital, or transferred through State Board of Charities). 1926. p. 19. **148**

14. Number of children discharged by the New York City Department of Public Welfare from child-caring institutions, by type of institution and cause of discharge **148**

CHILDREN, DEPENDENT OR NEGLECTED (*continued*)

Source Number

14. *(continued)* (application of parents; reinvestigated; etc.). 1926. p. 19.

15. Children who were public charges classified by religion (Catholic; Jewish; Protestant) and type of care (private family; institution for blind; etc.). Dec. 31, 1926. p. 20. **148**

16. Children committed by the New York City Department of Public Welfare to child-caring institutions whose cases were reinvestigated: number of children; number of families of children; number of children approved to remain as public charges, by reason for approval; number of children disapproved by cause. 1926. p. 20. **148**

17. Roman Catholic child-caring Homes: children cared for during year; children under care at end of year; staff (religious; lay). Each Home. Manhattan; Bronx. 1928. p. 24. ***40**

18. Roman Catholic specialized child-caring agencies: children cared for during year; staff (religious; lay). Each agency. Manhattan; Bronx. 1928. p. 24. ***40**

19. Jewish children in orphan and infant asylums: number of Jewish children under care by type of organization with which placed (orphan asylum; day nursery; temporary shelter; etc.); by sex and organization with which placed; age, each orphanage; source of admission (New York City Department of Public Welfare; court; private arrangement; free list); parental condition; occupation of parents; age distribution in orphanages classified according to length of stay; distribution of problem children, by problem; physical development; mental status; etc. May 1, 1926. p. 7, 22–23, 140–183. **26**

20. Jewish children committed by the court and by the New York City Department of Public Welfare to Jewish orphan and infant asylums. Each year, 1914–1926. Appendix, p. 143. **26**

CHILDREN, DEPENDENT OR NEGLECTED *(continued)*

Source Number

21. Jewish children committed by the court to Jewish institutions (for normal children; for delinquent children). Each year, 1914–1926. Appendix, p. 144. **26**

22. Children committed to child-caring institutions (Jewish; non-Jewish): (a) by the court, (b) by the New York City Department of Public Welfare. Each year, 1914–1921. Appendix, p. 68. **22**

23. Census of children under care of Jewish organizations accepting presumably normal dependent children: number of children by type of organization, each organization; number of families represented; sex distribution; age; length of stay; source of admission; parental condition; occupation of parents; previous care; health problem children; behavior problem children. May 1, 1926. **28**

24. Number of commitments and number of admissions of children to orphan asylums and placing-out organizations belonging to the Federation for the Support of Jewish Philanthropic Societies of New York City. Each year, 1914–1925. p. 22. **28**

See also: *Boarding homes for children* 3
Child Welfare, Board of (entire)
Courts 109, 110, 115, 117, 118, 122
Deaths and death rate 53, 54
Delinquents, Juvenile 1
Negroes 7
Outdoor relief 1

CHILD WELFARE

See: *Baby health stations*
Boarding homes for children
Camps
Child-caring institutions
Children, Dependent or neglected
Child Welfare, Board of
Clinics, Preschool age
Day nurseries
Open air classes

CHILD WELFARE, BOARD OF

Source Number

1. Allowances of the Board of Child Welfare of New York City: new applicants during year; new allowances given during year; families receiving allowances at end of year; average allowance per month per family and per child. 1927, 1928. p. 9. **115**

2. Work of the Board of Child Welfare of New York City: new applicants; applicants refused by cause; discontinued cases by cause; allowances given. Each month, 1928. p. 17–21. Same, but not in such complete detail. Each year, 1916–1928. p. 22. **115**

3. Families aided; minor children aided; applications (a) received, (b) denied; allowances made to (a) families, (b) children; average allowance (a) per family, (b) per child. Each year, 1926–1928. p. 7, 23. **115**

4. New applicants receiving allowances; families discontinued; total families on payroll; additional children, new cases, cared for; children in families discontinued and decreased; children on payroll. Subdivided under amendments: widowed citizens; wives of insane husbands; deserted mothers; etc. Each month, 1928. p. 14–16. **115**

5. Case records (8640) from the files of the New York City Board of Child Welfare, classified by number of children in family: number of families; family expenditure; wage-earning children; family income; city allowances. Mar., 1923. p. 104–106. **158**

See also: *Outdoor relief* 1

CHRONICALLY ILL PERSONS

1. Number of institutions under Jewish auspices for the chronic sick; number of beds. [1928]. p. 4. **32**

2. Chronic cases in municipal institutions, (a) discharged in 1926, and (b) in hospitals on census day, 1927: total patients; Jewish patients; per cent Jewish patients; Jewish cases classified by type of chronic illness (Class A, requiring medical care; Class B, requiring **32**

CHRONICALLY ILL PERSONS *(continued)*

Source Number

2. *(continued)* nursing care; Class C, requiring custodial care). Each hospital, and by groups (general hospitals of the Department of Public Welfare; chronic hospitals of the Department of Public Welfare; Bellevue and Allied Hospitals). p. 15.
3. Chronic cases in Jewish general hospitals, classified by type of illness (A, B, C, as in 2), each hospital, census day, 1927; number of chronic Jewish patients discharged from five of the Department of Public Welfare hospitals, by sex, each hospital, 1926. p. 20–21. **32**

NOTE: Statistics collected in a census of chronically ill persons in New York City are now being compiled in the Research Bureau of the Welfare Council of New York City.

See also: *Dependents, Age* 4
Hospitals 17, 18, 20

CHURCHES

1. Contributing members, Sunday school members, total amount of money raised, and value of church property. Each denomination, each church. Each borough. [Jan., 1929]. p. 195–216. **20**
2. Churches by religion (Jewish; Protestant; Roman Catholic): number of churches; families; Sunday school members. Each borough. 1928. p. 30. ***17**
3. Number of churches: by borough; by denomination. 1927. p. 45. **226**
4. Number of churches by denomination. Manhattan and Bronx, combined; Brooklyn; Queens; Richmond. [1921]. p. VIII. **68**

See also: *Building* 1, 2, 4, 6, 9–11, 13, 15–17
Fires 3, 9
Recreation 4, 5
Tax exemption 1, 2

Other allied topic: *Religion of population*

CITIZENSHIP OF POPULATION

Source Number

1. Aliens and total population in the 1920 area of New York City. Each decade, 1825–1875; 1892; each decade, 1905–1925. p. 13. **206**

2. Foreign-born persons by citizenship. Each borough. 1920. p. 842. **285**

3. Foreign-born white persons, by citizenship and sex, 1920; foreign-born white males, 21 years and over, by citizenship, 1900, 1910, 1920; foreign-born white females, 21 years and over, by citizenship, 1920. Each borough. p. 842–845. **285**

4. Foreign-born white persons, by citizenship and country of birth. Each borough. 1920. p. 856–857. **285**

5. Foreign-born white persons, 21 years and over, by citizenship, sex, and country of birth. Each borough. 1920. p. 866–867, 876–877. **285**

6. Foreign-born white persons 21 years of age and over who were naturalized citizens, by sex. Each assembly district and each borough. 1920. p. 63–68. **288**

7. White aliens without first papers by age (under 21; 21 and over) and sex. Each tabulation tract (one or more sanitary districts having a total population of 1000 or more). 1920. p. 2–819. **51**

See also: *Population and population estimates, not including 1930 and later* 5
Richmond, Borough of 2, 6

Other allied topic: *Naturalization*

CLINIC FEES

1. Per cent of fees in clinics and out-patient departments that were (a) under 10 cents, (b) 10–24 cents, (c) 25 cents, (d) over 25 cents. 1916, 1923, 1927. p. 1. **233**

2. Special fees in out-patient departments and clinics by type of service rendered (anaesthesia; bacteriological; **233**

CLINIC FEES *(continued)*

Source Number

2. *(continued)*
bandages; crutches; etc.): institutions reporting sub-divided as to fees or no fees charged; fees charged classified as maximum, minimum, and most frequent. [1927].

CLINICS

1. Clinics and health stations in New York City, classified by type of service: anti-rabic; arthritis; asthma; baby health; cancer; cardiac; etc. [Jan., 1929]. Inside back cover. **44**
2. Number of organizations maintaining clinics; number of places at which clinics are located, with the clinics subdivided as attached (municipal; non-municipal), and unattached (municipal; non-municipal), non-municipal unattached clinics being further subdivided as to type of organization maintaining them; number of clinics maintained; estimated number of patients; approximate number of visits to clinics. [1929]. Inside front cover. **44**
3. Service of licensed dispensaries (public; private) in greater New York: (a) treatments given; (b) patients admitted to the clinics in the dispensaries. 1926, 1927. p. 35. **157**
4. Dispensary cases and visits to dispensaries: (a) non-municipal hospitals by type (general; women's and children's; chronic and convalescent; special); (b) municipal hospitals, each hospital. 1927. p. 36–37. ***272**
5. Clinics (except industrial clinics) subdivided as (a) outpatient departments (municipal; non-municipal) and (b) unattached clinics (municipal; non-municipal): number of clinics; number of organizations maintaining these clinics; estimated number of patients; approximate number of visits. [1926]. **273**
6. Number of "old-fashioned dispensaries"; number of unattached clinics established by the New York City Department of Health; number of unattached clinics **274**

CLINICS (*continued*)

Source Number

6. (*continued*)
established under private auspices. Manhattan. 1900, 1904, 1909, 1914, 1919, 1924. p. 22. Chart only.

7. Dispensary service: (a) dispensaries by class of patients received (all races; white only; Negro only); (b) dispensaries by method of operation (hospital; independent); (c) visits by patients during year, by method of operation. Each borough. 1922. p. 40. **289**

8. Patients of public dispensaries: number of patients; total visits by patients; visits to patients in their homes. Each dispensary: (a) Bellevue and Allied Hospitals; (b) New York City Department of Health, each borough; (c) New York City Department of Public Welfare. 1927. p. 212–213. **157**

9. Patients treated at dispensaries belonging to the New York City Department of Public Welfare. Each dispensary. 1926. p. 31. **148**

10. Number of dispensaries, number of individuals served, and number of visits: for (a) attached clinics, (b) unattached clinics, (c) New York City Department of Health clinics. Brooklyn. 1925. p. 7. **19**

11. Visits by patients to out-patient departments of Jewish hospitals. Each hospital and by borough. Each year, 1921–1927. p. 4–5. **31**

12. Clinic sessions in Jewish out-patient departments, by time of session (morning; afternoon; evening) and by kind of clinic (asthma; baby health; cancer; etc.). By borough: Manhattan; Bronx; Brooklyn. 1927. p. 11. **31**

13. Comparison of per cent of Jewish population in the borough and of visits to Jewish out-patient departments. By borough: Manhattan; Bronx; Brooklyn. 1921, 1927. p. 7. **31**

NOTE: A health inventory of all health services in New York City exclusive of activities of the New York City Department of Health has been completed under the **329**

CLINICS *(continued)*

Source Number

NOTE: *(continued)*
auspices of the Welfare Council of New York City. This study includes an analysis of the following types of services: cancer; cardiac; child health; eye; health education; health examination; maternity; mental hygiene; tuberculosis; venereal disease. (For dental services, see source number 235). Each type of service is analyzed as to volume of clinic work, clinic personnel, etc. The data are based on the year 1927 or 1928.

See also: *Health service* (entire)
Heart disease 6, 7, 10, 11
Hospitals 6, 26
Sanitary districts 2
Settlements 3
Tuberculosis 4, 19, 27–33
Venereal disease 11

CLINICS, BABY HEALTH

See: *Baby health stations*

CLINICS, DENTAL

1. Licensed dental clinics and unlicensed dental clinics by type of supporting institution (hospital; charitable organization; church; etc.): (a) number of clinics; (b) number of visits reported. [1927]. p. 23–24. **235**
2. Dental service available in institutions, by type of institution (hospital; charitable organization; church; etc.): (a) type of service; (b) number of dental clinics. [1927]. p. 8, 10. **235**
3. Dental chairs and chair hours: (a) by type of supporting institution (hospital; charitable organization; church; etc.); (b) each borough. [1927]. p. 14–15. **235**
4. Service hours of dental chairs by number of chairs: (a) in hospital clinics; (b) all other clinics except college clinics. [1927]. p. 17. **235**
5. Potentially available chair hours not in use in (a) hospital clinics and (b) non-hospital clinics. [1927]. p. 18. **235**

CLINICS, DENTAL *(continued)*

Source Number

6. Dental clinics in Brooklyn: number of clinics; number of dentists; etc. 1925. p. 8. **19**

7. Dental clinics conducted in schools by the New York City Department of Health: number of children examined; new patients registered and patients reregistered; revisits; patients discharged (cured; dropped); treatments given. 1928. p. 48, 50. **131**

See also: *Clinics* 1, 12
Health service (entire)
Nurses 3

CLINICS, EYE

1. Eye clinics conducted in schools by the New York City Department of Health: number of clinics; new patients registered and patients reregistered, by type of disorder (medical; refraction); total visits, by type of disorder; patients discharged (cured; dropped) by type of disorder; treatments by type of disorder. 1928. p. 46–47. **131**

See also: *Clinics* 1, 12, Note
Nurses 3

CLINICS, MATERNITY

See: *Clinics, Prenatal*

CLINICS, PRENATAL

1. Prenatal clinics of the New York City Department of Health: number of clinics by borough; number of mothers and number of babies registered; mothers' visits to clinics; visits to homes; number of clinic sessions held and attendance; mothers' meetings held and attendance; stillbirths; miscarriages; premature births; work of medical inspectors. 1928. p. 32–34. **131**

See also: *Clinics* 1, 12, Note.
East Harlem 13
Health service (entire)

CLINICS, PRESCHOOL AGE

Source Number

1. Preschool age clinics in New York City: number of clinics; number of organizations operating these clinics; number of children; average attendance; clinic visits; children immunized; clinics giving special examination to children entering school; clinics having full time nurse; home visits; clinic visits. Each clinic. 1928. ***48**

See also: *Clinics* 1, Note
Health service (entire)

CLOTHING, COST OF

1. Average minimum retail price of selected articles of wearing apparel and accessories, by item of clothing. Each borough. 1926. p. 56–59. **102**
2. Average minimum cost of clothing for one year, by article of clothing, for a married male industrial worker living at a fair American standard; his wife; 12-year-old son; 8-year-old daughter; 2-year-old son. Data collected Aug.–Oct., 1927. p. 66–75. **103**

See also: *Cost of living* 1, 3, 4

COLOR OF POPULATION

1. Persons by color: white; Negro; Indian; Chinese; Japanese; all other. Each borough. 1900, 1910, 1920. p. 47, 55, 76. **285**
2. Persons by color: white; Negro; other. Each borough section, each borough. 1910, 1920. p. XXXI–XXXIII. **51**
3. Persons by color: white (native; foreign); Negro. Each district, each borough. 1920. Separate sheet for each district. **241**
4. Persons 21 years of age and over by color (white; Negro) and sex. Each assembly district and each borough. 1920. p. 63–68. **288**
5. Persons 10 years of age and over by color (white; Negro). Each assembly district and each borough. 1920. p. 63–68. **288**

COLOR OF POPULATION *(continued)*

Source Number

See also: *Age of population* 2–4, 6–8
Birthplace of population 2, 7–13
Citizenship of population 3–7
Country of origin of population (entire)
Density of population 8, 9
Education 1–3, 5
Illiteracy 1, 2, 4–6
Immigration 3–5
Language 1–7
Marital condition of population (entire)
Marriages and marriage rate 4
Nativity 2–6
Negroes 1–6
Occupations, Children engaged in 2
Occupations, Persons engaged in 5–9
Ownership of homes 1
Population and population estimates, not including 1930 and later 11
Religion of population 1
Richmond, Borough of 1–3, 5–11
Sex of population (entire)

COMMUNITY CENTERS

1. Community centers, baths, and lectures under the supervision of the Division of Extension Activities of the public schools: (a) number of centers; (b) number of sessions; (c) aggregate attendance; (d) average attendance. Each type of activity: evening community centers (official; non-official; occasional use); day community centers (after-school playgrounds; afternoon centers); baths (day; evening); lectures (radio; all others). Current month; corresponding month of preceding year; preceding month of current year. **123**
2. Evening community centers (official; non-official) under the supervision of the Division of Extension Activities of the public schools: (a) centers; (b) sessions; (c) aggregate attendance; (d) average attendance. Each borough. 1926/27, 1927/28. p. 716. **124**

COMMUNITY CENTERS *(continued)*

Source Number

3. Occasional use of public school buildings (afternoon centers; evening centers) by organizations outside the school system: (a) centers; (b) sessions; (c) aggregate attendance. Each borough, 1926/27, 1927/28. p. 717–718. **124**

See also: *Recreation* 3, 5

COMPENSATION

See: *Workmen's compensation*

CONTINUATION SCHOOLS

See: *Education*

CONVALESCENT CARE

1. Number of beds in institutions in or near New York City that are regarded as serving strictly convalescent patients: for adults by sex; for children classified as babies, boys, girls. [1925]. p. 4. **39**

2. Number of Jewish convalescent homes in or near New York City, and bed capacity of each home, by age of patient served: adult; children; both. 1928. p. 11–12. **34**

3. Number of patients admitted to Jewish convalescent homes in or near New York City, classified by age (adults; children) and medical type (surgical; cardiac; nerve; etc.). Each home. 1926. p. 16–17. **34**

4. Total patients, Jewish patients, and non-Jewish patients admitted to Jewish convalescent homes in or near New York City, by age and sex: men; women; boys; girls. Each home. 1926. p. 18–21. **34**

5. Per cent of utilization of Jewish convalescent homes in or near New York City, by age of patients admitted (adults; children; both): number of beds; maximum days; actual days; per cent utilization. Each home. 1926. p. 23–24. **34**

CONVALESCENT CARE *(continued)*

Source Number

6. Average length of stay in Jewish convalescent homes in or near New York City, by age of patient received (adults; children; both). Each home. 1926. p. 26. **34**

7. Part pay cases, free cases, and city cases by age of patients received (adults; children; both) in 10 of the 12 Jewish convalescent homes in or near New York City. Each home. 1926. p. 27–28. **34**

8. Patients in Roman Catholic convalescent homes; days of convalescent care. Each home. Archdiocese of New York (Manhattan, Bronx, and portion of Westchester County). 1928. p. 56. ***40**

See also: *Family service* 2
Heart disease 14
Negroes 11
Settlements 4

CORRECTION

NOTE: Institutions have been listed as city, county, and State and in alphabetical order within a given group.

INSTITUTIONS OF THE NEW YORK CITY DEPARTMENT OF CORRECTION

Total and Miscellaneous Groups of Institutions

1. Admissions, by sex and type: from courts (direct; indirect); violating parole (direct; transfer); interdepartmental transfer; return of escaped prisoners. Each institution: City Prison, Manhattan, Brooklyn, Queens, each prison; Second, Third, Fourth, Fifth, Sixth, Seventh, Eighth, Twelfth District Prisons, each prison; Traffic Detention; Detention of Witnesses; New York County Penitentiary; New York City Workhouse; Correction Hospital; Reformatory Prison, Hart's Island; Municipal Farm, Riker's Island; New York City Reformatory; New York City Reformatory Branch, Warwick; Women's Farm Colony, Greycourt; Construction Camp, Greycourt. 1928. p. 85. **121**

CORRECTION *(continued)*

Source Number

INSTITUTIONS OF THE NEW YORK CITY DEPARTMENT OF CORRECTION *(continued)*

Total and Miscellaneous Groups of Institutions *(continued)*

2. Admissions, by sex and type: commitments; admissions from other sources. Each institution (as in 1). Year ending June 30, 1928. p. 563. **162**

3. Prisoners received on commitment by sex: (a) by color; (b) by religious instruction; (c) by nativity; (d) by age (16 and under 21; 21–30; over 30); (e) by "social relations" (marital condition); (f) by education; (g) by offense. Each institution: City Prison, Manhattan, Brooklyn, Queens, each prison; Second, Third, Fourth, Fifth, Sixth, Seventh, Eighth, Twelfth District Prisons, each prison; Traffic Detention; Detention of Witnesses; New York County Penitentiary; New York City Workhouse; New York City Reformatory. Year ending June 30, 1928. p. 563–567. **162**

4. Prisoners received on commitment. Each institution (as in 3). Each year ending June 30, 1919–1928. p. 497. **162**

5. Prisoners received from the courts, and prisoners per 100,000 estimated population. Each year, 1915–1923. p. 42. **249**

6. Admissions on commitment, by sex. By institution: New York County Penitentiary; New York City Reformatory; New York City Workhouse. Each month, 1927. p. 12. **143**

7. Federal prisoners received on commitment: (a) total, year ending June 30, 1926, 1927, p. 13; (b) by sex, each institution (City Prison, Manhattan, Brooklyn, Queens, each prison; Second District Prison; New York City Workhouse), year ending June 30, 1928, p. 565. **162**

8. Male prisoners received on commitment: (a) total, and prisoners aged 16–21 by age (16–20 years; 21 years), each institution (City Prison, Manhattan, Brooklyn, **163**

CORRECTION *(continued)*

Source Number

INSTITUTIONS OF THE NEW YORK CITY DEPARTMENT OF CORRECTION *(continued)*

Total and Miscellaneous Groups of Institutions *(continued)*

8. *(continued)* Queens, each prison; New York City Reformatory; New York City Workhouse; New York County Penitentiary; Traffic Detention; Detention of Witnesses; Second, Third, Fourth, Fifth, Sixth, Seventh, Eighth, Twelfth District Prisons, each prison); (b) prisoners aged 16–21, by age (each year), by institution (City Prison, Manhattan, Brooklyn, Queens, each prison; New York City Reformatory; New York City Workhouse; New York County Penitentiary). Year ending June 30, 1928. p. 1–2.

9. Finger prints taken during year: (a) by sex of prisoners, 1927; (b) by sex of prisoners and by institution (New York City Workhouse; City and District Prisons, combined; New York County Penitentiary; New York City Reformatory), 1928; (c) by sex of prisoners and number of times prisoners had served terms in institutions. 1928. p. 70–71. **121**

10. Persons fingerprinted, excluding duplicates, by sex; number of times such persons were received during the year, by sex. 1928. p. 70–71. **121**

11. Prisoners by sex. Institutions combined. June 30, 1927; June 30, 1928; Dec. 31, 1928. p. 29. **162**

12. Prisoners by sex. Institutions combined. Dec. 31, 1927, 1928. p. 85. **121**

13. Prisoners by sex and cause of confinement (awaiting trial; convicted of crime; witnesses). Each institution: City Prison, Manhattan, Brooklyn, Queens, each prison; Second, Third, Fourth, Fifth, Sixth, Seventh, Eighth, Twelfth District Prisons, each prison; Detention of Witnesses; New York County Penitentiary; **162**

CORRECTION *(continued)*

Source Number

INSTITUTIONS OF THE NEW YORK CITY DEPARTMENT OF CORRECTION *(continued)*

Total and Miscellaneous Groups of Institutions *(continued)*

13. *(continued)*
New York City Workhouse; Correction Hospital; Reformatory Prison, Hart's Island; Municipal Farm, Riker's Island; New York City Reformatory; New York City Reformatory Branch, Warwick; Women's Farm Colony, Greycourt. June 30, 1928. p. 563.

14. Prisoners by cause of confinement: charged with crime and awaiting trial; convicted of crime; detained as witnesses; debtors. June 30, each year, 1919–1928. p. 496. **162**

15. Prisoners by sex. Year ending June 30, 1918, 1927, 1928. p. 497. **162**

16. Average daily census of prisoners by sex. Each year, 1910–1928. p. 86. **121**

17. Average daily number of prisoners by sex. Each institution: Second District Prison; Seventh District Prison; City Prison, Manhattan, Brooklyn, Queens, each prison; New York City Workhouse; New York County Penitentiary; Correction Hospital; Municipal Farm, Riker's Island; Reformatory Prison, Hart's Island; New York City Reformatory; Warwick Farms; Construction Camp, Greycourt; Women's Farm Colony, Greycourt; Male Detention (Witness). Each month, 1928. p. 87. **121**

18. Prisoners, by sex: by age (each year); by occupation; by nativity, with State of birth for native-born and country of birth of foreign-born; by color. 1928. p. 88–92, 95. **121**

19. Prisoners: total; 16–21 years, inclusive. 1914, 1916, 1920, each year, 1923–1928. p. 37. **121**

CORRECTION *(continued)*

Source Number

INSTITUTIONS OF THE NEW YORK CITY DEPARTMENT OF CORRECTION *(continued)*

Total and Miscellaneous Groups of Institutions *(continued)*

20. Prisoners by sex, each offense. 1928. p. 93–94. **121**

21. Estimated number of prisoners transported to and from courts, jails, and other penal institutions of New York City. 1928. p. 35. **121**

22. Average daily number of prisoners in custody, and number of prisoners per 100,000 estimated population. Each year, 1915–1923. p. 44. **249**

23. Prisoners: (a) number, each institution or group of institutions (City Prisons, combined; eight District Prisons, combined; Penitentiary and Workhouse, combined; City Reformatory; Women's Hospital and Workhouse, combined); (b) number per 100,000 estimated population. Sept. 30, each year, 1915–1923. p. 46. **249**

24. Prisoners: (a) largest number during period, Sept. 30, 1915–Sept. 30, 1923; (b) average number during same period; (c) average number, year ending Sept. 30, 1923; (d) normal capacity of institutions, Sept. 30, 1923. City Prison, Manhattan, Brooklyn, Queens, each prison; eight District Prisons, combined; New York County Penitentiary and Workhouse (male), combined; Women's Hospital and Workhouse (female), combined; Women's Farm Colony. Each institution or group of institutions. p. 47. **249**

25. Persons on parole, by sex: (a) persons on parole at beginning of year; (b) persons released on parole during year; (c) cases on parole ended during year (conditional release from supervision; enlisted U.S. Army; etc.); (d) persons on parole at end of year. Each institution: New York County Penitentiary; New York City Reformatory; New York City Workhouse. 1927. p. 12. ***143**

CORRECTION *(continued)*

Source Number

INSTITUTIONS OF THE NEW YORK CITY DEPARTMENT OF CORRECTION *(continued)*

Total and Miscellaneous Groups of Institutions *(continued)*

26. Persons released on parole: (a) by sex, each month; (b) by sex and result (conditional release from supervision; enlisted in U.S. Army; etc.); (c) by sex and color; (d) by sex and age; (e) by sex and "civil condition" (marital condition); (f) by sex and habits (alcohol; drugs; prostitution; etc.); (g) by sex and type of school attended; (h) by sex and country of birth; (i) by country of birth of each parent; (j) by number of previous convictions; (k) by sex and court by which committed (City Magistrates' Court; Court of Special Sessions; Court of General Sessions and County Court; Supreme Court of the State of New York), by county, and for cases committed to the Reformatory, by method by which convicted (plea; trial). Each institution: New York County Penitentiary; New York City Reformatory; New York City Workhouse. 1927. p. 13–21. ***143**

27. Length of time which had been served by persons released on parole, by sex: (a) longest; (b) shortest; (c) average. Each institution: New York County Penitentiary; New York City Reformatory; New York City Workhouse. 1927. p. 14, 19, 21. ***143**

28. Prisoners discharged, by sex and type of discharge: discharged; transferred from Department institutions; etc. Each institution (as in 1). 1928. p. 85. **121**

29. Prisoners discharged, by sex and type of discharge: parole; expiration of sentence; etc. Each institution (as in 1). Year ending June 30, 1928. p. 564. **162**

City Prisons

30. Male prisoners admitted: (a) total (committed, by occupation; admitted from other sources); (b) boys under **162**

CORRECTION *(continued)*

Source Number

INSTITUTIONS OF THE NEW YORK CITY DEPARTMENT OF CORRECTION *(continued)*

City Prisons *(continued)*

30. *(continued)* 21 who were committed and increase over preceding year. City Prison, Manhattan. Year ending June 30, 1928. p. 113.

31. Prisoners admitted by sex: (a) total; (b) number under 21 years of age. City Prison, Brooklyn. Year ending June 30, 1928. p. 115–116. **162**

32. Prisoners admitted yearly. City Prison, Queens. Estimated, Nov. 3, 1928. p. 118. **162**

33. Prisoners distributed by number of cells in the tiers of cells. City Prison, Manhattan. Oct. 17, 1928. p. 112. **162**

34. Maximum, minimum, and average day census of prisoners during the year. City Prison, Manhattan. Year ending June 30, 1928. p. 112. **162**

35. Maximum, minimum, and average day census of prisoners by sex, year ending June 30, 1928; average day census by sex, year ending June 30, 1927. City Prison, Brooklyn. p. 115. **162**

36. Prisoners by sex. City Prison, Brooklyn. Oct. 18, 1928. p. 114. **162**

37. Maximum and minimum day census of prisoners. City Prison, Queens. Year ending June 30, 1928. p. 118. **162**

38. Prisoners: (a) total by sex and reason for detention (examination; grand jury; etc.); (b) boys under 21 years of age. City Prison, Queens. Nov. 3, 1928. p. 118. **162**

See also: *Correction* 1–4, 7, 8, 13, 17, 23, 24, 28, 29
Courts 31, 41, 85

CORRECTION *(continued)*

Source Number

INSTITUTIONS OF THE NEW YORK CITY DEPARTMENT OF CORRECTION *(continued)*

Correction Hospital

39. Admissions of women, by type of sentence: New York County Penitentiary (indefinite); New York City Workhouse (definite; indefinite); New York County Penitentiary, violators of parole; New York City Workhouse, violators of parole; miscellaneous; direct; drug addicts, self-committed. 1928. p. 105. **121**

40. Estimated per cent of women admitted who were prostitutes. 1928. p. 46. **121**

41. Prisoners by sex. Dec. 31, 1928. p. 105. **121**

42. Prisoners discharged (paroles; fines; etc.); prisoners transferred, by institution to which transferred. 1928. p. 105. **121**

43. Prisoners released on parole, by sex, each offense. 1927. p. 22. ***143**

See also: *Correction* 1, 2, 13, 17
Drug laws, Violation of 5

District Prisons

44. Prisoners by sex. By prison: Second, Third, Fourth, Fifth, Sixth, Seventh, Eighth, Twelfth District Prisons. On a given day in the period July–Dec., 1928. p. 120–126. **162**

See also: *Correction* 1–4, 7, 8, 13, 17, 23, 24, 28, 29
Courts 31

Municipal Farm, Riker's Island

45. Admissions, classified as penitentiary inmates and working inmates. 1928. p. 107. **121**

46. Prisoners. Jan. 1 and Dec. 31, 1928. p. 107. **121**

47. Prisoners by occupation (excavating and leveling; farm work; etc.). Dec. 5, 1928. p. 106. **162**

CORRECTION *(continued)*

Source Number

INSTITUTIONS OF THE NEW YORK CITY DEPARTMENT OF CORRECTION *(continued)*

Municipal Farm, Riker's Island *(continued)*

48. Prisoners transferred: (a) to Penitentiary for reclassification and discharge; (b) to tubercular ward, Reformatory Prison, Hart's Island. 1928. p. 107. **121**

See also: *Correction* 1, 2, 13, 17, 28, 29
Drug laws, Violation of 5

New York City Reformatory

49. Prisoners: (a) total; (b) number employed by type of employment. Mar. 15 and Aug. 14, 1928. p. 99, 101. **162**

50. Persons released on parole, each offense for which they had been committed. 1927. p. 14. ***143**

See also: *Correction* 1–4, 6, 8, 9, 13, 17, 23, 25–29, 51, 52
Courts 24, 37
Mental disease 5

New York City Workhouse

See: *Correction* 1–4, 6–9, 13, 17, 25–29, 39, 51, 52, 79
Courts 24, 25, 41, 58, 81, 82, 85, 130
Drug laws, Violation of 6
Mental disease 5
Prostitution 2
Traffic regulations, Violation of 4
Venereal disease 9

New York County Penitentiary

51. Prisoners admitted: (a) by institution to which committed (New York County Penitentiary; New York City Workhouse; New York City Reformatory; miscellaneous; and parole violators classified as Penitentiary, Workhouse, and Reformatory); (b) by physical classification (alcoholic ward; drug addicts; normal; etc.); (c) per cent distribution by occupational ability (unskilled; skilled; clerical). 1928. p. 73, 77. **121**

CORRECTION *(continued)*

Source Number

INSTITUTIONS OF THE NEW YORK CITY DEPARTMENT OF CORRECTION *(continued)*

New York County Penitentiary *(continued)*

52. Bertillon department: (a) prisoners handled, by institution to which committed (New York County Penitentiary; New York City Workhouse; New York City Reformatory; and parole violators returned); (b) finger prints taken; (c) photographs taken. 1928. p. 75. **121**

53. Prisoners. Jan. 1 and Dec. 31, 1928. p. 72. **121**

54. Persons released on parole during year, by sex, each offense for which person had been committed. 1927. p. 19–20. ***143**

See also: *Correction* 1–4, 6, 8, 9, 13, 17, 25–29, 39, 45, 48, 79
Courts 24, 58, 108
Drug laws, Violation of 1
Mental disease 5
Venereal disease 9

Reformatory Prison, Hart's Island

55. Prisoners: (a) total; (b) number who were employed, by type of employment (tailor shop; cemetery gang; etc.). Dec. 21, 1928. p. 104. **162**

56. Prisoners: maximum, minimum, and average day census. Year ending June 30, 1928. p. 104. **162**

See also: *Correction* 1, 2, 13, 17, 28, 29, 48

Women's Farm Colony, Greycourt

57. Prisoners. Aug. 14, and Sept. 8, 1928. p. 109. **162**

See also: *Correction* 1, 2, 13, 17, 24, 28, 29

COUNTY JAILS

58. Prisoners by sex: (a) by "social relation" (marital condition); (b) by education (literacy); (c) by color; (d) by nativity; (e) by religious instruction; (f) by age (under 16; 16 and under 21; 21 and not over 30; **162**

CORRECTION *(continued)*

Source Number

COUNTY JAILS *(continued)*

58. *(continued)*
over 30); (g) by occupation before conviction; (h) by cause of detention (sentenced to imprisonment after conviction; committed for examination or trial; etc.); (i) by selected offenses. Each county. Year ending June 30, 1928. p. 550–557, 559, 562.

59. Federal prisoners received on commitment. Each county. Year ending June 30, 1928. p. 558. **162**

60. Prisoners admitted, by sex. New York County Jail. Year ending June 30, 1928. p. 251. **162**

61. Male prisoners received on commitment, and age (each year, 16–21). By jail: Bronx County Jail; Richmond County Jail. Year ending June 30, 1928. p. 3. **163**

62. Prisoners by sex: maximum, minimum, and average day census. Each county. Year ending June 30, 1928. p. 549. **162**

63. Prisoners by sex and cause of confinement: awaiting trial; convicted of crime; etc. Each county. June 30, 1928. p. 547. **162**

64. Number of days' work performed by prisoners in custody. Each county. Year ending June 30, 1928. p. 561. **162**

65. Prisoners: (a) by sex; (b) by offense. New York County Jail. Nov. 21, 1928. p. 250. **162**

66. Prisoners: maximum and minimum day census, Jan. 1–Nov. 21, 1928; maximum, minimum, and average day census, year ending June 30, 1928. New York County Jail. p. 251. **162**

67. Prisoners by sex, age (adults; minors), and cause of confinement: awaiting court action; serving sentence; civil prisoners. Bronx County Jail and Bronx County Jail Annex, combined, May 23, 1928, p. 197; Bronx County Jail and Bronx County Jail Annex, separately, Nov. 10, 1928, p. 200. **162**

CORRECTION *(continued)*

Source Number

COUNTY JAILS *(continued)*

68. Maximum and average day census, Jan. 1–Nov. 10, 1928; maximum day census, year ending June 30, 1928. Bronx County Jail and Bronx County Jail Annex, combined. p. 200–201. **162**

69. Prisoners by sex and age (adults; minors). Bronx County Jail Annex. Mar. 23, 1928. p. 198. **162**

70. Prisoners by sex and offense: material witnesses; alimony cases; judgment debtor cases. Kings County Jail. Oct. 27, 1928. p. 238. **162**

71. Maximum and minimum day census, by sex, Jan. 1–Oct. 27, 1928; maximum, minimum, and average day census, year ending June 30, 1928. Kings County Jail. p. 238. **162**

72. Prisoners by charge (alimony case; civil action), Nov. 3, 1928; maximum and minimum day census, Jan. 1–Nov. 3, 1928. Queens County Jail. p. 278. **162**

73. Prisoners by sex, age (under 21; 21 or over), and cause of detention: awaiting trial; awaiting grand jury; civil cases; serving time. Richmond County Jail. Nov. 24, 1928. p. 280. **162**

74. Prisoners by sex: maximum and minimum day census. Richmond County Jail. Jan. 1–Nov. 24, 1928. p. 280. **162**

75. Prisoners: (a) maximum day census by sex; (b) total number of prisoners 16–21 years of age, by age (each year) and sex. Richmond County Jail. Year ending June 30, 1928. p. 280. **162**

76. Discharges by sex. Each county. Year ending June 30, 1928. p. 548. **162**

77. Transfers to State Hospitals, by sex. Each county. Year ending June 30, 1928. p. 548. **162**

See also: *Courts* 31
Violence, Crimes of 3

CORRECTION *(continued)*

Source Number

STATE HOSPITALS FOR THE CRIMINALLY INSANE

78. Patients admitted by sex. Matteawan State Hospital. From each county. Year ending June 30, 1926. p. 273. **201**

79. Prisoners discharged by sex and disposition (to custody of New York County Sheriff; to New York County Penitentiary; to New York City Workhouse): (a) discharged recovered; (b) discharged because found not insane. Matteawan State Hospital. Year ending June 30, 1926. p. 285, 289. **201**

See also: *Mental disease* 5

STATE PENITENTIARIES

80. Prisoners committed from New York City to Westchester County Penitentiary (male prisoners only), by county in which convicted. Year ending June 30, 1928. p. 545. **162**

STATE PRISONS

81. Prisoners committed, by sex, and by county in which convicted. Each prison: Auburn; Clinton; Sing Sing. Year ending June 30, 1928. p. 516. **162**

82. Commitments to Sing Sing Prison. From each county. Year ending June 30, each year, 1922–1926. p. 21. **201**

83. Crimes committed by prisoners born in New York City compared with crimes committed by other prisoners, in a group of 5000 in Sing Sing prison: per cent distribution of each offense, according to birth place (New York City; United States, outside of New York City; foreign countries) and color of prisoners (white; black). [1928]. p. 35. **170**

84. Crimes committed by prisoners born in New York City compared with crimes committed by a group of other prisoners in Sing Sing prison: per cent distribution by offense of (a) 500 prisoners of English stock born in New York City, (b) 500 foreign-born prisoners of **170**

CORRECTION *(continued)*

Source Number

STATE PRISONS *(continued)*

84. *(continued)*
English stock, (c) 500 prisoners of English stock born in rural United States, (d) 500 prisoners of Negro stock born in New York City, (e) 500 foreign-born prisoners of Negro stock, (f) 500 prisoners of Negro stock born in rural United States. Sing Sing Prison. [1928]. p. 36.

85. Fifty inmates born and bred in New York City compared with 50 inmates born in other counties of New York State: (a) chronological age; (b) nativity; (c) religious creed; (d) institutional history; (e) marital condition; (f) loss of parents; (g) order of birth (oldest; youngest); (h) median mental age; (i) median weight; (j) occupation. Auburn Prison. 1920. p. 531–541, 544, 549. **319**

STATE REFORMATORIES

86. Prisoners committed from New York City, by sex and county in which convicted. Each institution: New York State Reformatory; Albion State Training School; New York State Reformatory for Women. Year ending June 30, 1928. p. 526. **162**

87. Prisoners committed to New York State Reformatory for Women, Bedford Hills, from each county. Year ending June 30, 1928. ***204**

See also: *Courts* 37
Prostitution 2

COST OF LIVING

1. Per cent of increase over Dec., 1914, in expenditure for: (a) food; (b) clothing; (c) rent; (d) fuel and light; (e) house furnishing goods; (f) miscellaneous. Specified months between Dec., 1915, and June, 1929. p. 23. **314** **Aug., 1929**

2. Per cent of change in cost of living from June, 1920, Dec., 1927, and June, 1928, to Dec., 1928. p. 179. **314** **Feb., 1929**

COST OF LIVING *(continued)*

Source Number

3. Average minimum cost (weekly; yearly) of maintaining a fair American standard of living for a family consisting of an industrial worker, his wife, and 2 children under 14: (a) total; (b) housing; (c) fuel; (d) food; (e) clothing; (f) sundries. Data collected Aug.–Oct., 1927. p. 51. **103**

4. Detailed cost of living for industrial workers and office workers, with and without families, for lodgings, fuel and light, food, clothing, sundries (transportation; recreation; etc.). Each borough. 1926. p. 73–127. **102**

5. Average weekly earnings of factory workers as compared with the cost of living, shown by index numbers. Dec., 1914–April, 1924. p. 11. Chart only. **91** **May 12, 1924**

6. Estimated average per cent of increase over July, 1914, in rents of wage earners' houses. Mar., July, Nov., each year, 1919–1925; Dec., 1925; Jan., 1926; Mar., 1926; each month, May, 1926–Dec., 1927. **104**

7. Average minimum cost per year for heat and light, by service required. Each borough. 1926. p. 43. **102**

8. Changes in cost for domestic use, of (a) gas and (b) electricity, shown by index numbers. July, 1914 (base); Nov., 1925; June, 1926; Jan., 1927; June, 1927. p. 123. **104**

9. Net price per kilowatt hour for electricity for household use. June and Dec., 1927 and 1928, and June, 1929. p. 215. **314** **Aug., 1929**

10. Net price per kilowatt hour for electricity for household use. Specified months between 1913 and 1926. p. 182. **314** **Aug., 1926**

11. Retail price of gas. Each year, 1913–1929. p. 211. **314** **Aug., 1929**

12. Average retail price of coal per ton, by kind of coal. Current month, corresponding month of preceding year, and preceding month of current year. **314**

13. Changes in retail price of coal in ton lots for domestic use, by kind of coal, shown by index numbers. July, 1914 (base); March, July, and Nov., each year, 1919–1927. p. 112–119. **104**

COST OF LIVING *(continued)*

Source Number

14. Average retail price of coal by kind of coal. Each month, 1926, 1927. p. 204. **311**

15. Average minimum cost of sundries (transportation, recreation, etc., itemized) for one week for a family consisting of an industrial worker, his wife, and two children under 14. Data collected Aug.–Oct., 1927. p. 48. **103**

See also: *Clothing, Cost of* (entire)
Food, Cost of (entire)
Rent (entire)

COUNTRY OF ORIGIN OF POPULATION

1. Foreign white stock, by country of origin, nativity, and parentage: foreign-born white (birthplace of father); native white of foreign or mixed parentage (both parents foreign; father foreign; mother foreign). Each borough. 1920. p. 941–942. **285**

2. Foreign white stock, by country of origin. Each borough. 1910, 1920. p. 926–929. **285**

3. Foreign white stock, by country of origin. Each borough. 1920. p. XXV. **51**
   NOTE: List of countries not the same as that in item 2.

4. White persons of foreign parentage classified by country of birth of parents. Each borough section, each borough. 1910. p. XXXIII. **51**

5. Foreign white stock by country of origin, according to pre-war map. 1910, 1920. p. XXVII. **51**

6. Foreign-born whites and native-born whites of foreign or mixed parentage, each by country of origin according to pre-war map, 1920; gain or loss, 1910–1920. p. XXIII. **51**

7. Foreign-born persons by color (white; colored) and "people" (Danish; Flemish; Serbian; etc.). 1920. p. XXVI. **51**

COUNTRY OF ORIGIN OF POPULATION *(continued)*

Source Number

8. Foreign-born white persons by sex and "people" (as in 7). 1920. p. xxvi. **51**

9. Native-born white persons of foreign parentage, by "people" (as in 7). 1920. p. xxvi. **51**

See also: *Language* 8

COURTS

NOTE: Courts have been listed from lowest to highest with divisions of City Magistrates' Courts in alphabetical order.

CITY MAGISTRATES' COURTS

Total and Miscellaneous Groups of Courts

1. Court summonses: (a) pending from preceding year; (b) issued during year, each court; (c) total during year, by action (answered; withdrawn; etc.). 1928. p. 5220–5221. ***118**

2. Court summonses: (a) pending from preceding year; (b) issued, each court, during year; (c) appeared, each court, during year; (d) total during year, by action (answered; withdrawn; etc.). 1927. p. 12, 49. ***117**

3. Warrants: (a) unexecuted from preceding year; (b) issued during year, each court; (c) total during year by action (executed; withdrawn; etc.). 1928. p. 5220–5221. ***118**

4. Warrants: (a) unexecuted from preceding year; (b) issued, during year, each court; (c) executed, during year, each court; (d) total, during year by action (executed; withdrawn; etc.). 1927. p. 12, 49. ***117**

5. Persons arraigned by sex, each process by which brought into court: arrest or no process; police summonses; warrants; court summonses; department summonses. 1928. p. 5221. ***118**

COURTS *(continued)*

Source Number

CITY MAGISTRATES' COURTS *(continued)*

Total and Miscellaneous Groups of Courts *(continued)*

6. Persons arraigned, all courts: (a) by sex, each process by which brought into court (arrest, or no process; police summonses; warrants; court summonses; departmental summonses), boroughs combined; (b) each process by which brought into court (as above), Manhattan and Bronx, Brooklyn, Queens, Richmond. 1927. p. 11, 52. ***117**

7. Persons arraigned, all courts, by sex: (a) by age (16–19; 20–24; 25–29; 30–39; 40–49; 50 and over); (b) by color; (c) native-born of native parents, by color; (d) native-born of foreign parents, by country of birth of parents; (e) foreign-born of foreign parents, by country of birth. 1928. p. 5224. ***118**

8. Persons arraigned, all courts, by sex: (a) by age (as in 7); (b) by color; (c) by nativity and parentage. Manhattan and Bronx; Brooklyn; Queens; Richmond. 1927. p. 91, 95, 99, 103. ***117**

9. Persons arraigned, by sex: (a) by age (as in 7); (b) by color; (c) by nativity and parentage. By court: Ninth (Women's) Court, Manhattan and Bronx; Family Court, Manhattan; Family Court, Bronx; Homicide Court, Manhattan; Homicide Court, Bronx; Chief Magistrate's Court, Manhattan; Women's Court, Brooklyn; Family Court, Brooklyn; Homicide and Traffic Court (Part 3), Brooklyn. 1927. p. 112, 114, 117, 123, 128–129, 132, 136, 141. ***117**

10. Corporations and companies arraigned, all courts. Manhattan and Bronx; Brooklyn; Queens; Richmond. 1927. p. 91, 95, 99, 103. ***117**

11. Arraignments by type of session: City Magistrates' Courts; Special Sessions held by magistrates. Each court. 1928. p. 5220. ***118**

COURTS *(continued)*

Source Number

CITY MAGISTRATES' COURTS *(continued)*

Total and Miscellaneous Groups of Courts *(continued)*

12. Arraignments in City Magistrates' Courts and Special Sessions held by magistrates, by sex of defendant and type of case (cases summarily disposed of; cases disposed of at Special Sessions held by magistrates; misdemeanors examined; felonies examined), each offense. Courts combined. 1928. p. 5221. ***118**

13. Arraignments in City Magistrates' Courts and Special Sessions held by magistrates, by type of case (cases summarily disposed of; cases disposed of at Special Sessions held by magistrates; misdemeanors examined; felonies examined), each offense. Courts combined. Each year, 1918–1927. p. 54–55. ***117**

14. Arraignments in City Magistrates' Courts and Special Sessions held by magistrates. Each Court. Each year, 1923–1927. p. 47. ***117**

15. Arraignments in City Magistrates' Courts and Special Sessions held by magistrates, by sex of defendant, for total cases and for each type of case (summary offenses, including misdemeanors tried at Special Sessions held by magistrates; misdemeanors transferred to be tried at Special Sessions held by magistrates; misdemeanors examined; felonies examined), each selected offense. Courts combined. Each year, 1918–1927. p. 56–63. ***117**

16. Arraignments in City Magistrates' Courts and Special Sessions held by magistrates and number held or convicted, by charge. Each year, 1900–1927. p. 509. ***244**

17. Pleadings in City Magistrates' Courts and Special Sessions held by magistrates, by sex of defendant, plea (guilty; not guilty or no plea), and type of case (cases summarily disposed of; cases disposed of at Special Sessions held by magistrates), each offense. 1928. p. 5222. ***117**

18. Action on first hearing in City Magistrates' Courts and Special Sessions held by magistrates, by sex of defendant, type of action (final disposition; adjournment), ***117**

COURTS *(continued)*

Source Number

CITY MAGISTRATES' COURTS *(continued)*

Total and Miscellaneous Groups of Courts *(continued)*

18. *(continued)*
and type of case (cases summarily disposed of; cases disposed of at Special Sessions held by magistrates; misdemeanors examined; felonies examined), each offense. Boroughs combined. 1928. p. 5221.

19. Action on first hearing in City Magistrates' Courts and Special Sessions held by magistrates, by type of action (final disposition; adjournment). By borough: Manhattan and Bronx; Brooklyn; Queens; Richmond. 1927. p. 52. *117

20. Cases held to appear and to answer in City Magistrates' Courts and Special Sessions held by magistrates, by sex of defendant, security (released on bail; transferred to Special Sessions held by magistrates; etc.), and disposition: held for summary disposition; held for disposition by magistrates at Special Sessions; etc. 1928. p. 5222. *117

21. Cases disposed of in City Magistrates' Courts and Special Sessions held by magistrates, by sex of defendant, general disposition (discharged; convicted or held; transferred to Special Sessions), and type of case (cases summarily disposed of; cases disposed of at Special Sessions held by magistrates; misdemeanors examined; felonies examined), each offense. 1928. p. 5223. *118

22. Cases disposed of in City Magistrates' Courts and Special Sessions held by magistrates, by sex of defendant, general disposition (discharged; convicted or held; transferred to Special Sessions), and type of case (cases summarily disposed of; cases disposed of at Special Sessions held by magistrates; misdemeanors examined; felonies examined), each offense. Courts combined, boroughs combined, p. 18–19; and courts combined, by borough, Manhattan and Bronx, Brooklyn, Queens, Richmond. p. 88–89, 92–93, 96–97, 100–101. 1927. *117

COURTS *(continued)*

Source Number

CITY MAGISTRATES' COURTS *(continued)*

Total and Miscellaneous Groups of Courts *(continued)*

23. Cases convicted or held in City Magistrates' Courts and Special Sessions held by magistrates, by sex of defendant, for total cases and for each type of case (summary offenses, including misdemeanors tried at Special Sessions held by magistrates; misdemeanors transferred to be tried at Special Sessions held by magistrates; misdemeanors examined; felonies examined), each selected offense. Courts combined. Each year, 1918–1927. p. 56–63. ***117**

24. Convictions in City Magistrates' Courts and Special Sessions held by magistrates, by sex of defendant, disposition (fined; New York City Workhouse; etc.), and type of case (cases summarily disposed of; cases disposed of at Special Sessions held by magistrates), each offense. Boroughs combined. 1928. p. 5223–5225. ***118**

25. Convictions in City Magistrates' Courts and Special Sessions held by magistrates, by sex of defendant, disposition (fined; New York City Workhouse; etc.), and type of case, each offense. By borough: Manhattan and Bronx; Brooklyn; Queens; Richmond. 1927. p. 90, 94, 98, 102. ***117**

26. Persons who were fingerprinted, by sex, number of times fingerprinted, and offense at latest conviction. 1927. p. 66. ***117**

27. Persons who were fingerprinted, by sex and offense at latest conviction. Each court. 1927. p. 67. ***117**

28. Cases fined in City Magistrates' Courts and Special Sessions held by magistrates, by result (fines paid, by amount; committed in default of payment; transferred for collection), and type of case (cases summarily disposed of; cases disposed of at Special Sessions held by magistrates), each offense. 1927. p. 22. ***117**

COURTS *(continued)*

Source Number

CITY MAGISTRATES' COURTS *(continued)*

Total and Miscellaneous Groups of Courts *(continued)*

29. Fines collected in City Magistrates' Courts and Special Sessions held by magistrates. Each court. Each year, 1923–1927. p. 48. *117

30. Fines collected in City Magistrates' Courts and Special Sessions held by magistrates, each offense. Courts combined. Each month, 1927. p. 50. *117

31. Fines collected after commitment, by City Magistrates' Courts and Special Sessions held by magistrates, by place of collection: City Magistrates' Courts, combined; Tombs Prison; District Prisons, combined; City Prison, Brooklyn; City Prison, Queens; Bronx County Jail; Richmond County Jail; New York City Workhouse or New York County Penitentiary. Each month, 1927. p. 51. *117

32. Workhouse sentences imposed by City Magistrates' Courts and Special Sessions held by magistrates, by type of sentence (fixed sentences, by length; indeterminate sentences) and type of case, each offiense. 1928. p. 5224. *118

33. Preliminary investigations of the Probation Department: (a) by result (placed on probation; sentence suspended; etc.), District Courts, combined, of Manhattan and Bronx, combined, and Ninth (Women's) Court, Manhattan; (b) by result (as above) and sex, District Courts, combined, by borough, Brooklyn, Queens, Richmond, and Women's Court, Brooklyn. 1927. p. 80–83. *117

34. Work of Probation Department: cases pending at beginning of year; cases received direct during the year, each offense; cases received by transfer; total cases under supervision in preceding year; increase in moneys collected for family support over such moneys collected during preceding year. Courts combined. 1927. p. 74. *117

COURTS *(continued)*

Source Number

CITY MAGISTRATES' COURTS *(continued)*

Total and Miscellaneous Groups of Courts *(continued)*

35. Work of Probation Department: probation officers, by sex; cases pending at beginning of year, by sex of officers; cases received during year, by sex of officers; cases finished, by sex of probationers and result (discharged with improvement; revoked and committed; etc.); home visits, by sex of officers; investigations, by sex of officers; moneys collected for family support. District Courts, combined, each borough; each Family Court; each Women's Court. 1927. p. 74–83. ***117**

36. Cases placed on probation during the year, by sex of probationer; average number of probation cases under supervision during the year; number of home visits. Courts combined. Year ending June 30, 1927. p. 34, 42. **161**

37. Cases committed to reformatory institutions, by City Magistrates' Courts and Special Sessions held by magistrates, by type of case (cases summarily disposed of; cases disposed of at Special Sessions held by magistrates), each offense. Each institution. Courts combined, by borough: Manhattan and Bronx; Brooklyn; Queens; Richmond. Women's Court, by borough: Manhattan and Bronx; Brooklyn. 1927. p. 26, 91, 95, 99, 103, 112, 131. ***117**

38. Cases pending at end of year, in City Magistrates' Courts and Special Sessions held by magistrates, by sex of defendant and type of case (cases summarily disposed of; cases disposed of at Special Sessions held by magistrates; misdemeanors examined; felonies examined), each offense. Manhattan and Bronx; Brooklyn; Queens; Richmond. 1927. p. 88–89, 92–93, 96–97, 100–101. ***117**

See also: *Correction* 26
Courts 101–104
Delinquents, Juvenile 8

COURTS *(continued)*

Source Number

CITY MAGISTRATES' COURTS *(continued)*

Total and Miscellaneous Groups of Courts *(continued)*

See also: *(continued)*
Drunkenness 4
Education 14, 15, 18
Traffic regulations, Violation of 7
Truants 3
Venereal disease 7

Chief Magistrate's Court

39. Arraignments by sex of defendant, each offense. 1927. p. 128. ***117**

40. Cases disposed of, by sex of defendant and disposition (convicted; discharged), each offense. 1927. p. 129. ***117**

41. Convictions, by disposition (City Prison; hospital; straight sentence; New York City Workhouse), each offense. 1927. p. 129. ***117**

See also: *Courts* 1–4, 9, 29

District Courts

42. Prisoners in District Court Pens: (a) number on a date between July 1 and Dec. 31, 1928, or (b) average daily number of prisoners in custody, estimated on a date between July 1 and Dec. 31, 1928, or (c) maximum daily number and minimum daily number, estimated on a date between July 1 and Dec. 31, 1928. Each specified pen. p. 131, 133–135, 139–140, 142–144, 147. **162**

43. Cases heard. Each specified court. For a period from Jan. 1 to a date after July 1, 1928. p. 131–134, 139–144, 146–148. **162**

44. Cases disposed of, by sex of defendant, general disposition (discharged; convicted or held; transferred to Special Sessions held by magistrates) and type of case: cases ***117**

COURTS (*continued*)

Source Number

CITY MAGISTRATES' COURTS (*continued*)

District Courts (*continued*)

44. (*continued*) summarily disposed of; cases disposed of at Special Sessions held by magistrates; misdemeanors examined; felonies examined. Each District Court. 1927. p. 104–110.

See also: *Adolescent offenders* (entire)
Courts 1–4, 27, 29, 33, 35
Traffic regulations, Violation of 9

Family Courts

45. Average day census of male prisoners in custody. Pens of Family Court, Brooklyn. Estimated Sept. 26, 1928. p. 138. **162**

46. Cases heard: (a) new cases; (b) rehearings. Family Court, Manhattan. Period Jan. 1–June 30, 1928, p. 133. **162**

47. Cases heard. Family Court, Brooklyn. Jan. 1–Sept. 26, 1928. p. 138. **162**

48. Arraignments by sex of defendant and type of case (arraignments before magistrates as such; arraignments at Special Sessions held by magistrates), each offense. Family Court, Brooklyn, and Special Sessions held by magistrates. 1927. p. 134. ***117**

49. Arraignments and adjusted applications, by sex of defendant and process (arraignments; applications adjusted by agreement), each offense. By court: Family Court, Manhattan; Family Court, Bronx. 1927. p. 113, 115. ***117**

50. Applications adjusted by reconciliations or otherwise, or pending. Family Court, Manhattan. 1927. p. 112. ***117**

51. Recurrent cases (or rearraignments). By court: Family Court, Manhattan; Family Court, Bronx. 1927. p. 113, 115. ***117**

COURTS *(continued)*

Source Number

CITY MAGISTRATES' COURTS *(continued)*

Family Courts *(continued)*

52. Cases disposed of, by sex of defendant and general disposition (convicted; dismissed; transferred), each offense. Each court: Family Court, Manhattan; Family Court, Bronx; Family Court, Brooklyn, and Special Sessions held by magistrates, combined. 1927. p. 113, 115, 135. ***117**

53. Convictions by sex of defendant and disposition (probation; released on bond to support; etc.), each offense. Each court: Family Court, Manhattan; Family Court, Bronx; Family Court, Brooklyn, and Special Sessions held by magistrates, combined. 1927. p. 113, 116, 135. ***117**

See also: *Courts* 1–4, 9, 29, 35

Homicide and Traffic Court (Part 3), Brooklyn

54. Cases heard (homicide; other). Period Jan. 1–July 20, 1928. p. 137. **162**

55. Arraignments in Court and in Special Sessions held by magistrates, by sex of defendant and type of case (arraignments before magistrates as such, (a) summary offenses, (b) misdemeanors, (c) felonies; arraignments at Special Sessions held by magistrates), each offense. 1927. p. 138. ***117**

56. Cases disposed of in Court and in Special Sessions held by magistrates, by sex of defendant, and general disposition (discharged; convicted or held), each type of case (cases summarily disposed of; cases disposed of at Special Sessions held by magistrates; misdemeanors examined; felonies examined), each offense. 1927. p. 139. ***117**

57. Cases held to answer by sex of defendant and security (bailed; bail not given; without bail), each offense. 1927. p. 140. ***117**

COURTS *(continued)*

Source Number

CITY MAGISTRATES' COURTS *(continued)*

Homicide and Traffic Court (Part 3), Brooklyn *(continued)*

58. Convictions, each type of case (cases summarily disposed of; cases disposed of at Special Sessions held by magistrates), by disposition (fined; New York City Workhouse; etc.), each offense. 1927. p. 140. *117

See also: *Courts* 1–4, 9, 29
Traffic regulations, Violation of 9

Homicide Courts

See: *Courts* 1–4, 29
Homicide 2, 3

Municipal Term Courts

59. Persons arraigned by sex and Department of City, each offense. By borough: Manhattan; Bronx; Brooklyn. 1927. p. 118, 124, 133. *117

60. Arraignments by sex of defendant and type: persons arraigned; cases transferred, and arraignments at Special Sessions held by magistrates. By borough: Manhattan; Bronx; Brooklyn. 1927. p. 117, 123, 132. *117

61. Cases disposed of in Municipal Term Courts and Special Sessions held by magistrates, by sex of defendant and disposition: discharged; fined; etc. By borough: Manhattan; Bronx; Brooklyn. 1927. p. 118, 124, 133. *117

62. Cases fined in Municipal Term Courts and Special Sessions held by magistrates, by result (fines paid, by amount; committed; transferred for collection), each City Department against which offenses were committed: Building; Education; etc. By borough: Manhattan; Bronx; Brooklyn. 1927. p. 119, 125, 134. *117

See also: *Courts* 1–4, 29

COURTS *(continued)*

Source Number

CITY MAGISTRATES' COURTS *(continued)*

Probation Courts

63. Arraignments, by disposition: honorably discharged; probation revoked; etc. Each court: Manhattan and Bronx; Brooklyn. 1927. p. 84. ***117**

64. Warrants issued, by disposition: revoked and committed; probation continued; etc. Each court: Manhattan and Bronx; Brooklyn. 1927. p. 84. ***117**

Traffic Courts

See: *Courts* 1–4, 29
Traffic regulations, Violation of 2–6, 8, 9

Women's Courts

65. Women in custody: (a) number, Sept. 28, 1928; (b) maximum day census, estimated Sept. 28, 1928. Women's Day Court Pens, Manhattan. p. 130. **162**

66. Women in custody: (a) number, Oct. 10, 1928; (b) average day census, estimated Oct. 10, 1928. Women's Day Court Pens, Brooklyn. p. 138. **162**

67. Arraignments, each offense. Ninth (Women's) Court, Manhattan and Bronx. 1927. p. 111. ***117**

68. Arraignments, each offense. Ninth (Women's) Court, Manhattan and Bronx. Each year, 1920–1927, p. 32. Each month, 1927, p. 35. Total, offenses combined, Jan. 1–Apr. 15, each year, 1920–1928, p. 34. ***54**

69. Arraignments: (a) total, Jan. 1–Sept. 28, 1928, and corresponding period, 1927; (b) each offense, 1927; (c) per cent comparison of 1927 with 1926 as regards prostitution cases, and wayward minor cases. Women's Day Court, Manhattan and Bronx. p. 130. **162**

70. Arraignments by time of sessions (day; night), each offense. Women's Court, Brooklyn. 1927. p. 130. ***117**

COURTS *(continued)*

Source Number

CITY MAGISTRATES' COURTS *(continued)*

Women's Courts *(continued)*

71. Cases heard: (a) period Jan. 1–Oct. 10, 1928; (b) cases tried, by offense, 1927. Women's Day Court, Brooklyn. p. 138. **162**

72. Persons arraigned, by type of residence: hotels; furnished room houses; tenements. Ninth (Women's) Court, Manhattan and Bronx. 1927. p. 41. ***54**

73. Jewish women arraigned: (a) by offense, 1928; (b) per cent which Jewish women arraigned for prostitution were of all women arraigned for prostitution, 1927, 1928; (c) Jewish women convicted or pleading guilty, 1928. Ninth (Women's) Court, Manhattan and Bronx. p. 34–35. **80**

74. Cases disposed of, by general disposition (discharged; convicted or held), each offense. Ninth (Women's) Court, Manhattan and Bronx. 1927. p. 111. ***117**

75. Lapse of time in weeks, between arrest and final disposition of first 100 cases arraigned during the year. Ninth (Women's) Court, Manhattan and Bronx. 1920. p. 372. **343**

76. Disposition of first 100 cases arraigned during year: (a) by type of disposition (defaulted; probation; etc.) and number of adjournments preceding final disposition; (b) by disposition (as above) and number of days between arrest and disposition; (c) for 78 women by number of adjournments and number of days between arrest and final disposition. Ninth (Women's) Court, Manhattan and Bronx. 1920. p. 498–500. **344**

77. Cases disposed of by general disposition (discharged; convicted or held), each offense. Women's Court, Brooklyn. 1927. p. 130. ***117**

COURTS *(continued)*

Source Number

CITY MAGISTRATES' COURTS *(continued)*

Women's Courts *(continued)*

78. Cases held to answer for misdemeanors, by security: released on bail; paroled; etc. Ninth (Women's) Court, Manhattan and Bronx. 1927. p. 111. ***117**

79. Cases held to answer, by security (released on bail; committed in default of bail), each offense. Women's Court, Brooklyn. 1927. p. 131. ***117**

80. Cases in which bail was taken and received, by purpose for which given (station house, for appearance; for examination; to answer; good behavior), each group of offenses: felonies; misdemeanors; summary offenses. Women's Night Bail Court, Brooklyn. 1927. p. 132. ***117**

81. Convictions by disposition (New York City Workhouse; reformatory institutions; etc.), each offense. Ninth (Women's) Court, Manhattan and Bronx. 1927. p. 111. ***117**

82. Convictions by disposition (fined; New York City Workhouse; etc.), each offense. Women's Court, Brooklyn. 1927. p. 131. ***117**

83. Jewish women on probation: (a) placed on probation during year, by nativity and by age (under 21, 21 and over); (b) continued on probation from preceding year; (c) received on probation from other district courts; (d) number discharged with improvement. Ninth (Women's) Court, Manhattan and Bronx. 1928. p. 34–35. **80**

See also: *Adolescent offenders* (entire)
Courts 1–4, 9, 27, 29, 33, 35, 37, 130
Prostitution (entire)
Sex offenses (entire)
Venereal diseases 8, 10
Wayward minors (entire)

COURTS *(continued)*

Source Number

CITY MAGISTRATES SITTING AS JUSTICES OF THE COURT OF SPECIAL SESSIONS

84. Cases before City Magistrates sitting as Justices of the Court of Special Sessions: (a) pending at beginning of year; (b) received during year; (c) disposed of during year, by disposition (pleas of guilty; convicted by trial; etc.); (d) actions pending at end of year. Each misdemeanor. Each county. 1928. p. 58–62, 64, 66–68. **122**

85. Convictions by disposition: sentence suspended; fine only; etc. Each county. 1928. p. 59, 61, 63, 65, 67, 69. **122**

86. Amount of fines, (a) imposed by Court, (b) paid to Clerk of Court. Each county. 1928. p. 59, 61, 63, 65, 67, 69. **122**

COURT OF SPECIAL SESSIONS

87. Warrants in criminal proceedings: (a) pending unexecuted at beginning of year; (b) issued during year; (c) executed during year; (d) pending unexecuted at end of year. Each county. 1928. p. 23–33. **122**

88. Prisoners by sex. Court of Special Sessions Pen, Manhattan. Dec. 14, 1928. p. 128. **162**

89. Prisoners: (a) by sex, period Jan. 1–Nov. 2, 1928; (b) by sex, Nov. 2, 1928; (c) average and maximum day census, estimated Nov. 2, 1928. Court of Special Sessions Detention Pens, Brooklyn. p. 136. **162**

90. Average daily number of male prisoners. Court of Special Sessions Pens, Bronx. Estimated Nov. 10, 1928. p. 143. **162**

91. Criminal actions for trial, by sex of defendant: (a) actions pending trial at beginning of year; (b) actions received during the year; (c) bond forfeitures restored during the year; (d) cases discharged on own recognizance which were restored during the year; (e) new trials ordered during the year. Each misdemeanor. Each county. 1928. p. 23–33. **122**

COURTS *(continued)*

Source Number

COURT OF SPECIAL SESSIONS *(continued)*

92. Criminal actions received during year, each misdemeanor: (a) sexes combined, each year, 1912–1924; and (b) by sex of defendant, each year, 1925–1928. p. 21. **122**

93. Criminal actions for trial disposed of, by sex of defendant and disposition: convicted, by plea of guilt; convicted by trial; etc. Each misdemeanor. Each county. 1928. p. 23–33. **122**

94. Cases tried. Court of Special Sessions, Brooklyn. Jan. 1–Nov. 2, 1928. p. 136. **162**

95. Cases tried. Court of Special Sessions, Queens. Period Jan. 1–Oct. 12, 1928. p. 146. **162**

96. Convictions pending sentence at beginning of year and convictions pending sentence at end of year, by sex of defendant, each misdemeanor. Each county. 1928. p. 23–33. **122**

97. Criminal cases sentenced, by sex of defendant and type of sentence (suspended sentence revoked; workhouse, city prison, or county jail, by length of sentence; etc.), each misdemeanor. Each county. 1928. p. 23–33. **122**

98. Amount of fines: (a) imposed; (b) paid. Each county. 1928. p. 23–33. **122**

99. Per cent distribution of criminal proceedings according to length of time between receipt of cases by Court and disposition by Court, by type of case (bail cases; prison cases). 1927, 1928. p. 14–15. **122**

100. Criminal actions for trial pending, at end of year, by sex of defendant, each misdemeanor. Each county. 1928. p. 23–33. **122**

101. Appeals taken during year to the Appellate Part of the Court of Special Sessions from decisions of the City Magistrates' Courts, by disposition (affirmed or modified; reversed; etc.), each offense. Manhattan and Bronx, combined; Brooklyn, Queens, Richmond, combined. 1927. p. 53. ***117**

COURTS *(continued)*

Source Number

COURT OF SPECIAL SESSIONS *(continued)*

102. Cases appealed to the Appellate Part of the Court of Special Sessions from decisions of the City Magistrates' Courts, by sex: (a) pending decision at beginning of year; (b) appeals filed during the year; (c) total cases on hand during the year, by disposition (affirmed; modified; etc.). Each offense. First Judicial Department (Manhattan and Bronx, combined); Second Judicial Department (Brooklyn, Queens, Richmond, combined). 1928. p. 35–37. **122**

103. Cases before the Appellate Part of the Court of Special Sessions, appealed from judgments of the City Magistrates' Courts: (a) on hand during the year, by disposition (affirmed; modified; etc.); (b) appeals argued and pending decision at end of year. 1927, 1928. p. 15. **122**

104. Certificates of reasonable doubt in cases appealed to the Appellate Part of the Court of Special Sessions from judgments of the City Magistrates' Courts, by sex of appellant and disposition (allowed; denied), each offense. Manhattan and Bronx, combined; Brooklyn, Queens, Richmond, combined. 1928. p. 35–37. **122**

    NOTE: Item 101 appears to cover practically the same group of data as items 102–104, but the statistics found in the two reports concerned do not agree.

105. Cases in Probation Department by sex of probationer: (a) investigations pending at beginning of year; (b) investigations ordered during year; (c) investigations completed during year, by disposition (sentence suspended, placed on probation; transferred to Children's Court; etc.); (d) investigations pending at end of year; (e) probation cases at beginning of year; (f) new cases admitted to probation during year; (g) cases restored to probation during year; (h) cases terminated during year, by cause (sentence after probation; discharged; etc.); (i) probation cases pending at end of year. Each offense. Each county. 1928. p. 45–55. **122**

COURTS *(continued)*

Source Number

COURT OF SPECIAL SESSIONS *(continued)*

106. Cases in Probation Department: (a) cases placed on probation during year, by age and sex of probationer; (b) by sex and color; (c) by sex and country of birth; (d) cases terminated during year by sex of probationer and duration; (e) funds collected, by purpose (restitution; paternity, New York City Department of Public Welfare; etc.). Each county. 1928. p. 45–55. **122**

107. Cases in Probation Department: (a) number received during year, by sex; (b) average number of probation cases under supervision during the year; (c) average number of home visits. Each county. Year ending June 30, 1927. p. 34, 42. **161**

108. Applications submitted by the Parole Commission, for release on parole of inmates of the New York County Penitentiary committed to the penitentiary for indeterminate sentence, by length of imprisonment before application for release on parole, and by action taken by the committing justices (approved; disapproved), each offense, 1928, p. 39; and the same, but with offenses combined, 1927, p. 14. **122**

See also: *Adolescent offenders* (entire)
Correction 26
Illegitimacy 4

CHILDREN'S COURT

109. Cases in Children's Court, by sex of child and type of case (delinquent children; neglected children; material witnesses; others): (a) pending at beginning of year; (b) new cases during year; (c) cases disposed of during year; (d) cases pending at end of year. 1928. p. 11. **116**

110. New cases by type of case (as in 109): (a) by sex of child and allegation, p. 12; (b) by petitioner (attendance officer; citizen; etc.) and sex of child, p. 12; (c) by type of arraignment (single; group of two; **116**

COURTS *(continued)*

Source Number

CHILDREN'S COURT *(continued)*

110. *(continued)*
group of three or more), each allegation, p. 16; (d) total, by sex of child, each county, p. 23; (e) by sex and number of times previously brought into court, p. 18; (f) by sex and age (2 years and under, and each year 3–15), p. 18; (g) by country of birth, each allegation, p. 20–21; (h) by country of birth of parents, each allegation, p. 21–22; (i) by color, p. 22. 1928.

111. Number of hearings: new cases; continued cases. Each month, 1928. p. 16. **116**

112. Jewish children before the Court. Manhattan and Bronx. Each year, 1921–1928. p. 45. **80**

113. Children brought before the Court, by cause (juvenile delinquency; special proceedings), and sex. Each year, 1916–1924. p. 28. **88**

114. Per cent distribution of boys brought to court, by home conditions: normal home, parents together; one parent dead; etc. Each year, 1921–1924. p. 9. **169**

115. Petitions by type of case (juvenile delinquency; neglected children; material witnesses; others) and disposition (petitions not taken; petitions dismissed; etc.), each allegation. 1928. p. 13, 15. **116**

116. Orders to parents to pay for the support of children committed to institutions, by amount per week. 1928. p. 19. **116**

117. Cases disposed of during year, by sex of child and type of case: delinquency; dependency or neglect. 1927. p. 29. ***298**

118. Cases investigated by Probation Department: (a) by disposition (placed on probation or supervision; paroled pending disposition; etc.) and sex of child, each county; (b) by sex of child and parental conditions (parents living together; father dead; etc.); (c) by type of case (juvenile delinquency; neglected children), number of children in family, and amount of **116**

COURTS *(continued)*

Source Number

CHILDREN'S COURT *(continued)*

118. *(continued)* family income; (d) by school attendance (regular classes, distributed by age and grade; holding working papers, employed; etc.). 1928. p. 29–32.

119. Cases on probation by sex of child: (a) cases handled during year (received from preceding year; received during year); (b) cases passing from supervision during year, by result (discharged with improvement; committed; etc.); (c) cases passing from supervision during year, by duration of probation; (d) cases on probation at end of year. Each county. 1928. p. 29–30. **116**
NOTE: Additional information by counties available at office of Chief Probation Officer of Children's Court. 1928. p. 32.

120. Cases placed on probation: (a) number during year by sex of child; (b) average number of probation cases under supervision during year; (c) number of home visits. Each county. Year ending June 30, 1927. p. 35, 44. **161**

121. Commitments by sex of child, each institution. 1928. p. 17. **116**

122. Cases in mental clinic of Children's Court: (a) by sex of child and place of examination (Brooklyn Court; Manhattan Court; Postgraduate Hospital); (b) each borough; (c) by nativity; (d) by color for native children of native parents; (e) by country of origin of native children of foreign parents; (f) by country of birth of foreign-born; (g) by race (Latin; Semitic; etc.); (h) by characteristics of family history (alcoholism; immorality; etc.); (i) by school attendance (as in 118) and age; (j) by age; (k) by mental age; (l) by intelligence quotient; (m) by allegation; (n) by allegation and clinical classification (normal; retarded; etc.); (o) by physical defects (defects found; defects not found; cases not examined); (p) by recommendation (probation; institution, by type; etc.); (q) by disposition (probation; institution, by type; etc.). 1928. p. 37–44. **116**

COURTS *(continued)*

Source Number

CHILDREN'S COURT *(continued)*

123. Cases examined in psychiatric clinic of Children's Court: (a) number found to have psychopathic personality; (b) number found to be constitutionally psychopathic inferiors; (c) number found to be emotionally unstable. Each year, 1920–1924. p. 13–14. **203**

See also: *Deliquents, Juvenile* 3–8
Education 16–18
Negroes 7
Truants 3

COUNTY COURTS

124. Prisoners in County Court Pens: average day census of male prisoners. Bronx County Court. Estimated Nov. 10, 1928. p. 143. **162**

125. Prisoners in County Court Pens: (a) average day census and maximum day census of male prisoners; (b) average weekly census of female prisoners. Kings County Court. Estimated Sept. 26, 1928. p. 135. **162**

126. Indictments in Court of General Sessions: (a) by disposition (convicted on plea or trial; acquitted; etc.), 1927; (b) ratio to indictments in the other county courts of New York City, period 1925–1927. p. 31. **153**

127. Probation cases investigated during the year: (a) by offense; (b) by age; (c) by religion; (d) by previous court record. Court of General Sessions. Current month. **154**

128. Cases placed on probation, by sex of probationer. Court of General Sessions, New York County. Year ended June 30, 1927. p. 35. **161**

129. Persons examined for probation by Catholic Charities Probation Bureau: (a) by sex; (b) per cent distribution by type of offense (crimes of acquisitiveness and violation of property rights; offenses against public order; offenses of pugnacity; crimes against sex); **268**

COURTS *(continued)*

Source Number

COUNTY COURTS *(continued)*

129. *(continued)*
(c) per cent distribution of cases charged with felonies, by age; (d) per cent distribution by number of arraignments and sex; (e) per cent who came from broken homes (cared for in orphanage or similar institution; cared for by remaining parent); (f) cases distributed by number of years of school attendance; (g) by characteristics of school work (normal; truant; backward); (h) by religious observances (regular; irregular or none); (i) by employment (employed [skilled; unskilled]; unemployed); (j) by marital status and number of children; (k) per cent of cases examined which were known to the Social Service Exchange of New York City; (l) per cent which were placed on probation; (m) estimated per cent of probationers who will be permanently adjusted. Court of General Sessions, New York County. Period Jan. 1, 1925–Sept. 1, 1926. p. 15, 34–37, 68.

130. Cases appealed before the Court of General Sessions from the Ninth (Women's) Court, Manhattan and Bronx: (a) by disposition (dismissed; affirmed; reversed), each offense; (b) by disposition in Court of General Sessions (as above) and disposition in Women's Court (probation; New York City Workhouse). Period Jan. 1–June 30, 1920. p. 496. **344**

See also: *Adolescent offenders* (entire)
Correction 26
Felonies 3, 7–10, 13, 14, 16–18
Homicide 4

COUNTY COURT AND SUPREME COURT OF THE STATE OF NEW YORK

131. Cases placed on probation: (a) number during year, by sex of probationer; (b) average number of cases under supervision during year; (c) number of home visits. County Court and State Supreme Court, combined. Bronx; Kings; Queens; Richmond. Year ending June 30, 1927. p. 35–36. **161**

COURTS *(continued)*

Source Number

SUPREME COURT OF THE STATE OF NEW YORK

See: *Correction* 26
Divorce 2–10
Guardians (entire)
Mental disease 4

COURTS OF RECORD

132. Convictions in Courts of Record: (a) by sex of defendant; (b) by type (convicted on trial; convicted on confession); (c) number of sentences suspended; (d) number of prisoners placed on probation; (e) convictions by number of times convicted (previously convicted; first conviction). Each county. Each year ending Oct. 31, 1924–1927. p. 29–30, 34–35. ***165**

CRIPPLES

1. Cripples, estimated. Each borough. 1920. p. 40. **219**

2. Survey of cripples in 6 typical districts: (a) cripples found, by place of treatment (or not treated) and age groups (under 15; 16–45; over 45), for Manhattan and Bronx district, and for Brooklyn district; (b) cripples by age groups and cause; (c) cripples by age (5-year groups) and sex; (d) age at onset; (e) education; (f) degree of support by sex; (g) public school classes. Period Nov., 1919–Mar., 1920. p. 41–63. **219**

3. Educational facilities for crippled children in 9 cities in New York State, including New York City: (a) place of instruction (home; school; hospital; etc.) by number of classes and pupils; (b) management of classes (Board of Education; private; county); (c) status of teachers; (d) curriculum; (e) transportation; (f) source of orthopedic and medical provision. 1925. p. 16–17. **214**

4. Beds for orthopedic cases in hospitals. Each hospital. Each borough. [1920]. p. 87. **219**

CRIPPLES *(continued)*

Source Number

See also: *Clinics* 1
Education 44, 45
Family service 2

DANCE HALLS

1. Dance halls in Manhattan: estimated attendance and average admission charges by type of dance place (restaurant; dance palace; closed hall, etc.). Winter 1923/24. p. 5, 7. **337**

See also: *Licenses* (entire)

DAYLIGHT SAVING

1. Result of a poll taken of representative workers in New York City as to their sentiments toward daylight saving time: (a) number of employees voting; (b) result of vote. Each organization, by type of business. Jan., 1921. p. 7. **91 Feb. 14, 1921**

DAY NURSERIES

1. Number of nurseries under permit from the Board of Health. 1928. p. 39. **131**
2. Day nurseries (49) belonging to the Association of Day Nurseries, New York City: days open; aggregate attendance; aggregate attendance by age (under 9 months; 9 months to 6 years; school children); average daily attendance; number of families represented; reason child is placed in nursery (child of widow or widower; parents both working; etc.); cost of maintenance. Each nursery. 1928. Statistical sheet. **7**
3. Number of children in nursery, by sex, Feb. 1, 1923; number received, by sex, Feb. 1 to Apr. 30, 1923; type of supervision of nursery, 1923; color or race of children accepted, 1923; age range of children admitted, 1923. Each nursery. Each borough. p. 221–224. **281**
4. Roman Catholic day nurseries: (a) capacity; (b) number of children cared for; (c) age range of children; (d) staff (religious; lay). Each day nursery. Manhattan; Bronx. 1928. p. 34. ***40**

See also: *Settlements* 4

DEAF PERSONS

Source Number

1. City day schools for the deaf, combined, and State schools for the deaf in New York City, each school: (a) instructors by sex; (b) pupils enrolled by sex and grade; (c) pupils graduated at end of year; (d) pupils enrolled by method by which taught (auricular; oral). 1926/27. p. 9, 15. **302**

See also: *Education, Public* 34, 44, 45

DEATHS AND DEATH RATE

PRIVATE SOURCES

1. Deaths from selected causes, each cause: diphtheria and croup; pulmonary tuberculosis; non-pulmonary tuberculosis; pneumonia; bronchitis; diarrhea, under 5 years; cancer; kidney diseases; heart disease; violence; puerperal diseases; typhoid fever. Each year, 1910–1927. p. 507. ***244**

2. Population, deaths and death rate, by standard age groups (under 5; 5–9; 10–14; 15–19; 20–24; 25–34; 35–44; etc., to 75 and over) and sex, for (a) New York City Jews, 1925, estimated, and (b) United States, 1923 (registration area of 1920, whites). p. 12–18, 22. **25**

3. Deaths and death rate of New York City Jews from causes on the "Abridged International List of Causes of Death." 1925. p. 34–35. **25**
   NOTE: See list, Appendix 1.

4. Deaths and death rate from major causes of death (tuberculosis, all forms; diseases of the heart; cancer; diabetes; nephritis; cerebral hemorrhage and softening of the brain; pneumonia, all forms), by standard age groups (see 2 above) for (a) New York City Jews (1925) and (b) United States (1923). Separate tables and chart for each disease. p. 25–33. **25**

5. Per cent of deaths from each of the major causes of death (see 4 above) by standard age groups (see 2 above) for (a) New York City Jews (1925) and (b) New York City non-Jewish whites (1925). p. 36–44. **25**

DEATHS AND DEATH RATE *(continued)*

Source Number

PRIVATE SOURCES *(continued)*

6. Deaths and death rate from principal causes of death in adult life (15–44 years) for (a) New York City Jews (1925) and (b) United States (1923), by sex and by disease: diseases of the heart; tuberculosis of the respiratory system; cancer and other malignant tumors; violent deaths (except suicide); lobar pneumonia; puerperal state; suicide; acute and chronic nephritis; appendicitis and typhlitis; bronchopneumonia; other epidemic and endemic diseases; influenza; diseases of the stomach (except cancer); non-cancerous tumors and other diseases of the female genital organs; hernia and intestinal obstruction; diabetes. Opposite p. 24. **25**
7. Crude death rate for principal diseases (diseases of the heart; cancer; pneumonia, all forms; nephritis; tuberculosis, all forms; diabetes; suicide; cerebral hemorrhage; puerperal state; venereal diseases), for (a) New York City Jews and (b) United States. [1925]. p. 20. **25**
8. Seasonal variations in mortality (1 year and over). Each month, 1920–1923, combined. p. 8. **95 May, 1924**

PUBLIC SOURCES

New York City

9. Deaths and death rate. Each week, last 13 weeks, and average for corresponding weeks of preceding 6-year period. Published weekly. **136**
10. Deaths and annual death rate. Each week, 1928. p. 142–143. **131**
11. Deaths and death rate: (a) each year, 1898–1928; (b) each borough, 1928. p. 133–134. **131**
12. Deaths and death rate. Each year, 1868–1928. p. 170. Chart only. **131**
13. Deaths, death rate, corrected death rate. Each borough. Current monthly through Dec., 1927. **133**

DEATHS AND DEATH RATE *(continued)*

Source Number

PUBLIC SOURCES *(continued)*

New York City *(continued)*

14. Crude, standardized, and corrected death rates. Each borough. 1910, 1920, 1926. p. 139. **136** **Aug. 20, 1927**

15. Deaths by sex: (a) each borough; (b) each month. 1928. p. 136–137. **131**

16. Deaths which occurred in borough, and death rate; deaths distributed to borough residence, and death rate. Each borough. 1928. p. 134. **131**

17. Deaths of non-residents: (a) each borough; (b) each month. 1928. p. 136–137. **131**

18. Deaths by location (dwellings; hotels, etc.; institutions; tenements; other). Each month, 1928. p. 137. **131**

19. Deaths by place of death: institutions (total; each selected institution); tenements; dwellings; hotels; other places. Each borough. 1928. p. 134, 154. **131**

20. Deaths of non-residents by place of death: hotels; institutions; tenements; dwellings; other places. 1928. p. 141. **131**

21. Deaths: (a) by country of birth of deceased; (b) by country of birth of parents of deceased. 1928. p. 156. **131**

22. Deaths by age: under 1 year; 1; 2; 3; 4; 5-year groups to 85 and over. Each borough. 1928. p. 3. **135**

23. Deaths by age: under 1; under 5; 5 to 65; 65 and over. Last 13 weeks. Published weekly. **136**

24. Deaths by age: under 1; under 5; 5 to 65; 65 and over. Each borough. Current week. **136**

25. Deaths by age: under 1; 1–2; under 5; 5–15; 15–25; 25–45; 45–65; 65 and over. Each borough. Current quarter year. **136**

DEATHS AND DEATH RATE *(continued)*

Source Number

PUBLIC SOURCES *(continued)*

New York City *(continued)*

26. Deaths by age: under 1 year (and death rate); under 5 years; 5 to 65 years; 65 years and over. Each week, 1928. p. 142–143. **131**

27. Deaths by age (under 1 year; 1–2 years; under 5 years; 65 years and over; total): (a) each borough; (b) each month. 1928. p. 136–137. **131**

28. Deaths by age: under 1; 1 to 2; under 5; 5 to 15; 15 to 25; 25 to 45; 45 to 65; 65 and over. Each borough. Current monthly through Dec., 1927. **133**

29. Death rate: (a) total population, each year, 1868–1923; (b) children under 5, each year, 1877–1923; (c) children under 1, each year, 1901–1923. p. 27–29. Charts only. **133 Feb., 1924**

30. Deaths and death rate of children under 5 years of age. Each year, 1910–1928. p. 159. **131**

31. Deaths of children under 5 years of age. Each ward, each borough. Current monthly through Dec., 1924. **133**

32. Population, deaths and death rate, of children under 5 years: (a) per year; (b) for June, July, and August, combined. Manhattan and Bronx. Each year, 1891–1924. **134**

33. Deaths of non-residents by age: under 1; 1–4; 5–14; 15–24; 25–44; 45–64; 65 and over. 1928. p. 141. **131**

34. Deaths by sex: (a) by color (white; negro; other); (b) by parentage (native; foreign; mixed; unknown); (c) by marital condition. 1928. p. 135. **131**

35. Deaths by color (colored; Chinese): (a) each borough; (b) each month. 1928. p. 136–137. **131**

36. Deaths by color (colored; Chinese). Current quarter year. **136**

DEATHS AND DEATH RATE *(continued)*

Source Number

PUBLIC SOURCES *(continued)*

New York City *(continued)*

37. Deaths by color (colored; Chinese). Each borough. Current monthly through Dec., 1927. **133**

38. Deaths by cause ("Detailed International List of the Causes of Death") and sex: (a) by age (under 1; 1; 2; 3; 4; 5–9; then 5-year groups to 85 and over); (b) by color (colored; Chinese; Japanese). 1928. p. 144–153. **131**
NOTE: See list, Appendix 1.

39. Deaths from principal causes: typhoid fever; malarial fever; smallpox; measles; scarlet fever; whooping-cough; diphtheria and croup; influenza; encephalitis lethargica; poliomyelitis; other epidemic diseases; tuberculosis pulmonalis; tuberculous meningitis; other forms of tuberculosis; cancer and other malignant tumors; simple meningitis; cerebrospinal meningitis; apoplexy and softening of the brain; diseases of the arteries; organic heart diseases; acute bronchitis; chronic bronchitis; pneumonia (except bronchopneumonia); bronchopneumonia; other respiratory diseases; diseases of the stomach (cancer excepted); diarrheal diseases (under 5 years); appendicitis and typhlitis; hernia and intestinal obstruction; cirrhosis of the liver; Bright's disease and nephritis; diseases of women (not cancer); puerperal septicemia; other puerperal diseases; congenital debility and malformation; old age; violent deaths (sunstroke; automobile fatalities; other accidents; homicide); suicide; all other causes; ill-defined causes. Each borough. Current week of current year, and corresponding week of preceding year. **136**

40. Deaths from principal causes: contagious diseases; pulmonary tuberculosis; cerebrospinal meningitis; influenza; lobar pneumonia; bronchopneumonia; diarrheal diseases (all ages; under 5 years); suicide; homicide; automobile fatalities; other accidents. Each borough. Current weekly through Apr. 27, 1929. **136**

DEATHS AND DEATH RATE *(continued)*

Source Number

PUBLIC SOURCES *(continued)*

New York City *(continued)*

41. (Same as 39). Each borough. For current quarter year and corresponding quarter of preceding year. **136**

42. Deaths from certain causes: acute infectious diseases; pulmonary tuberculosis; influenza; lobar pneumonia; bronchopneumonia; cancer; automobile fatalities. Each week, last 13 weeks. Published weekly. **136**

43. Deaths: (a) all causes; (b) selected causes (acute infectious diseases; pulmonary tuberculosis; influenza; lobar pneumonia; bronchopneumonia; cancer; automobile fatalities). Each week, 1928. p. 142–143. **131**

44. Deaths from principal causes (typhoid fever; typhus; malarial fevers; smallpox; measles; scarlet fever; whooping-cough; diphtheria and croup; influenza; lethargic encephalitis; poliomyelitis; other epidemic diseases; tuberculosis pulmonalis; tuberculous meningitis; other tuberculosis; cancer and other malignant tumors; simple meningitis; cerebrospinal meningitis; diseases of the arteries; apoplexy and softening of the brain; organic heart disease; acute bronchitis; chronic bronchitis; pneumonia, except bronchopneumonia; bronchopneumonia; other respiratory diseases; diseases of the stomach, except cancer; diarrheal diseases, under 5 years; appendicitis and typhlitis; hernia and intestinal obstruction; cirrhosis of the liver; Bright's disease and acute nephritis; diseases of women, not cancer; puerperal septicemia; other puerperal diseases; congenital debility and malformations; old age; sunstroke; other accidents; homicide; suicide; other causes): (a) each borough; (b) each month. 1928. p. 136–137. **131**

45. Deaths and death rate: (a) from all causes; (b) from selected causes, each cause (typhoid fever; measles; scarlet fever; diphtheria; whooping-cough; epidemic meningitis; pulmonary tuberculosis; other tuberculosis; **131**

DEATHS AND DEATH RATE *(continued)*

Source Number

PUBLIC SOURCES *(continued)*

New York City *(continued)*

45. *(continued)* influenza; acute bronchitis; pneumonias; other respiratory diseases; diarrhea under 5 years; cancer; Bright's disease and nephritis; chronic heart disease; puerperal diseases; vehicular accidents; other accidents). Each year, 1910–1928. p. 159–164.

46. Deaths (from same causes as in 39, except automobile fatalities omitted). Each borough. Current month of current year and corresponding month of preceding year. Current through Dec., 1927. **133**

47. Deaths and death rate by color (white; Negro; other): (a) all causes; (b) selected causes, each cause (pulmonary tuberculosis; pneumonia; cancer; heart disease; Bright's disease and nephritis; violence). 1925. p. 75. **136** **May 8, 1926**

48. Death rate of white population from selected causes, each cause: pulmonary tuberculosis; cancer; heart disease; pneumonias; Bright's disease and nephritis; violence. 1900, 1925. p. 97–98. **136** **June 19, 1926**

49. Deaths: (a) all causes; (b) certain infectious diseases by disease (typhoid fever; smallpox; measles; scarlet fever; diphtheria and croup; pulmonary tuberculosis; lobar pneumonia; bronchopneumonia; diarrheal diseases). Each ward, each borough. Current monthly through Dec., 1924. **133**

50. Deaths and death rate, by principal causes: typhoid fever; measles; scarlet fever; diphtheria and croup; whooping-cough; cerebrospinal meningitis; pulmonary tuberculosis; other tuberculosis; influenza; acute bronchitis; pneumonia; other respiratory diseases; diarrhea; cancer; Bright's disease; nephritis; heart diseases; puerperal diseases; violence. Each year, 1898–1923. Opposite p. 42. **133** **Feb., 1924**

DEATHS AND DEATH RATE *(continued)*

Source Number

PUBLIC SOURCES *(continued)*

New York City *(continued)*

51. Deaths by age groups (under 10; 10-19; 20-29; etc.) from (a) heart disease, (b) Bright's disease, (c) apoplexy. 1920. p. 60. **133 Mar., 1922**

52. Deaths of non-residents: (a) total causes; (b) each selected cause (typhoid fever; pulmonary tuberculosis; other tuberculosis; cancer; alcoholism; heart disease; acute respiratory diseases; diarrheal diseases; appendicitis; cirrhosis of the liver; diseases of women; congenital debility; accidents; suicides; other causes). 1928. p. 141. **131**

53. Deaths in child caring institutions under the jurisdiction of the Division of Institutional Inspection of the New York City Department of Health (New York Foundling Hospital; New York Nursery and Child's Hospital; other institutions). 1921; and each month, 1922. p. 57. **133 Mar., 1923**

54. Deaths in child caring institutions, by principal causes. Each month, 1921, 1922. p. 58-61. **133 Mar., 1923**

New York State

55. Deaths and death rate; infant death rate; deaths by age (under 1 year; 1 to 4; 65 and over). Current month. **179**

56. Deaths: (a) death rate; (b) death rate of infants under one year. Annual average, period 1921-1925, and each year, 1925, 1926. p. xvi, xx. ***176**

57. Deaths and death rate by age: under 1; 1; 2; 3; 4; 5-year age periods to 85 and over. 1926. p. 22. ***176**

58. Deaths by age: under 1 year; 1-4; 5-9; 10-14; 15-19; 20-29; 30-39; 40-49; 50-59; 60 and over; age unknown. Each month, 1926. p. 29. ***176**

59. Deaths: (a) by sex; (b) by color (white; Negro; Indian; other); (c) by marital condition; (d) by nativity. 1926. p. 22. ***176**

60. Deaths, each cause and class of causes on "Detailed International List of Causes of Death." Current month. **179**
 NOTE: See List, Appendix 1.

DEATHS AND DEATH RATE *(continued)*

Source Number

PUBLIC SOURCES *(continued)*

New York State *(continued)*

61. Deaths, each cause on "Detailed International List of Causes of Death." 1926. p. 23–28. •176
    NOTE: See List, Appendix 1.

62. Deaths from certain important causes: typhoid and paratyphoid fever; smallpox; measles; scarlet fever; whooping-cough; diphtheria; influenza; acute anterior poliomyelitis; meningococcus meningitis; tuberculosis; tuberculosis of the respiratory system and acute disseminated tuberculosis; tuberculosis of the meninges and central nervous system; tuberculosis of the intestines and peritoneum, of the vertebral column, of other organs, and chronic or unspecified disseminated tuberculosis; cancer; diabetes mellitus; alcoholism; cerebral hemorrhage and apoplexy; heart disease; diseases of the arteries; bronchitis; bronchopneumonia; pneumonia; diarrhea and enteritis (under 2 years of age); appendicitis and typhlitis; hernia and intestinal obstruction; cirrhosis of the liver; nephritis; puerperal septicemia; accidents of pregnancy, puerperal hemorrhage, and other accidents of labor; other puerperal diseases and conditions; congenital malformations; congenital debility; premature birth (not stillborn); injury at birth (not stillborn), other diseases peculiar to early infancy, and lack of care; senility; violent deaths (suicide, homicide, and infanticide excepted); accidental drowning; railroad accidents; automobile accidents; suicide; homicide and infanticide. Each month, 1926. p. 30–33. •176

63. Deaths and death rate: acute poliomyelitis; cerebrospinal meningitis; tuberculosis (all forms); influenza; bronchitis; pneumonia (all forms); cancer; apoplexy and cerebral hemorrhage; diseases of the heart; diseases of the arteries; diarrhea and enteritis (under 2 years); acute and chronic nephritis; malformations and diseases of early infancy; all puerperal causes; •176

DEATHS AND DEATH RATE *(continued)* Source Number

PUBLIC SOURCES *(continued)*

New York State *(continued)*

63. *(continued)*
puerperal septicemia; suicide; homicide; accidents. Each year, 1900–1926, excepting homicide and accidents, for which data begin in 1907, and acute poliomyelitis, for which data begin in 1912. p. 12–18.

64. Deaths and death rate: typhoid fever; measles; scarlet fever; whooping-cough; diphtheria; pulmonary tuberculosis. Each year, 1898–1926. p. 8–11. ***176**

65. Death rate by sex and age from selected causes: (a) from syphilis (under 1; under 10; 10–14; ten-year periods to 75 and over); (b) from measles (under 1; 1; 2; 3; 4; 1–4; 5–9; 10 and over); (c) scarlet fever (age as in measles); (d) whooping-cough (age as in measles); (e) diphtheria (age as in measles); (f) influenza (under 1; 1–4; 5–14; ten-year periods to 75 and over); (g) acute poliomyelitis (under 1; 1; 2; 3; 4; 5–9; 10–14; 15–19; 20–24; 25 and over); (h) meningococcus meningitis (age as in acute poliomyelitis); (i) homicide (under 1; 1–14; ten-year periods to 75 and over); (j) hernia (age as in homicide); (k) nephritis (under 25; ten-year periods to 75 and over); (l) cirrhosis of the liver (age as in nephritis); (m) cancer (age as in nephritis); (n) diabetes (age as in nephritis); (o) alcoholism (age as in nephritis); (p) cerebral hemorrhage and apoplexy (age as in nephritis); (q) diseases of the heart (age as in nephritis); (r) diseases of the arteries (age as in nephritis); (s) bronchitis (under 1; 1–4; 5–9; 10–14; 15–19; 20–24; ten-year periods to 75 and over); (t) pneumonia (age as in bronchitis); (u) drowning (age as in bronchitis); (v) appendicitis (under 5; ten-year periods to 75 and over); (w) accidents (age as in appendicitis); (x) suicide (under 15; ten-year periods to 75 and over). Annual average, period 1921–1925, and 1926. p. XXX–LXVII. ***176**

66. Deaths from external causes. Current month. **179**

DEATHS AND DEATH RATE *(continued)*

Source Number

PUBLIC SOURCES *(continued)*

United States

67. Total deaths and death rate, infant deaths and infant death rate. Each borough. Current week, and for corresponding week of preceding year (except infant death rate). **299**

68. Total deaths and death rate, infant deaths and death rate. Current week. Also total death rate and infant deaths for corresponding week of preceding year. Each borough. **317**

69. Total deaths, death rate, and infant deaths, each borough, 1927, 1928; provisional infant death rate for 1928, and infant death rate for 1927, each borough. Published annually. p. 134. **317 Jan. 18, 1929**

70. Total deaths and death rate; deaths and death rate of residents only. Each borough; further subdivided by color (white; colored) for Manhattan, for Brooklyn, and for New York City. 1926. p. 7. ***293**

71. Crude and refined death rates. Each borough. 1924, 1925. p. 31. ***292**

72. Deaths from important causes, each cause: typhoid and paratyphoid fever; malaria; smallpox; measles; scarlet fever; whooping-cough; diphtheria; influenza; dysentery; erysipelas; lethargic encephalitis; meningococcus meningitis; tuberculosis of the respiratory system; other forms of tuberculosis; diabetes mellitus; cerebral hemorrhage, apoplexy, and softening of the brain; organic heart disease; bronchitis; bronchopneumonia; pneumonia; diarrhea and enteritis (under 2 years of age); diarrhea and enteritis (2 years and over); nephritis; puerperal septicemia; other puerperal diseases and conditions; suicide; automobile accidents; railroad accidents; street-car accidents. Each borough; fuither subdivided by color (white; colored) for Manhattan, for Brooklyn, and for New York City. Each month, 1926. p. 353–355. ***293**

DEATHS AND DEATH RATE *(continued)* — Source Number

PUBLIC SOURCES *(continued)*

United States *(continued)*

73. Deaths by important causes, each cause: typhoid and paratyphoid fever; malaria; smallpox; measles; scarlet fever; whooping-cough; diphtheria; influenza; erysipelas; meningococcus meningitis; tuberculosis of the respiratory system; tuberculosis of the meninges; other forms of tuberculosis; cancer and other malignant tumors; rheumatism; diabetes mellitus; cerebral hemorrhage and softening of the brain; diseases of the heart; bronchitis; pneumonia (all forms); diarrhea and enteritis (under 2 years); appendicitis and typhlitis; hernia; cirrhosis of the liver; nephritis; puerperal septicemia; other puerperal causes; congenital malformation and diseases of early infancy; suicide; homicide; automobile accidents; other external causes; unknown or ill-defined diseases. Each borough; further subdivided by color (white; colored) for Manhattan, for Brooklyn, and for New York City. 1926. p. 78–79. **•293**

74. Deaths from important causes, by age groups (under 1; 1; 2; 3; 4; 5–9; 5-year groups to 34; 10-year groups to 75 and over), each cause: typhoid and paratyphoid fever; measles; scarlet fever; whooping-cough; diphtheria; influenza; meningococcus meningitis; tuberculosis of the respiratory system; other forms of tuberculosis; cancer; diabetes mellitus; cerebral hemorrhage, apoplexy, and softening of the brain; organic heart disease; bronchitis; bronchopneumonia; pneumonia; diarrhea and enteritis; appendicitis and typhlitis; hernia and intestinal obstruction; cirrhosis of the liver; nephritis; non-cancerous tumors and other diseases of the female genital organs; puerperal septicemia; other puerperal diseases and conditions; suicide; homicide and infanticide; automobile accidents; railroad accidents; street-car accidents. Each borough; further subdivided by color (white; colored) for Manhattan, for Brooklyn, and for New York City. 1926. p. 302–304. **•293**

DEATHS AND DEATH RATE *(continued)*

Source Number

PUBLIC SOURCES *(continued)*

United States *(continued)*

75. Death rate, each selected cause: typhoid and paratyphoid fever; malaria; smallpox; measles; scarlet fever; whooping-cough; diphtheria; influenza and pneumonia; acute anterior poliomyelitis; tuberculosis (all forms); tuberculosis of the respiratory system and acute disseminated tuberculosis; cancer and other malignant tumors; diabetes mellitus; diseases of the heart; pneumonia (all forms); diarrhea and enteritis (under 2 years); acute and chronic nephritis; puerperal septicemia; suicide; homicide; automobile accidents. Each borough. 1920, 1924, 1925. p. 47, 49, 51, 54, 58, 62, 66, 68, 70, 77, 79, 86, 107, 112, 114, 118, 122, 135, 140, 142, 147. ***292**

76. Annual death rate among white persons by sex and age: 0; 1; 2; each fifth year to 92. Period 1919–1920. p. 12–15. **295**

77. Deaths out of 100,000 white persons born alive, by sex and age: 0–1; 1–2; 5-year periods to 92–97. Period 1919–1920. p. 20–23. **295**

PRIVATE AND PUBLIC SOURCES, COMBINED

See also: *Accidents* (entire)
Accidents, Elevator (entire)
Accidents, Highway (entire)
Accidents, Motor vehicle (entire)
Accidents, Street railway 1–3
Alcoholism 1
Anthrax 1–3
Apartments 5
Asphyxiation (entire)
Beaches, Bathing 2
Bellevue-Yorkville district 6–14, 18, 20
Bronx, Borough of 1, 2
Burns (entire)
Cancer (entire)

DEATHS AND DEATH RATE *(continued)*

PRIVATE AND PUBLIC SOURCES, COMBINED *(continued)*

DEATHS AND DEATH RATE *(continued)*

Source Number

PRIVATE AND PUBLIC SOURCES, COMBINED *(continued)*

See also: *(continued)*
Tuberculosis 1–3, 5–18, 20–24
Tularemia (entire)
Typhoid fever 1–7, 9–11
Typhus 1, 2
Undulant fever (entire)
Vital statistics (entire)
Whooping-cough 2–5

Other allied topics: *Funeral costs*
Interments
Mortuary, City

DEFECTIVE DELINQUENTS

See: *Delinquents, Defective*

DEFECTIVES

1. Applicants to the New York City Department of Public Welfare for admission to private institutions for the care of the physically defective, by disposition of case (approved; disapproved) and type of defect; reinvestigation of cases of inmates by disposition of case and type of defect. 1926. p. 22–23. **148**

See also: *Blind persons* (entire)
Cripples (entire)
Deaf persons (entire)
Delinquents, Defective (entire)
Epileptics (entire)
Handicapped persons (entire)
Mental defectives (entire)

Other allied topic: *Tuberculosis*

DEFECTIVES, MENTAL

1. State institutions for mental defectives: (a) first admissions by sex, and rate per 100,000 population, year **200**

DEFECTIVES, MENTAL *(continued)*

Source Number

1. *(continued)* ending June 30, 1928; (b) total patients under treatment by sex, and rate per 100,000 population, June 30, 1928. From each county. p. 294.
2. Mental defectives and epileptics applying to the New York City Department of Public Welfare for care in municipal or state institutions: (a) number of cases by diagnosis; (b) recommendations for care. 1926. p. 24–25. **148**

See also: *Education* 44, 45

DELINQUENTS, DEFECTIVE

1. Prisoners committed from New York City to the Institution for Defective Delinquents, Napanoch, by county. Year ending June 30, 1928. p. 530. **162**

DELINQUENTS, JUVENILE

1. Children in institutions for juvenile delinquents who were delinquents and who were non-delinquents, by sex: (a) children present, Jan. 1, 1923; (b) children admitted first six months of 1923; (c) children discharged first six months of 1923. Each institution in New York City. p. 352. **281**
2. Delinquent children in private institutions for juvenile delinquents, by sex: (a) present, Feb. 1, 1923; (b) admitted, period Feb. 1–Apr. 30, 1923; (c) discharged (placed in free family homes; returned to parents; otherwise discharged or passed from care), period Feb. 1–Apr. 30, 1923. Each institution in New York City. p. 376–377. **281**
3. Children adjudged delinquent in Children's Court, by sex and disposition (suspended sentence in first instance; placed on probation; committed to institutions; fined), each allegation: assault; burglary; corporation ordinances, violation of; desertion of home; disorderly conduct; peddling or begging; railroad law, violation of; robbery; stealing; truancy; ungovernable or wayward minor; unlawful entry; unclassified. 1928. p. 14. **116**

DELINQUENTS, JUVENILE *(continued)*

Source Number

4. Cases brought before the Children's Court, for juvenile delinquency (from a selected area in Brooklyn): (a) by sex of child, and age (each year), each allegation for delinquent children, p. 18; (b) number of girls detained as material witnesses, by age, p. 18; (c) delinquency ratio for boys computed on 1920 population data, by sanitary districts of the selected area, arranged by location (new commercial section; along waterfront; center of area studied), p. 20, 22. 1926. **167**

5. Cases brought before the Children's Court for juvenile delinquency: (a) by type of arraignment (single; group of two; group of three or more), each allegation for delinquent children, boroughs combined, 1925; (b) by type of arraignment and classification of delinquency (offenses against the person; offenses against property; offenses against property or public peace, combined; offenses against the peace), by borough, Manhattan, Brooklyn, 1922, 1923, 1924. p. 39–40. **167**

6. Boys brought before the Children's Court as delinquents: (a) by age (each year, 6–15), New York City Children's Courts, combined, each year, 1921–1925, p. 32; and (b) boys arraigned as delinquents in Children's Court, Manhattan, each court district, each year, 1920–1924. p. 15–16. **168**

7. Juvenile delinquents in a portion of District 1 of the Manhattan Children's Court: (a) foreign-born white population, by country of birth, each sanitary district, 1920; (b) estimated total population, 1925; (c) children arraigned in Manhattan Children's Court, by sex, age, and complaint, 1926; (d) boys referred to Police Welfare Lieutenants (not including cases referred by police to City Magistrates' Court and Children's Court), by disposition (City Magistrates' Court; Children's Court; placed under police supervision), each precinct, 1926; (e) cases, by sex, supervised by the Jewish Board of Guardians, 1926; (f) per cent of boy population, 7–15 years of age, combined, who were **168**

DELINQUENTS, JUVENILE *(continued)*

Source Number

7. *(continued)*
delinquent, each sanitary district, 1926; (g) each offense committed by boys referred to the Police Welfare Department, by age and disposition of case, each month, 1926; (h) boys arraigned in City Magistrates' Court, 1925, and Children's Court, 1926, combined, by age; (i) average number of delinquent children, per block, 1926, and number of delinquent children in 1926 in four blocks examined by the Reconstruction Commission in 1920, and in five blocks having largest number of delinquents, 1926; (j) delinquent boys, distributed as in gangs or as single delinquents, 1926; (k) spare time activities observed on street, by age and number of participants, one hour, Sunday afternoon in May, 1926; (l) spare time activities reported by 185 school children making normal progress in grades 6, 7, and 8, 1926; (m) violations of street trading regulations by children, three nights, May, 1926; (n) commercial and non-commercial amusements in area, 1926; (o) membership, by age, in settlements and neighborhood houses, 1926; (p) attendance at parks, playgrounds, and school centers, 1926.

8. Boys 7–18 years of age in District 1 of the Manhattan Children's Court, who were arraigned as delinquents: (a) each year, 7–15, in Children's Court; (b) each year, 16–18, in City Magistrates' Court; (c) age group, 7–15, each sanitary district of District 1; (d) age group 16–18, each sanitary district of District 1. 1925. p. 4, 7. **13**

9. Children 7–15 years of age who were arrested, classified by nationality. Manhattan. 1920. p. 150. **270**

10. Sanitary districts contributing the most numerous cases of juvenile delinquency (numbers 4; 6; 10; 16; 26; 30; 34; 40; 18; 28; 32; 38; 29; 43; 47; 49; 67; 123; 129; 156; 164; 172; 182; 212; 230; 232): (a) density per acre of child population; (b) racial composition; (c) index of juvenile delinquency. Each specified sanitary district, Manhattan. 1920. p. 152–159. **270**

DELINQUENTS, JUVENILE *(continued)*

Source Number

11. Industrial schools for delinquents: (a) staff (teachers; assistants not teachers) by sex; (b) inmates by sex and color; (c) inmates by sex and nativity; (d) native-born inmates by sex and parentage; (e) average pupils enrolled during year by sex; (f) persons committed during year by sex and literacy (unable to read or write; able to read second reader but unable to write); (g) inmates discharged during year by sex and ability to read and write; (h) inmates receiving instruction in school classes by sex; (i) average enrollment in school classes by sex; (j) inmates learning some trade or occupation. Each institution in New York City. 1926/27. p. 15, 20. **304**

See also: *Arrests and summonses* 1, 4
Arson (entire)
Children, Dependent or neglected 21
Correction 58
Courts 109, 110, 113, 115, 117, 118, 122
Negroes 7
Police welfare department 1
Recreation 6, 7
Truants 1

Other allied topics: *Adolescent offenders*
Wayward minors

DENGUE

1. Cases, deaths. 1927. p. 6. **317 Supp. # 70**

DENSITY OF POPULATION

1. Relative density of New York City and contiguous territory according to United States Census figures. 1850, 1900, 1920. p. 20–22. Maps only. **261**
2. Persons per acre. Each ward; each borough. 1920. (Last published in Dec., 1924, issue). p. 283–284. **133 Dec., 1924**
3. Persons per acre. Each tabulation tract (one or more sanitary districts having a total population of 1000 or more). 1920. p. 834–837. **51**

DENSITY OF POPULATION *(continued)*

Source Number

4. Tabulation tracts by density of population (over 100 per acre; under 100 per acre): (a) maps showing each tabulation tract of 1910 and each tabulation tract of 1920; (b) area in acres of tracts of 1910 and of 1920; (c) population in 1910 of tabulation tracts of 1910 and gain or loss 1905–1910; (d) population in 1920 of tabulation tracts of 1920 and gain or loss 1915–1920. p. x–xi. **51**

5. Sanitary districts with a population of 100 or more persons per acre, classified according to density (100–199; 200–218; 219–299; 300–399; 400–499; 500–599; 600–799; 800 and over): (a) number of districts, 1910, 1920; (b) area in acres, 1910, 1920; (c) population in 1910 of sanitary districts of 1910 and gain or loss, 1905–1910; (d) population in 1920 of sanitary districts of 1920 and gain or loss 1910–1920 and 1915–1920. p. xxi. **51**

6. Sanitary districts with a population of 16 or more persons per acre, classified according to degree of density (16–35; 36–99; 100–199; 200–219; 220–299; 300–399; 400–499; 500–599; 600 and over): (a) area in acres, 1920; (b) population, 1920, and gain or loss, 1910–1920 and 1915–1920; (c) number of persons per acre, 1920. Each district, each borough. p. xiv–xix. **51**

7. Sanitary districts with a population of fewer than 16 persons per acre: (a) number of districts, 1920; (b) area in acres, 1920; (c) population, 1920, and gain or loss, 1910–1920 and 1915–1920. p. xix. **51**

8. Foreign-born white persons in sanitary districts having a total population of 300 or more persons per acre, classified by country of birth and by density of total population: 300–399; 400–499; 500–599; 600 and over. Each sanitary district. 1920. p. xii–xiii. **51**

9. Density of population (a) white, (b) Negro, per acre. Manhattan. 1925. p. 79. **338**

See also: *Area* 7, 8
Birthplace of population 11
Recreation 9

DEPENDENTS, AGED

Source Number

1. Public and private Homes for the Aged within a radius of 50 miles of New York City which admit New York City residents, not including Homes exclusively for the blind, the deaf, and the incurable, respectively: number of Homes and number of beds, (a) by type of Home (public; private), sex and marital status of residents, and financial requirement of Homes, (b) by type of Home and sex and marital status of residents, and location of Homes. Each Home. June 30, 1929, and compiled currently. **324**

2. Private Homes for the Aged (as in 1): (a) controlling religious denomination and financial requirement, (b) controlling religious denomination and location. Each Home. June 30, 1929, and compiled currently. **324**

3. Private Homes for the Aged (as in 1) which report data monthly to the Welfare Council of New York City: residents (a) first day of month, (b) admitted during month, (c) withdrawing during month, by cause (deaths; dismissals; etc.), (d) last day of month; vacancies; capacity of Homes. Compiled monthly. **324**

   NOTE: The group reporting does not include all Homes eligible for reporting, but includes a large proportion of such Homes.

4. Bed capacity in Jewish Homes for the Aged: (a) total beds; (b) number of beds which are available to the chronic sick, each Home. Manhattan; Brooklyn; Bronx. 1927. p. 42. **32**

5. Aged poor outside institutions who received material relief from family welfare societies, from selected relief agencies, and from selected Protestant churches: (a) persons assisted by sex, with amount of relief, for churches combined, and each society; (b) by age and sex; (c) by marital status and sex; (d) by sex and living arrangements (alone; with spouse; etc.); (e) by nativity, sex, and color; (f) by nativity, sex, and age; (g) foreign-born persons by sex and country of birth; (h) by sex, naturalization status, and length of time in the United States; (i) naturalized persons by sex and length of time since naturalization; (j) naturalized **2**

DEPENDENTS, AGED *(continued)*

Source Number

5. *(continued)*
persons by sex and country of birth; (k) persons assisted, by sex and employment status; (l) persons employed, by sex, age, and present occupation; (m) persons gainfully employed distributed by weekly wages and sex; (n) by amount of relief, living arrangements, and sex; (o) persons assisted who received $300 and over distributed by amount of relief and sex, with average amount of relief; (p) organizations grouped according to number of aged persons assisted per organization, with number of persons assisted by each group. Data for a fiscal year ending in 1928 or for the year 1927. p. 213–224.

See also: *Public Charges* 5, Note

DESERTION

See: *Non support or neglect of family.*

DIABETES MELLITUS

1. Deaths. Current month. **179**
2. Deaths and death rate. Each year, 1920–1925. p. 51. **136 Mar. 27, 1926**

See also: *Deaths and death rate* 4–7, 38, 60–62, 65, 72–75

DIARRHEAL DISEASES

1. Deaths (diarrhea and enteritis under 2 years, combined). Current month. **179**
2. Deaths and death rate of children under 5 years of age from diarrheal diseases. Each year, 1868–1928. p. 171. **131**

See also: *Baby health stations* 1
Bellevue-Yorkville district 6–8, 10, 15, 16
Bronx, Borough of 1
Deaths and death rate 1, 3, 38–41, 44–46, 49, 50, 52, 54, 60–63, 72–75
East Harlem 6–10
Infant deaths and death rate 2, 8, 9, 12, 13, 15
Vital Statistics Note

DIPHTHERIA

	Source Number
1. Cases, and estimated expectancy of cases. Current week.	**317**
2. Cases and deaths. Current month.	**179**
3. Cases, deaths, and death rate. Each year, 1873–1928. p. 27.	**136** Jan. 26, 1929
4. Cases and deaths. Each month, 1927, 1928. p. 172.	**131**
5. Deaths and death rate from diphtheria and croup combined. Each year, 1868–1928. p. 173.	**131**
6. Cases and deaths. Each week, Jan. 1, 1921–Oct. 27, 1928. p. 201.	**136** Oct. 27, 1928
7. Cases and deaths, case rate and death rate, fatality rate, estimated expectancy. 1927. p. 7.	**317** Supp. # 70
8. Deaths and death rate. By borough: Manhattan; Bronx; Brooklyn. Each year, 1915–1925. p. 126.	**136** Aug. 7, 1926
9. Deaths and death rate, cases and case rate. By borough: Queens; Richmond. Each year, 1915–1925. p. 154.	**136** Sept. 25, 1926
10. Deaths and death rate, cases and case rate, case fatality, cultures, place of treatment (hospital; home). Each borough. For current quarter year and corresponding quarter of preceding year.	**136**
11. Sex and age distribution (single years to 20; 5-year groups to 45 and over) of 10,040 cases reported. Each borough. 1920. p. 147.	**133** July, 1921
12. Cases: (a) primary and secondary cases, and carriers; (b) place of treatment; (c) deaths; (d) age incidence (single years to 15; 15 and over). Richmond borough, subdivided into districts. Jan. 1–Aug. 15, 1923. p. 291.	**136** Sept. 15, 1923
13. Number of children given immunizing toxin antitoxin injections by the New York City Department of Health. 1928. p. 43.	**131**
14. Testing of children in public and parochial schools by Schick test: (a) number of schools and number of children tested, Manhattan and Bronx, combined; (b) same for Brooklyn, Queens, and Richmond, combined, with	**133** May, 1923

DIPHTHERIA *(continued)*

Source Number

14. *(continued)* addition of number of children and adults tested in institutions. 1922. p. 98. (Same as (a) for 1923 in Sept., 1924, issue. p. 206).

15. Diphtheria and croup mortality rates, combined, in (a) East Harlem District, (b) Manhattan, (c) New York City. Each year, 1916–1927. p. 5. **60**

16. Number of cases and number of deaths from diphtheria occurring in the East Harlem District by age and sex of patient. By sanitary area. Each year, 1921–1927. p. 12–13. **60**

See also: *Bellevue-Yorkville district* 6–8, 10, 15, 19
Bronx, Borough of 1, 3
Deaths and death rate 1, 3, 38, 39, 41, 44–46, 49, 50, 54, 60–62, 64, 65, 72–75
Diseases, Transmissible 1–12
East Harlem 6–10
Heart disease 13
Infant deaths and death rate 9
Nurses 3
Nursing service 1
Serums (entire)
Vital statistics 12, Note

DISEASES, OCCUPATIONAL

1. Cases of occupational diseases, by disease: anthrax; lead poisoning; occupational eczema; dermatitis; caisson disease; poisoning (a) arsenical, (b) benzol, (c) sulphuric. 1923. p. 171. **136 June 7, 1924**

2. Cases of occupational diseases, by disease. 1920. p. 39. **133 Feb., 1921**

3. Occupation and disease of the patients in 6 representative hospitals in New York City: (a) age and sex of patients by occupational groups; (b) causes of hospitalization by occupational groups. 1923. p. 35–36. **57**

DISEASES, OCCUPATIONAL *(continued)*

Source Number

4. Median age of workers that were patients in 6 representative New York City hospitals by occupation and sex. 1923. p. 273. **58**
   NOTE: Part of same study as above.

See also: *Anthrax* (entire)
Silicosis (entire)

DISEASES, TRANSMISSIBLE

1. Cases of reportable infectious diseases, by disease: tuberculosis; diphtheria; measles; scarlet fever; chicken pox; influenza; pneumonia; typhoid fever; whooping-cough; syphilis; gonorrhea; poliomyelitis; cerebrospinal meningitis. Each week, last 13 weeks. Published weekly. **136**

2. Cases and deaths, case, death, and fatality rates, for reportable diseases: anthrax; botulism; chicken pox; cholera (Asiatic); diphtheria (membranous croup); dysentery (amebic and bacillary); epidemic encephalitis; epidemic cerebrospinal meningitis; epidemic or streptococcus (septic) sore throat; erysipelas; German measles; glanders; malaria; measles; mumps; ophthalmia neonatorum; paratyphoid fever; plague; pneumonia (a) broncho or lobular, (b) acute lobar; poliomyelitis (acute anterior); puerperal septicemia; rabies; scarlet fever; smallpox; tetanus; trachoma; tuberculosis; typhoid fever (except paratyphoid); typhus fever; Vincent's angina; whooping-cough; syphilis; gonorrhea; chancroid. Current month. **179**

3. Cases of infectious diseases reported, each disease: typhoid fever; typhus; malaria; smallpox; measles; scarlet fever; whooping-cough; diphtheria and croup; leprosy; mumps; German measles; chicken pox; glanders; anthrax; rabies; tetanus; pellagra; pulmonary tuberculosis; other tuberculosis; syphilis; gonorrhea; cerebrospinal meningitis; poliomyelitis; hook-worm; trichinosis; influenza; pneumonia. Each borough. Current quarter year and corresponding quarter of preceding year. **136**

DISEASES, TRANSMISSIBLE *(continued)*

Source Number

4. Cases of reportable infectious diseases, by disease: tuberculosis; diphtheria; measles; scarlet fever; chicken pox; influenza; pneumonia; typhoid fever; whooping-cough; syphilis; gonorrhea; poliomyelitis; cerebrospinal meningitis. Each week, 1928. p. 142–143. **131**

5. Cases of reportable infectious diseases, each disease (as in 4). Each year, 1914–1928. p. 165–166. **131**

6. Cases of selected diseases reported and cases which were hospitalized at hospitals of the New York City Department of Health, each disease: diphtheria; scarlet fever; measles; pertussis. Each year, 1926–1928. p. 94. **131**

7. Cases of infectious diseases, by disease: typhoid fever; typhus; malaria; smallpox; measles; scarlet fever; whooping-cough; diphtheria and croup; leprosy; mumps; German measles; chicken pox; glanders; anthrax; rabies; tetanus; pellagra; pulmonary tuberculosis; other tuberculosis; syphilis; gonorrhea; cerebrospinal meningitis; poliomyelitis; hook-worm; trichinosis; influenza; pneumonia. Each borough. Current month of current year and corresponding month of preceding year. Published monthly through Dec., 1927. **133**

8. Cases and deaths, and case, death, and fatality rates, by disease: measles; diphtheria; poliomyelitis; scarlet fever; typhoid fever; whooping-cough. Average, period 1922–1926, and 1927. p. 112–125. ***177**

9. New cases of communicable diseases reported and morbidity rates, by disease: typhoid fever; typhus; malaria; smallpox; measles; scarlet fever; whooping-cough; diphtheria and croup; leprosy; mumps; German measles; chicken pox; glanders; anthrax; rabies; tetanus; pellagra; pulmonary tuberculosis; tuberculous meningitis; other tuberculous diseases; syphilis; gonorrhea; cerebrospinal meningitis; poliomyelitis; hookworm; trichinosis; influenza; pneumonias; encephalitis lethargica. Each borough. 1925, 1926, 1927. Supplementary sheet. **231**

DISEASES, TRANSMISSIBLE (*continued*)

Source Number

10. Cases and deaths, case rate and death rate, for certain diseases: diphtheria; scarlet fever; measles; whooping-cough; meningococcus meningitis; typhoid fever. Each borough. 1920, 1921. p. 178–188. **133** Aug., 1922

11. Major contagious diseases found in schools, by disease: diphtheria; scarlet fever; measles; mumps; German measles; chicken pox; whooping-cough. Each borough, first three months of 1922, 1923, 1924. p. 187. **136** June 21, 1924

12. Children excluded from school on account of contagious diseases, by disease: diphtheria; scarlet fever; measles; chicken pox; whooping-cough; mumps. 1915, 1920, 1922. p. 130. **133** June, 1923

13. Contagious eye and skin diseases found in schools, by disease (pediculosis; trachoma; acute conjunctivitis; follicular conjunctivitis; ringworm; scabies; impetigo; favus; molluscum contagiosum); number of inspections of pupils made. 1927, 1928. p. 42. **131**

See also: *Anthrax* (entire)
Baby health stations 1
Chicken pox (entire)
Deaths and death rate 1, 3–7, 38–50, 52, 54, 60–65, 72–75
Diphtheria (entire)
Encephalitis lethargica (entire)
Hospitals 17, 20, 24, 25
Infant deaths and death rate 2, 9, 12, 13, 15, 16
Influenza (entire)
Leprosy (entire)
Malaria (entire)
Measles (entire)
Meningitis (entire)
Mumps (entire)
Nursing service 2
Overcrowding (entire)
Physical examinations 11
Poliomyelitis (entire)
Rabies (entire)

DISEASES, TRANSMISSIBLE *(continued)*

Source Number

See also: *(continued)*
Scarlet fever (entire)
Smallpox (entire)
Tetanus (entire)
Tuberculosis (entire)
Tularemia (entire)
Typhoid fever (entire)
Typhus (entire)
Undulant fever (entire)
Venereal disease (entire)
Whooping-cough (entire)

Other allied topic: *Rats*

DISORDERLY CONDUCT

See: *Arrests and summons* 1, 4
Correction 2, 20, 43, 50
Courts 12, 13, 15, 17, 18, 21–28, 30, 32, 34, 37–41, 55, 56, 58, 70, 77, 82, 101, 102, 104, 110, 115, 122
Delinquents, Juvenile 3, 5
Felonies 19
Mendicants (entire)
Negroes 7

DISPENSARIES

See: *Clinics*

DIVORCE

1. Marriages and divorces, each county, 1925, 1926; annulments, each county, 1926. p. 80. ***290**
2. Alimony cases in Supreme Court of the State of New York, First Judicial Department, Special Term for Trials, each referee. New York and Bronx Counties, combined. 1928. p. 26. ***207**
3. Undefended matrimonial causes referred to official referees, each year, 1924–1928, p. 27; motions in matrimonial causes to confirm referee's report, 1928, p. 21. ***207**

DIVORCE *(continued)*

Source Number

3. *(continued)*
Supreme Court of the State of New York, First Judicial Department, Special Term for Trials. New York County.

4. Undefended matrimonial causes heard by the official referees, in which proof was made, by nature of causes: annulments; divorces; separations; dissolutions. Supreme Court of the State of New York, First Judicial Department, Special Term for Trials. New York County; Bronx County. 1928. p. 26. *207

5. Contested matrimonial actions disposed of during year, distributed as follows (tried, proof by all parties; in judgment, proof made; dismissed on default; settled and discontinued; abated; settled during trial, or still pending); number of minor children concerned. Supreme Court of the State of New York, First Judicial Department, Special Term for Trials. New York County. 1928. p. 24. *207

6. Judgments in trials and in hearings in matrimonial causes, distributed for plaintiff and defendant, by sex, and by type of judgment: (a) judgments granted on motion on referee's reports (defended divorces); (b) judgments granted on motion on verdict of jury, i.e., framed issues (defended annulments; defended divorces); (c) judgments granted after trial by the Court (defended annulments; defended divorces; defended separations; undefended divorces; undefended separations; undefended dissolutions). Supreme Court of the State of New York, First Judicial Department, Special Term for Trials. New York County. 1928. p. 25. *207

7. Decisions in undefended matrimonial causes in accordance with reports of official referees, by type of cause: annulments; divorces; separations; dissolutions. Supreme Court of the State of New York, First Judicial Department, Special Term for Trials. New York County; Bronx County. 1928. p. 25. *207

DIVORCE *(continued)*

Source Number

8. Judgments in matrimonial causes after trial, distributed as defended and undefended, by plaintiff and defendant, and as tried in 1928 or prior to 1928. Supreme Court of the State of New York, First Judicial Department, Special Term for Trials. New York County. 1928. p. 27. ***207**
9. Minor children concerned in matrimonial causes which were tried and heard. Supreme Court of the State of New York, First Judicial Department, Special Term for Trials. New York County. 1928. p. 25. ***207**
10. Matrimonial actions, distributed as defended and undefended by type: divorce; annulment; separation. Supreme Court of the State of New York, First Judicial Department, Special Term for Trials. Bronx County. Each term of Court, 1928. p. 34. ***207**

See also: *Correction* 65, 70, 72

Other allied topics: *Marital condition of population*
Marriages and marriage rate

DOG BITES

See: *Rabies*

DRIVING WHILE INTOXICATED

See: *Highway law, Violation of*

DROWNING

1. Accidental drownings. Each month, Jan., 1927–May, 1929. p. 198. **136** **June 22, 1929**
2. Deaths from drowning, by cause or place. Each borough. 1928. p. 9. **114**
3. Deaths by drowning: (a) each borough, each year, 1918–1926, and period Jan.–June, 1927; (b) each month, 1922–1926, and Jan.–June, 1927. p. 134. **136** **Aug. 13, 1927**
4. Deaths by drowning, by sex and age: under 1; 1–9; 10–19; 20–34; 35–59; 60–80. 1923, 1924, 1925. p. 166. **136** **Oct. 16, 1926**

See also: *Accidents* 1, 2, 4
Deaths and death rate 38, 60–62, 65
Suicide 1–3

DRUG ADDICTION

Source Number

See: *Drug laws, Violation of*

DRUG LAWS, VIOLATION OF

1. Drug addicts received at the New York County Penitentiary, by institution to which committed: total and number who were self-committed (New York City Reformatory; New York City Workhouse; New York County Penitentiary. 1928. p. 81. **121**

2. Persons arrested on drug charges: (a) by type (addicts; sellers) and number of times previously arrested; (b) 100 who were sellers by number of previous convictions of felonies; (c) 100 who were sellers by number of previous convictions of misdemeanors; (d) 100 who were sellers by number of previous convictions in Federal Courts for violations of the Harrison Act and the Miller-Jones Act. Period Apr.–June, 1928. p. 11–12. **122**

3. Arrests for drug addiction; total discharges and discharges of cases of drug addiction from (a) hospitals of the New York City Department of Public Welfare, and (b) Bellevue and Allied Hospitals. Each year, 1914–1927. p. 509. ***244**

4. Arrests and commitments, combined, of drug addicts to correctional institutions, and cases sent to hospital, each year, 1921, 1922, 1923, and the period Jan.–June, 1924; number of self-committed addicts, by sex, 1922, 1923, and the period Jan.–June, 1924. p. 10–11. **202**

5. Confinement of drug addicts: (a) commitments for drug addiction of men at Men's Hospital, Riker's Island, and of women at Correction Hospital, each institution, each year, 1917–1923; and (b) average number of drug addicts in custody, Riker's Island, each year, 1918–1923. p. 51–52. **249**

6. Prisoners committed to New York City Workhouse for drug treatment: (a) number of previous sentences served in a correctional institution and by section of the code under which committed (self-committed through **77**

DRUG LAWS, VIOLATION OF *(continued)*

Source Number

6. *(continued)*
   Department of Health; self-committed through City Magistrates' Court; committed by judge, usually of the Court of Special Sessions), 1920; (b) number of times treatment had previously been received at the Workhouse, and by section of code under which committed (as above), 1920; (c) sex and section of code under which committed (as above), each month, 1920, and all months combined, 1919. p. 355–356.

DRUNKEN DRIVING

DRUNKENNESS

1. Arrests for drunkenness. Each year, 1898–1927. p. 7. Chart only. ***98**
2. Arrests for intoxication and total arrests. Each year, 1913–1923. **341**
3. Arrests for intoxication and total arrests. Each year, 1910–1922. **340**
4. Persons arrested for intoxication: (a) arrests, each year, 1910–1922; (b) arraignments in City Magistrates' Court by sex, each year, 1911–1921; (c) convictions for intoxication, by sex, each year, 1916–1922. p. 2. **339**

DWELLINGS (according to definition of United States Bureau of the Census)

Source Number

NOTE: "A dwelling, for census purposes, is a place in which one or more persons regularly sleep. It need not be a house in the usual sense of the word, but may be a hotel, boarding house, institution, or the like. A boat, a tent, a freight car, or a room in a factory, store, or office building, although occupied by only one person, is also counted as a dwelling, while, on the other hand, an entire apartment house, although containing many families, constitutes but one dwelling." p. 1265. **285**

1. Dwellings. Manhattan and Bronx; Brooklyn; Queens; Richmond. 1920 and estimate for 1927. p. 202. **245**
2. Dwellings and families. Each borough. 1900, 1910, 1920. p. 1268. **285**
3. Dwellings and families. By district, each borough. 1920. Separate sheet for each district. **241**
4. Dwellings and families. Each assembly district and each borough. 1920. p. 63–68. **288**
5. Number of dwellings. Each tabulation tract of 1920 (one or more sanitary districts having a total population of 1000 or more). 1910, 1920. p. 2–819. **51**

See also: *East Harlem* 4
Families 2

Other allied topics: *Housing*
Ownership of homes

EAST HARLEM

1. Persons in East Harlem District: (a) in 1920 (Federal Census); (b) 1925 (State Census); and (c) estimated number of persons, each year, 1921–1927. By sanitary areas (# 162, 170, 178, 180, 188, 192, 194, 202). p. 2. **60**
2. Estimated age distribution of population: under 1; 1–4; 5–9; 10–14; 15–19; 20 and over. Each year, 1921–1927. p. 7. **60**

EAST HARLEM *(continued)*

Source Number

3. Persons in the area covered by the East Harlem Nursing and Health Demonstration (Sanitary Areas # 180 and 188), by age groups: under 1 year; 1–5; 6–15; 16–20; 21–44; 45 and over. 1920. p. 6. **65**

4. Dwellings, families, individuals, nativity of population, illiterates: in (a) sanitary area # 180; (b) sanitary area # 188. 1920. p. 6. **65**

5. Births and birth rate in the East Harlem District. By sanitary area. Each year, 1921–1927. p. 2. **60**

6. Estimated population; births and birth rate; stillbirths and stillbirth rate; number and rate of deaths under 1 year; total deaths from selected causes, by cause: pneumonia; organic heart disease; pulmonary tuberculosis; diarrhea and enteritis; influenza; accidents; Bright's disease and nephritis; cancer; diphtheria and croup; measles; whooping-cough; puerperal state; scarlet fever; typhoid fever. By sanitary area. Each year, 1920–1925. p. 28–29. **63**

7. Deaths and death rate in the East Harlem District by leading causes (typhoid fever; measles; scarlet fever; whooping-cough; diphtheria and croup; influenza; pulmonary tuberculosis; cancer; organic heart disease; pneumonia; diarrhea and enteritis; Bright's disease; puerperal disease; accidents; all other causes); also births; stillbirths; infant deaths; maternal deaths. Period 1916–1920, and each year, 1921–1927. Tables 3A, 3B, 4A, 4B. **64**

8. Deaths in the East Harlem District by age groups, for total causes and each leading cause: typhoid fever; measles; scarlet fever; whooping-cough; diphtheria and croup; influenza; pulmonary tuberculosis; cancer; organic heart disease; pneumonia; diarrhea and enteritis; Bright's disease; puerperal disease; accidents. 1927. Table 2. **64**

9. Per cent change in rate of deaths: (a) all causes; (b) each leading cause (pneumonia; pulmonary tuberculosis; cancer; organic heart disease; diarrhea and **67**

EAST HARLEM *(continued)*

Source Number

9. *(continued)* enteritis; external causes); also number and per cent of total deaths from acute communicable diseases (typhoid fever; measles; scarlet fever; whooping-cough; diphtheria and croup). For (a) East Harlem Nursing and Health Demonstration area (sanitary areas # 180 and 188); (b) East Harlem District (sanitary areas # 162, 170, 178, 180, 188, 192, 194, 202); (c) Manhattan; (d) New York City. Period 1923–1925 and period 1920–1922. p. 15, 17.

10. Average annual morbidity rate, and per cent change, for all causes of death and each leading cause: typhoid fever; measles; scarlet fever; whooping-cough; diphtheria and croup; influenza; pulmonary tuberculosis; cancer; organic heart disease; pneumonia; diarrhea and enteritis; Bright's disease; puerperal disease; accidents. East Harlem District; Manhattan; New York City. Period 1916–1920, and period 1921–1927. Tables 5 and 6. **64**

11. Morbidity services given by the East Harlem Nursing and Health Demonstration: (a) number of morbidity cases nursed, and number of visits to nursed cases, each year, 1923–1927; (b) nature of illness and fatality, by disease, 1927; (c) sex and age by disease (pneumonia; bronchitis; measles; influenza; tuberculosis; organic heart disease), 1927; (d) cost of morbidity service by leading causes of illness, each year, 1923–1927. Demonstration area (sanitary areas # 180 and 188). **67**

12. Persons attending periodic health examination clinic: (a) age groups, (b) sex, (c) source of referral, each year, 1921–1927; also defects and disease conditions noted by age and sex, for the period 1925–1927. Tables I, II, IV. **62**

13. Original maternity service (East Harlem Nursing and Health Demonstration) in East Harlem District: antepartum cases; postpartum cases; home visits; conference visits; class visits; cases under care of the Demonstration as compared with total births reported for the **66**

EAST HARLEM *(continued)*

Source Number

13. *(continued)*
district; length of antepartum care; antepartum complications; cases by place of delivery and person by whom delivered. Each year, 1923–1927. Also infant mortality; stillbirths. 1927.

14. Location from which clients came to the East Harlem Health Center. By sanitary area. [1925]. p. 225. Map only. **61**

See also: *Diphtheria* 15, 16

EDUCATION

PRIVATE AND PUBLIC SCHOOLS

1. Persons attending school: (a) by age (7–20; 7–13) and color (white; Negro); (b) white population attending school, by age (as above), nativity, and parentage (native; foreign or mixed). Each borough. 1910, 1920. p. 1082–1084. **285**

2. Persons attending school: (a) by age (under 7; 7–13; 14 and 15; 16 and 17; 18–20; 21 and over), sex, and color (white; Negro); (b) white population attending school, by age (as above), sex, nativity, and parentage. Each borough. 1920. p. 1111–1112. **285**

3. Persons attending school: (a) by age (each year, 5–20), and sex; (b) by age (each year, 5–20), and color (white; Negro); (c) white persons by age (each year, 5–20), nativity, and parentage. Each borough. 1920. p. 1134–1135. **285**

4. Persons attending school by age: 7–13; 14–15; 16–17; 18–20. Each assembly district and each borough. 1920. p. 63–68. **288**

5. Persons 5–20 years of age who were in school and who were out of school: (a) by age (5; 6; 7–9; 10–13; 14; 15; 16–19; 20), color (white; Negro; other), and sex; (b) white persons 5–20 years of age who were in school and who were out of school, by age (as above), sex, **51**

EDUCATION *(continued)*

Source Number

PRIVATE AND PUBLIC SCHOOLS *(continued)*

5. *(continued)* nativity and parentage. Each tabulation tract (one or more sanitary districts having a total population of 1000 or more). 1920. p. 2–819.

6. Boys registered in day schools: (a) number by age (each year 9–18), in public schools, (regular grade elementary schools; junior high schools; day high schools; special classes); (b) estimated per cent of boys aged 9–13 who were in school (public; parochial); (c) estimated per cent of boys aged 14–18 (each year), who were in public school. 1925/26. p. 16–17. **88**

7. Work of officers of Bureau of Attendance: (a) investigations closed; (b) hearings; (c) court prosecutions; (d) convictions; (e) commitments. Each attendance district and each borough. 1927/28. p. 263–264. **124**

8. Investigations made by the Bureau of Attendance. Each attendance district. Each week, 1918/19–1928/29. **125**

9. Investigations made by the Bureau of Attendance of cases which were "unlawful": (a) by source of case and cause of absence of pupil; (b) by cause of absence and disposition; (c) by age, grade, and sex; (d) by type of case (truancy; unlawfully detained; unlawfully employed). Each school year, 1918/19–1924/25; Oct., Dec., 1926, and Feb., Apr., June, 1927; Sept., Nov., 1927, and Jan., Mar., May, 1928. **125**

10. Investigations made by the Bureau of Attendance of cases which were "lawful," by disposition of case. Sept.–Jan., 1918/19; Feb.–June, 1919/20; Sept.–Jan., 1920/21; Dec.-Apr., 1922/23; Sept.–Jan., 1923/24; Sept.–Jan., 1924/25; Oct., Dec., 1926, and Feb., Apr., June, 1927; Sept., Nov., 1927, and Jan., Mar., May, 1928. **125**

11. Investigations made by the Bureau of Attendance of cases which were "lawful": (a) by source of case and cause of absence; (b) by cause of absence and disposition; **125**

EDUCATION *(continued)*

Source Number

PRIVATE AND PUBLIC SCHOOLS *(continued)*

11. *(continued)*
(e) by age, grade, and sex; (d) illness cases (included in preceding) by age, grade, and sex. Feb.–June, 1919/20; Sept.–Jan., 1920/21; Dec.–Apr., 1922/23; Sept.–Jan., 1923/24; Sept.–Jan., 1924/25; Oct., Dec., 1926, and Feb., Apr., June, 1927; Sept., Nov., 1927, and Jan., Mar., May, 1928.

12. Investigations made by the Bureau of Attendance of cases which were "lawful," by cause, age, and sex. Sept.–Jan., 1924/25; Oct., Dec., 1926, and Feb., Apr., June, 1927. **125**

13. Hearings held by the Bureau of Attendance: (a) total each borough, each school month, 1918/19–1921/22; (b) by age, grade, and sex, each year, 1918/19–1921/22; (c) by classification (truants; unlawfully detained; unlawfully employed; violation of newsboy law), each year, 1918/19–1921/22, 1923/24; (d) by age, grade, sex, and classification, each year, 1922/23, 1925/26, 1927/28; (e) by classification and disposition, 1922/23, 1925/26; (f) by classification, disposition, and specific cause, 1927/28; (g) number of truants, each borough, 1926/27; (h) number of hearings held on each case, each borough, 1922/23, 1925/26, 1927/28; (i) children placed on probation, each year, 1918/19–1921/22, 1922/23, 1925/26, 1927/28. **125**

14. Prosecutions made by the Bureau of Attendance in the City Magistrates' Court: (a) by complaint and cause of absence, each year, 1918/19–1922/23, 1924/25; (b) by complaint and disposition, each year, 1918/19–1922/23; (c) by age, grade, and sex, each year, 1918/19–1922/23, 1924/25. **125**

15. Prosecutions made by the Bureau of Attendance in the City Magistrates' Court: (a) number; (b) convictions (imprisonments; cases fined); (c) amount of fines. Each attendance district. Each school week, Sept., 1921, to current week. **125**

EDUCATION *(continued)*

Source Number

PRIVATE AND PUBLIC SCHOOLS *(continued)*

16. Prosecutions made by the Bureau of Attendance in the Children's Court: (a) by age, sex, and complaint; (b) by complaint and disposition. Each year, 1918/19–1922/23. **125**

17. Prosecutions made by the Bureau of Attendance in the Children's Court: (a) number; (b) convictions. Each attendance district. Each school week, Sept., 1921, to current week. **125**

18. Commitments executed as result of action of the Bureau of Attendance, by committing authority (Director of Bureau; City Magistrates' Court; Children's Court). Each attendance district. Each school week, Sept., 1921, to current week. **125**

19. Institutions of higher education: (a) registration (undergraduate, by classes; undergraduate, by courses; unclassified; graduate); (b) degrees conferred on completion of course; (c) higher degrees conferred during year; (d) persons graduated without degrees; (e) honorary degrees conferred. Each item by sex. Each group and each institution: universities; graduate departments; colleges for men; colleges for women; colleges for men and women; colleges of theology; colleges of education; and the following schools: law; medicine; chiropody; dentistry; dental hygiene; pharmacy; veterinary medicine; optometry; librarianship; accountancy; architecture; engineering and technology; art and journalism; music; agriculture; others. 1926/27. p. 276–347. ***174**

See also: *Bellevue-Yorkville district* 22
Blind persons 3
Boy population (entire)
Bronx, Borough of 4
Building 1, 2, 9–11, 13, 16, 17
Clinics, Dental 7
Clinics, Eye (entire)

EDUCATION *(continued)*

Source Number

PRIVATE AND PUBLIC SCHOOLS *(continued)*

See also: *(continued)*
Correction 20
Courts 37, 48, 52, 53, 59, 62, 84
Cripples 3
Delinquents, Juvenile 11
Diseases, Transmissible 11–13
Employment certificates (entire)
Finances, City 5
Homework of children (entire)
Malnutrition (entire)
Nurses 3
Nursing service 2
Physical examinations 1, 4–9
Playgrounds 2–4
Recreation 5
Richmond, Borough of 8, 9
Ringworm (entire)
Tax exemption 1, 2
Truants (entire)

PRIVATE SCHOOLS

20. Private high schools and academies: (a) religious influence; (b) years in course; (c) pupils, by sex; (d) graduates, by sex. Each institution. 1925/26. p. 29. ***301**

21. Academic departments of private academies: (a) registration, each year of course; (b) registration, by sex; (c) average daily attendance, by sex; (d) graduates, by sex; (e) graduates entering higher institutions (colleges; normal schools and normal colleges; professional and technical schools). Each academy. 1926/27. p. 220–229. ***174**

22. Private commercial and business schools which enrolled 100 or more students: (a) teachers, by sex; (b) students enrolled by sex (in day courses; in night courses only); (c) average daily attendance (day school; night school). Each school. 1924/25. p. 21–22. **300**

EDUCATION *(continued)*

Source Number

PRIVATE SCHOOLS *(continued)*

23. Roman Catholic schools: (a) pupils, by sex; (b) teachers, by type (religious; lay; special); (c) classes. By borough: Manhattan; Bronx; Richmond. Sept., 1929. **218**

24. Attendance in Roman Catholic schools: (a) pupils and teachers in elementary schools, each year, 1918–1927; (b) pupils in high schools, by sex, each year, 1923–1927; (c) pupils in diocesan high schools, by sex, each year, 1923–1927; (d) pupils, by sex, and teachers (religious; lay), each school and each type of school (elementary schools; elementary academies; elementary institutions; diocesan high schools; parish high schools; community high schools; colleges), data as of Oct., 1927. Brooklyn and Queens. ***15**

25. Number of elementary school graduates from Roman Catholic Schools, by sex. June, 1927, and Jan., 1928. Brooklyn and Queens. ***15**

26. Jewish religious schools (commercial schools; congregational schools; Sunday schools; Yiddish schools; parochial schools): (a) pupils registered (free; part-pay; full-pay); (b) teachers; (c) classes; (d) sessions per week; (e) income (tuition fees; other); (f) expenditures (teachers' salaries; principals and clerks; other); (g) number of rooms, library, gymnasium, etc. Each school; each type of school; each district of Jewish Education Association; each borough. 1928. **81**

27. Increase and decrease in the register of Jewish religious schools: weekday schools; Sunday schools; Yiddish schools; parochial schools. Each school; each type of school; each borough. 1916, each year, 1923–1928. ***85**

28. Attendance in Jewish schools: (a) number of schools and children enrolled, by type of school (weekday schools [communal; congregational and synagogue]; Sunday schools; Sunday departments of weekday schools; parochial schools; Yiddish schools), 1927, and increase, 1927 over 1916; (b) per cent of children of Jewish-school age **36**

EDUCATION *(continued)*

Source Number

PRIVATE SCHOOLS *(continued)*

28. (*continued*)
attending, each borough, 1927; (c) number in weekday schools and per cent which they were of pupils in all Jewish schools, 1916, 1927; (d) decrease or increase in enrollment and number of schools, each type of school, 1927 over 1916; (e) per cent of Jewish child population enrolled in each type of school, 1927; (f) number and per cent of Jewish children not in Jewish schools, 1916, 1927; (g) estimated number enrolled in private schools and receiving instruction privately at home, 1927; (h) estimated number of Jewish children (7–13) who will have been entered in a Jewish school during the 7-year school-age period. p. 2–8.

29. Income and expenditures of 76 of the largest Jewish religious schools (parochial; Talmud Torah; congregational; center): (a) total income and income per pupil, by source (parents; synagogue; earnings; local contributions; community agencies); (b) total expenditures and expenditures per pupil, by purpose (current expenses; capital outlay; debt service). 1926/27. **82**

See also: *Fires* 3, 9
Salaries and wages 15
Settlements 4, 5

PUBLIC SCHOOLS

30. Persons attending public day schools: (a) average daily register; (b) average daily attendance; (c) whole register (whole time, regular schedule; whole time, special schedule; short time). Each type of school: elementary (kindergarten; kindergarten-elementary, 1A–1B; 2A–6B; 7A–8B; special miscellaneous; special handicapped); junior high (special handicapped; all others); high; training; vocational; truant. Each borough. Current month; corresponding month of preceding year; preceding month of current year. **123**

EDUCATION *(continued)*

Source Number

PUBLIC SCHOOLS *(continued)*

31. Per cent which average daily attendance was of pupils enrolled: (a) all day schools, by type of school (elementary; junior high; high; trade; continuation), each borough; (b) each elementary school, each borough; (c) elementary schools, each attendance district, each borough; (d) each junior high school, each borough; (e) each trade school; (f) each continuation school; (g) each high school, each borough. Each month of the school year; summary for school year by term (spring; fall), compared with preceding year by term. Also comparison with corresponding month of the preceding year for the following: all day schools, by type; elementary schools, each attendance district, each borough. **125**

32. Per cent of pupils in average daily attendance at day schools. Each school (elementary; continuation; high) and each borough. Each school year, 1921/22–1928/29; and junior high, trade school, and truant school, separately, each year, 1925/26–1928/29. **125**

33. Number of public schools and pupils registered by type of school: elementary; junior high; high; training schools for teachers; vocational. Each borough. Sept., 1928. p. 31. ***17**

34. Regular day schools: (a) number of schools by classification (training schools for teachers; high schools; vocational and trade schools; elementary schools, including junior high schools; school for the deaf; parental school), July 1, 1927, 1928; (b) average daily register and average daily attendance, by classification of schools (as above, but with elementary schools subdivided as regular grades, junior high schools, and kindergartens), each year, 1926/27 and 1927/28; (c) average daily register for all schools combined, each year, 1907/08–1927/28; (d) average daily register and average daily attendance, by classification of schools (as in (b) above), each borough, 1927/28; (e) register, **124**

EDUCATION *(continued)*

Source Number

PUBLIC SCHOOLS *(continued)*

34. (*continued*)
by classification (elementary schools, including junior high and parental schools; high schools; training schools; vocational schools), on specified days, 1927/28. p. 439, 441, 443, 447–448.

35. Pupils in day schools placed on school suspense registers and pupils removed from such registers, by cause (temporary disability; quarantine; failure to seek admission): (a) by school district, 1925/26, 1926/27, 1927/28; (b) by type of school (elementary and junior high; high; trade; continuation), 1925/26, 1926/27, 1927/28; (c) each elementary school, continuation school, and high school, 1926/27, 1927/28; (d) by borough, 1926/27, 1927/28. **125**

36. Children committed to truant or parental schools, by type of offender (truant; insubordinate or disorderly). Period 1913/14–1927/28. p. 240. **124**

37. Number of day elementary schools: (a) schools maintained, June 30, 1927; (b) organized, 1927/28; (c) abandoned or consolidated, 1927/28; (d) in operation, June 30, 1928; (e) number of schools by size of school, June 30, 1928. Each borough. p. 448, 454. **124**

38. Persons attending day elementary schools: (a) average daily register and average daily attendance by classification of schools (kindergarten; regular grades; junior high; parental), each year, 1926/27 and 1927/28; (b) average daily register and average daily attendance, each borough, each year, 1917/18–1927/28; (c) average daily attendance, each borough, 1927/28; (d) average daily register, by sex and classification of schools (as above), each borough, 1927/28; (e) pupils on register, by regular schedule, special schedule, and short time, Oct. 31, 1927; Mar. 31, 1928; and June 30, 1928; (f) pupils on register, by part time and full time, June 30, each year, 1909–1928; (g) pupils on register, by regular schedule, special schedule, and **124**

EDUCATION *(continued)*

Source Number

PUBLIC SCHOOLS *(continued)*

38. (*continued*) short time, each borough, June 30, 1928; (h) pupils on register, by double session or short time, each borough, June 30, each year, 1919–1928. p. 456, 462, 466, 467, 469, 471, 475, 477.

39. Promotion of pupils in day elementary schools: (a) pupils promoted and per cent of total, each grade or class, Jan. 31 and June 30, 1928; (b) pupils promoted during the term, each grade or class, terms ending Jan. and June, 1928, each term; (c) rate of promotion, each grade or class, each borough, Jan. and June, 1928; (d) rate of promotion, each grade or class, June 30, each year, 1918–1928; (e) pupils by age and grade, Sept., 1927; (f) pupils who were under age, normal age, and over age, each grade in regular grades and junior high schools, Sept., 1927; (g) per cent of pupils in regular grades who were under age, normal age, and over age, Sept., each year, 1923–1927; (h) pupils by grade and number of terms in school, regular grades and junior high schools, Sept., 1927; (i) per cent of pupils in regular grades who made slow, rapid, and normal progress, Sept., each year, 1922–1927. p. 501–504, 511, 516, 522, 524, 525, 536, 539, 544, 547, 554, 556. **124**

40. Pupils completing elementary course in day schools: (a) by sex, each borough; (b) by sex and age; (c) by sex and number of terms in school; (d) by age standard (under age; normal age; over age) and progress (rapid; normal; slow). Jan. 31 and June 30, 1928. p. 561, 565, 567–568. **124**

41. Pupils completing junior high school course: (a) by sex, each borough; (b) by sex and age; (c) by sex and number of terms in school; (d) by age standard (under age; normal age; over age) and progress (rapid; normal; slow). Jan. 31 and June 30, 1928. p. 570, 572–574. **124**

EDUCATION *(continued)*

Source Number

PUBLIC SCHOOLS *(continued)*

42. Pupils discharged from elementary day schools: (a) by sex and grade; (b) by sex and age; (c) by sex and cause. Each borough. 1927/28. p. 579–581. **124**

43. Pupils discharged from elementary day schools: (a) by age, sex, and cause, each year, 1920/21–1922/23, 1927/28, 1928/29; (b) by age, grade, and sex, each year, 1920/21–1922/23; (c) by individual cause, grade, age, and sex, each borough, each year, 1923/24–1925/26, and each term, 1926/27; (d) by grade, sex, and cause, 1928/29. **125**

44. Children attending special classes for the mentally and physically handicapped: (a) register; (b) average register; (c) average attendance. Each type of class: blind; cardiopathic; crippled; deaf; hospital; open air; sight conservation; tubercular; ungraded. Current month; corresponding month of preceding year; preceding month of current year. **123**

45. Number of classes for handicapped and exceptional children by size of class and type of class (blind; cardiac; cripple; deaf; hospital; open air; parental; probationary; sight conservation; tubercular; ungraded; miscellaneous). Oct. 31, 1927, and Mar. 31, 1928. p. 497. **124**

46. Open air classes in public schools: pupils by sex; per cent of children gaining weight; per cent of children gaining in scholarship. 1928. p. 47. **131**

47. Open air classes: pupils remaining at end of year and pupils discharged during year (a) by sex, (b) by weight record, (c) by scholarship, (d) by age groups. 1926/27 and 1927/28. p. 583. **137 Nov., 1928**

48. Number of day high schools. Each borough. Each year, 1926/27 and 1927/28. p. 583. **124**

49. Persons attending day high school: (a) average daily register and average daily attendance, each year, **124**

EDUCATION *(continued)*

Source Number

PUBLIC SCHOOLS *(continued)*

49. *(continued)*
1907/08–1927/28; (b) average daily register and average daily attendance, each borough, each year, 1917/18–1927/28; (c) average daily register and average daily attendance, by sex, each borough, each year, 1926/27 and 1927/28, and each school, 1927/28; (d) pupils on regular schedule, special schedule or short time, Jan. 31 and June 30, 1928; (e) pupils on short time, double session, or special schedule, June 30, each year, 1923/24–1927/28; (f) pupils on register, by sex, grade, and course, June 30, 1928. p. 589, 592–597.

50. Average daily register in day high schools. Each borough. Each year, 1919/20–1925/26. p. 18. **88**

51. High school registration. Each borough. Each year, 1898–1925. **222**

52. Promotion of pupils in day high schools: (a) pupils by sex, age, and grade, Sept. 30, 1927; (b) pupils by sex, who were under age, normal age, and over age, each grade, Sept., 1927; (c) per cent of pupils who were under age, normal age, and over age, Sept. 30, each year, 1924–1927; (d) pupils by sex, grade, and number of terms in school, Sept., 1927; (e) per cent of pupils who made slow, rapid, and normal progress, Sept., each year, 1924–1927. p. 601–603, 605–609. **124**

53. Pupils graduated from day high schools: (a) by sex, course, and length of course (four-year; three-year); (b) by sex, age, and length of course; (c) by sex, length of course, and number of terms in school. Jan., 1928, June, 1928. p. 645, 647, 649. **124**

54. Pupils discharged from day high schools: (a) by grade, each borough; (b) by age, boroughs combined; (c) by cause, each borough. 1927/28. p. 651–653. **124**

EDUCATION *(continued)*

Source Number

PUBLIC SCHOOLS *(continued)*

55. Pupils discharged from day high schools and vocational and trade schools: (a) each school, each month, 1918/19; (b) by cause, grade, and sex, each borough, 1918/19, 1921/22, 1922/23, and for boroughs combined, 1919/20, 1920/21; (c) by cause, age, and sex, each borough, 1918/19; (d) by cause and age, each borough, 1919/20, 1920/21; (e) by cause, age, and sex, each borough, 1921/22, 1922/23, and for boroughs combined, each term, 1928/29; (f) by cause, each school and each borough, 1920/21, 1921/22, 1922/23, and each school, each year, 1924/25–1927/28; (g) by grade and sex, each borough, 1919/20; (h) by grade, each school and each borough, 1920/21, 1921/22, 1922/23, and each school, each year, 1924/25–1927/28; (i) by individual cause, age, grade, and sex, each borough, each year, 1923/24–1927/28. **125**

56. Persons attending training schools for teachers: (a) average daily register and average daily attendance, by sex, each year, 1903/04–1927/28; (b) pupils by sex and grade, each school, June 30, 1928; (c) pupils admitted, each school, Sept., 1927, and Feb., 1928; (d) pupils by age, grade, and sex, Sept., 1927. p. 656, 659–661. **124**

57. Pupils in training schools for teachers by grade, sex, and number of terms in school. Sept. 30, 1927. p. 663. **124**

58. Graduates of training schools for teachers: (a) by age and sex, each training school, Jan., June, 1928; (b) graduates by sex and number of terms in training school, Jan., June, 1928. p. 668–669. **124**

59. Persons attending vocational and trade schools: (a) average daily register and average daily attendance, by sex, each school, 1926/27 and 1927/28; (b) average daily register and average daily attendance, each year, 1917/18–1927/28; (c) pupils on register, by age, each school, Sept., 1927. p. 670–672. **124**

EDUCATION *(continued)*

Source Number

PUBLIC SCHOOLS *(continued)*

60. Pupils discharged from vocational and trade schools: (a) by grade, each borough; (b) by age, boroughs combined; (c) by cause, each borough. 1927/28. p. 673–674. **124**

61. Persons attending continuation schools and classes: (a) register; (b) average register; (c) average attendance. Each type of schools and classes: compulsory schools; compulsory annexes (regular centers); industrial centers; general improvement; voluntary (not supported by Board of Education); day classes for adults in English and citizenship. Current month; corresponding month of preceding year; preceding month of current year. **123**

62. Number of compulsory continuation schools. Each borough. June 30, 1928. p. 675. **124**

63. Persons attending compulsory continuation schools: (a) enrollment, by sex, each school, 1926/27, 1927/28; (b) average daily register and average daily attendance, each school, 1926/27 and 1927/28; (c) pupils on register, by sex and age, June 30, 1927, 1928. p. 676–678. **124**

64. Pupils discharged from continuation schools: (a) by age and cause, each term, 1928/29; (b) by cause, each school and each borough, each term, 1928/29; (c) by age and cause, each school and each borough, Feb.–June, 1928. **125**

65. Persons attending evening schools: (a) register; (b) average register; (c) average attendance. Each type of school and subject: elementary (academic and commercial subjects of elementary grade; commercial subjects of high-school grade; trade subjects); high (academic; commercial; trade); trade (academic; commercial; trade). Current month; corresponding month of preceding year; preceding month of current year. **123**

EDUCATION *(continued)*

Source Number

PUBLIC SCHOOLS *(continued)*

66. Number of evening elementary schools. Each borough. 1926/27, 1927/28. p. 680. **124**

67. Persons attending evening elementary schools: (a) average register and average attendance, by sex, each borough; (b) aggregate attendance and number of sessions, by subject. 1926/27, 1927/28. p. 680, 682. **124**

68. Pupils enrolled in evening elementary schools: (a) pupils enrolled, by country of birth, sex, and subject (English and citizenship; other subjects), 1927/28; (b) pupils receiving instruction in English and citizenship, who were unable at registration to read English and to write English, by sex, 1926/27, 1927/28; (c) pupils receiving instruction in English and citizenship, by sex and citizenship, 1926/27, 1927/28. p. 686–687, 689, 691. **124**

69. Pupils in evening elementary schools who received (a) diplomas and (b) certificates, by sex and subject. 1926/27, 1927/28. p. 691. **124**

70. Schools offering evening instruction in high school subjects, by type (evening high; evening trade; evening elementary) and subject (academic and commercial; commercial). 1926/27. Each borough, 1927/28. p. 692–693. **124**

71. Persons attending schools offering evening instruction in high school subjects: (a) average register and average attendance, by subject (academic and commercial; commercial) and sex, each school, each type (evening high; evening trade; evening elementary), 1926/27 and 1927/28; (b) enrollment, by sex, subject, and year of course, each evening high school and each evening trade school), 1927/28. p. 694–698. **124**

72. Pupils graduated from schools offering evening instruction in high school subjects, by length of course (4-year; 3-year) and sex: (a) receiving diplomas; (b) receiving certificates. Each borough. 1927/28. p. 699. **124**

EDUCATION *(continued)*

Source Number

PUBLIC SCHOOLS *(continued)*

73. Schools offering evening instruction in trade courses and subjects by type of school: evening trade; evening high; evening elementary. 1926/27, 1927/28. p. 700. **124**

74. Persons attending schools offering evening instruction in trade subjects: (a) average register and average attendance, by sex, each school, each type (evening trade; evening high; evening elementary), 1926/27, 1927/28; (b) enrollment by type of school and sex, each trade, 1927/28. p. 701–703, 706–708. **124**

75. Pupils receiving (a) diplomas and (b) certificates from schools offering evening instruction in trade subjects, by sex and type of school. 1926/27, 1927/28. p. 708. **124**

76. Vacation elementary schools: (a) schools; (b) average register; (c) average attendance; (d) classes. Each borough. Summer, each year, 1927, 1928. p. 722. **124**

77. Summer junior high schools: (a) schools; (b) average register by sex; (c) average attendance by sex. Each borough. Summer, each year, 1927, 1928. p. 723. **124**

78. Pupils attending summer high schools, by sex: (a) enrollment; (b) average daily register; (c) average daily attendance. Each borough. Summer, each year, 1927, 1928. p. 724. **124**

79. Estimated number of Jewish children, aged 5–14, in public day schools (elementary; junior high; high; vocational and trade). Each school; each district of the Jewish Education Association; each borough. 1928. ***83**

See also: *Americanization* (entire)
Bronx, Borough of 3
Community centers (entire)
Deaf persons (entire)
Employment of children 4
Epileptics 2
Fires 3, 9
Heart disease 12, 13

EDUCATION *(continued)*

Source Number

PUBLIC SCHOOLS *(continued)*

See also: *(continued)*
Libraries 2
Physical examinations 2
Playgrounds 5–9
Recreation 3, 10
Salaries and wages 13, 14
Savings banks 5
Vocational guidance (entire)

ELEVATED TRAINS

See: *Street railways*
Transportation

EMPLOYMENT

1. Factory employment: number of employees; total payroll; average weekly earnings. By type of industry: (a) metals, machinery, and conveyances; (b) brass, copper, and aluminum; (c) machinery and electrical appliances; (d) instruments and appliances; (e) wood manufactures; (f) furs, leather, and rubber goods; (g) shoes; (h) printing and bookmaking; (i) clothing; (j) men's clothing; (k) women's clothing; (l) food products; (m) bread and other bakery products; (n) confectionery and ice cream; (o) tobacco products. For current month, for corresponding month of preceding year, and for preceding month of current year. **188**

2. Employment of shop workers in representative factories in New York City: number of employees and amount of payroll, by sex and industry (11 principal divisions [stone, clay, and glass; metals and machinery; wood manufactures; fur, leather, and rubber goods; chemicals, oils, paints, etc.; pulp and paper; printing and paper goods; textiles; clothing and millinery; food and tobacco; water, light, and power] and subdivisions). For current month. Index numbers, based on Jan., 1923. **188**

EMPLOYMENT (continued)

Source Number

3. Employment in representative factories, by type of industry: (a) employees and amount of payroll, Aug., 1927; (b) changes in employees and amount of payroll from June, 1914, to Aug., 1926, July, 1927, Aug., 1927, (index numbers); (c) average weekly earnings, Aug., 1926, July, 1927, Aug., 1927. p. 351. **188** Sept., 1927

4. Seasonal fluctuations (employees) of various industries, by industry. By month. [1926]. Opposite p. 12. Chart only. **318**

5. Course of employment in various industries: beverages; boots and shoes; men's clothing; furs; laundering; etc. Each month, 1921-1925. p. 42-54. Charts only. **318**

6. Changes in factory employment. Index numbers. Each month, 1914-1925. Part II, p. 210. **41**

7. Estimated number of factory workers, and actual number of employees in factories reporting, by sex. Each industry and type of industry. June, 1925. p. 157-160. **194**

8. Changes in employment in factories by industries (11 divisions and principal subdivisions) and sex. Index numbers, June, 1923 (base), June, 1924, June, 1925. p. 165. **194**

9. Number of persons gainfully employed, Jan., 1920; number unemployed, Mar. 15, 1922. By type of industry. p. 135. **314** June, 1922

10. Location of plants with 20 or more employees, by type of product made and by number of employees, for the following industries: (a) wood plants, p. 54-55; (b) textile plants, p. 58-59; (c) tobacco plants, including those with fewer than 20 employees, p. 48, 50-51; (d) food plants, p. 63-65; (e) metal plants, p. 77-79; (f) women's clothing, p. 82-86; (g) men's clothing, p. 88-93; (h) chemical plants, p. 96-97; (i) printing plants, p. 74-75. New York and its environs. 1900, 1922. Maps only. **256**

EMPLOYMENT *(continued)*

Source Number

11. Wage earners in factories employed fifteenth day of each month. Each borough. 1919. p. 978. **287**
12. Average number of wage earners in factories, by prevailing hours of labor per week. 1914, 1919. p. 983. **287**
13. Factories and wage earners in factories, by average number of wage earners employed in each factory. 1919. p. 985. **287**
14. Industrial map of Brooklyn: each of 8 concentrated industrial districts is shown by a series of bars, each bar representing an industry, the bars being in proportion to the number of persons employed in each industry and the total number employed in the borough. [1923]. **18**

See also: *Candy industry* (entire)
Chemical industry 1
Employment of children (entire)
Employment of prisoners (entire)
Family service 1
Food products industry 1
Garment industry (entire)
Homework 1–3, 5, 7–9
Hours of work 2
Laundries (entire)
Manufactures (entire)
Metal industry (entire)
Paper box industry (entire)
Printing industry (entire)
Stores 6
Textile industry (entire)
Tobacco products industry (entire)
Wood industry (entire)

Other allied topics: *Agriculture*
Housework
Occupations, Children engaged in
Occupations, Persons engaged in
Strikes
Trade unions
Unemployment

EMPLOYMENT BUREAUS

Source Number

1. Non-profit-making employment bureaus reporting to the Research Bureau of the Welfare Council of New York City: (a) registered applicants (newly registered; formerly registered); (b) referrals to jobs; (c) applicants placed; (d) placements (positions lasting one week or more; positions lasting less than one week). Each preceding item by age (14–16; 17 and over) and sex, and the following by sex only: (a) openings for workers, including re-openings; (b) openings for workers, excluding re-openings. Each bureau. Data compiled each month. The same data for a constant group of seven bureaus, each month. The same data for a constant group of ten bureaus, each month. **325**
   NOTE: The group reporting does not include all bureaus eligible for reporting, but includes a large proportion of such bureaus.
2. Work of the New York State Employment office: (a) workers registered, workers called for, places filled, by sex, current month; (b) number of workers registered for each hundred places open, current month, corresponding month of preceding year, preceding month of current year. **188**
3. Public employment offices of New York State: persons registered; cases renewed; help wanted; applicants referred; applicants placed. Each office, Bronx, Brooklyn, Manhattan, year ending June 30, 1927. p. 367. ***187**
4. State and municipal employment services cooperating with the United States Employment Service (combined): registrations received; requests for help; applicants referred; applicants placed. By borough: Manhattan; Bronx; Brooklyn. Current five calendar weeks. **316**
5. Number of persons registered, referred, and placed, by the Industrial Aid Bureau of New York City. 1922. **140**
6. Number of persons registered, referred, and placed by the Employment Division of the Industrial Aid Bureau, of New York City. Sept. 19–30, 1921, and each month, Oct., 1921–Feb., 1922. p. 9. **141**

See also: *Handicapped persons* (entire)
Licenses (entire)

Source Number

EMPLOYMENT BY THE CITY OF NEW YORK

1. Number of city employees, by Department in which they are employed and amount of compensation provided. 1926. p. 73. **226**

EMPLOYMENT CERTIFICATES

1. Children receiving general employment certificates issued on first application: (a) by age and grade, 1921/22; (b) by age, grade, and sex, each year, 1922/23–1928/29. **125**
2. General employment certificates issued (first application; application for reissuance); vacation work permits issued (first application; application for reissuance); certificates of age. Each borough. 1928/29. **125**
3. Employment certificates reissued (general and vacation, combined); vacation employment certificates. Each year, 1921/22–1928/29. **125**
4. Newsboy permits issued, by age. Each year, 1921/22–1928/29. **125**
5. Children receiving regular employment certificates for the first time, by age groups (14 and 15; 16); also the per cent of children of each age group who had completed at least the eighth grade before receiving first regular certificates. 1926, 1927. p. 19–20, 22, 24. ***298**
6. Employment certificates issued: (a) regular certificates to children 14 years and under 16 years; (b) regular certificates to children 16 years and under 17 years; (c) vacation employment certificates to children 14 years and under 16 years. Each year, 1910–1927 (or for as many years as the certificate has been obtainable). p. 279. **188** June, 1928
7. Boys by age (14; 15) and grade in school, who received employment certificates. 1922, 1925. p. 21. **88**
8. Employment certificates issued (regular; vacation). Each year, 1910–1923. p. 3. **192**

EMPLOYMENT CERTIFICATES (*continued*)

Source Number

9. Children between 14 and 16 years of age receiving regular employment certificates for the first time, each year, 1922–1923; and per cent of increase or decrease compared with preceding year. p. 115. **314** **May, 1924**

10. Number of work permits issued to 6th, 7th, and 8th grade children; also number of high school drop outs. 1922/23. p. 49. Chart only. **49**

11. Certifications of physical fitness made by the New York City Department of Health to the New York City Department of Education in connection with the regular and special vacation employment certificates for children; also certificates permanently or temporarily withheld by cause. Each borough. 1922. p. 132. **133** **June, 1923**

See also: *Employment of children* 2, 3
Physical examinations 13

EMPLOYMENT OF CHILDREN

1. Children 14 to 16 years of age found employed in (a) factories and (b) mercantile establishments: number of establishments; number of children by sex. Each borough. Year ending June 30, 1927. p. 132, 151. **•187**

2. Children found illegally employed in (a) factories, (b) mercantile establishments: number of establishments employing children; number of employed children under 14 years of age by sex; number of children 14 to 16, by sex, working (a) without certificates, (b) illegal hours, (c) both. Each borough. Year ending June 30, 1927. p. 130, 149. **•187**

3. Number of children found illegally employed in tenement living rooms: number of tenements; number of apartments; number of children under 14, by sex; number of children 14–16 working without certificates, by sex. Each borough. Year ending June 30, 1927. p. 136. **•187**

4. Children (412) in continuation school: nativity; home conditions; age; reason for going to work; school grade; **193**

EMPLOYMENT OF CHILDREN *(continued)*

Source Number

4. *(continued)*
method of obtaining employment; occupation; wages; hours; health; etc. [Period Feb.–June, 1924].

See also: *Homework of children* (entire)

Other allied topics: *Occupations, Children engaged in*
Occupations, Persons engaged in

EMPLOYMENT OF PRISONERS

See: *Correction* 45, 47, 49, 55, 64

EMPLOYMENT PRACTICE

1. Office hours and practice of 78 large bank, insurance, and mercantile offices: general office hours; opening and closing hours; summer schedules; lunch periods; overtime practice; vacation policies. By type of organization (bank; insurance; mercantile). Feb., 1924. p. 5–6. **91** Mar. 24, 1924

2. Vacations given, working hours (office; factory), and holidays observed. Queensboro (based on 46 business concerns). 1924. p. 134. **251** Mar., 1924

3. Holiday practices of 805 offices, stores, and factories, (representing almost every line of business), for each holiday, by type of business. 1925. **92**

ENCEPHALITIS LETHARGICA

1. Cases and deaths. Current week. p. 148. **317**

2. Cases, deaths, and case fatality. Each year, 1919–1927 and period Jan.–June, 1928. p. 65. **136** June 30, 1928

3. Cases and deaths, case rate and death rate, fatality rate. 1927. p. 10. **317** Supp. # 70

4. Cases of encephalitis by age groups. 1926 and 1927 combined. p. 82–83. **136** July 14, 1928

ENCEPHALITIS LETHARGICA *(continued)*

Source Number

5. Cases and deaths, each week, first 8 weeks, each year, 1921–1923; cases and deaths by age groups and sex, period Jan. 1–Feb. 27, 1923; cases and deaths, each month, Jan.–May, each year, 1921, 1922, and each month, Jan., Feb., 1923. p. 98–99. **136** Mar. 31, 1923

6. Cases and deaths per month, 1919, 1920; cases and deaths by sex and age groups, 1920. p. 89. **136** Mar. 19, 1921

See also: *Deaths and death rate* 38, 39, 41, 44, 46, 60, 61, 72
Diseases, Transmissible 2, 9

EPILEPTICS

1. Movement of population at Craig Colony by sex: (a) present at beginning of year; (b) received; (c) discharged; (d) died; (e) present at end of year. Each county. Year ending June 30, 1928. p. 14–15. ***164**

2. Cases of epilepsy in the public schools reported to the Bureau of Attendance: (a) by age, grade, and sex of pupils; (b) cases which were diagnosed by physicians as epileptics, by age, grade, and sex; (c) school status of total number, each school district; (d) number reported as having major attack, each school district. Period Sept., 1926–Dec., 1927. **125**

See also: *Deaths and death rate* 38, 60, 61
Defectives, Mental 2

EVENING SCHOOLS

See: *Education*

EXPECTATION OF LIFE

1. Survivors out of 100,000 white persons born alive, by sex and age: 0; 1; 2; each fifth year to 92. Period 1919–1920. p. 16–19. **295**

2. Number of years of life expected among white persons, by sex and age: 0; 1; 2; each fifth year to 92. Period 1919–1920. p. 24–27. **295**

See also: *Deaths and death rate* 76, 77

FALLS

Source Number

1. Deaths from falls, by place of fall: fire escape; scaffold; etc. Each borough. 1928. p. 8. **114**

See also: *Accidents* 1, 2, 4
Deaths and death rate 38, 60, 61
Workmen's compensation (entire)

FAMILIES

1. Population and number of families. Manhattan and Bronx; Brooklyn; Queens; Richmond. 1920 and estimate for 1927. p. 202. **245**

2. Families per dwelling. Each borough. 1920. p. 10. **221**

3. Families. Each tabulation tract of 1920 (one or more sanitary districts having a total population of 1,000 or more). 1910, 1920. p. 2–819. **51**

See also: *Bronx, Borough of* 3
Dwellings 2–4
East Harlem 4
Richmond, Borough of 11
Standard of living 1, 4–8

Other allied topic: *Boy population*

FAMILY SERVICE

1. Family service agencies which report monthly data to the Research Bureau of the Welfare Council of New York City: (a) major care cases (cases carried from last month; intake [new; reopened]; active cases [relief; service only]; inactive cases [attention needed; observation only; waiting to be closed]; cases closed); (b) minor care cases (cases interviewed; report only; out-of-town inquiry; other); (c) staff (supervisory personnel; visitors; etc.); (d) per cent change from preceding month of major care cases (relief cases; intake; active cases); (e) per cent change from last month of relief cases (major care cases [allowance; other]; minor care cases); (f) amount of relief (major **323**

FAMILY SERVICE (continued)

Source Number

1. *(continued)*
care cases [allowance; other]; minor care cases); (g) families in which persons were unemployed and seeking work (major care cases [carried from last month; intake]; minor care cases); (h) families in which persons were underemployed, classified as above. Each agency. The same data for a constant group of six agencies. Compiled monthly.
NOTE: The group reporting does not include all agencies eligible for reporting but includes a large proportion of such agencies.

2. Financial trends of family service agencies: (a) gross amounts received from all sources of income by type (gross earnings, with subdivisions; dividends, interest, and rent; contributions, with subdivisions); (b) functional expenditures by function (relief; administration and service; wages and other expenditures for the blind, for the crippled, and for the physically and mentally handicapped; shelter for the homeless and employment for the indigent; health education; nursing service; convalescent care; hospitals and clinics; protective and correctional activities; summer camps and vacation houses; all other). Each year, 1910–1926. **330**

3. Family service agencies which report monthly data to the New York School of Social Work: (a) major care cases (cases carried from last month; intake [new; recurrent]; open during month; closed and transferred during month; open at end of month); (b) minor care cases open during month. Four societies, each society: Association for Improving the Condition of the Poor; Catholic Charities; Charity Organization Society; Jewish Social Service Association. Each health area, Manhattan. Compiled monthly. **225**

4. Division of Families of Catholic Charities: (a) families served; (b) individuals served; (c) money expended. Each office. Manhattan; Bronx. 1928. p. 13. ***40**

NOTE: The Jewish Social Service Association cares for all the Jewish applicants for aid in Manhattan and the

FAMILY SERVICE *(continued)*

Source Number

NOTE: *(continued)*

Bronx, and the unpublished annual statistical report for this organization gives a detailed analysis of the families aided.

See also: *Child Welfare, Board of* (entire)
Dependents, Aged 5
Outdoor relief (entire)

FARM AND FARMERS

See: *Agriculture*

FEEBLEMINDED PERSONS

See: *Mental defectives*

FELONIES

1. Cases of felony reported to the Police Department, by type. Period Jan.–June, each year, 1928, 1929. p. 43. **146**

2. Cases of felony reported, by disposition (arrest; pending; other) and type of felony. Each county. Period Jan.–June, 1929. p. 44–49. **146**

3. Indictments and convictions for felonies in the county courts, each offense. Court of General Sessions, Manhattan, each year, 1900–1927; County Court, Brooklyn, each year, 1912–1927. p. 508. ***244**

4. Cases arraigned for felonies (in the inferior court, grand jury room, or court of records, combined), each charge: (a) cases; (b) median age. Period July 1–Dec. 31, 1926. p. 38. **171**

5. Arrests, by disposition (eliminated in preliminary hearing; eliminated in grand jury; etc.), each charge. Period July 1–Dec. 31, 1926. p. 70–71. **171**

6. Cases arrested for felonies: (a) eliminated in preliminary hearing, with median number of days from arraignment to elimination; (b) eliminated in the **171**

FELONIES (*continued*)

Source Number

6. (*continued*)
grand jury, with median number of days from arraignment in the inferior court to disposition in preliminary hearing, and from disposition in preliminary hearing to elimination in grand jury. Period July 1–Dec. 31, 1926. p. 105.

7. Cases of felonies in County Courts, by plea (guilty of offense charged; guilty of other offense; etc.) and disposition (acquitted; convicted of offense charged; etc.), each charge. Period July 1–Dec. 31, 1926. p. 81, 86. **171**

8. Cases of felonies in County Courts: median number of days from entrance in County Court to disposition, by disposition (eliminated; guilt established), each plea: guilty of offense charged; guilty of other offense; etc. Period July 1–Dec. 31, 1926. p. 64. **171**

9. Cases of felonies in County Courts, by disposition (eliminated in County Courts; punished by suspended sentence; punished by death, imprisonment, or fine): (a) median number of days from arraignment in inferior court to disposition in preliminary hearing; (b) from disposition in preliminary hearing to grand jury action; (c) from grand jury action to arraignment in trial court; (d) from arraignment in trial court to final disposition; (e) from arraignment at preliminary hearing to final disposition. Period July 1–Dec. 31, 1926. p. 105–106. **171**

10. Cases of felonies in County Courts: (a) per cent distribution of cases tried by jury, according to disposition (convicted; acquitted), p. 13; (b) cases in County Courts in which guilt of a felony was established, by disposition (sentence suspended; imprisoned or fined), p. 19; (c) cases in County Courts in which guilt of a felony was established, by type of sentence (sentence suspended; life; etc.) and charge in indictment, p. 96; (d) cases in County Courts in which guilt of a felony was established, by type of sentence (as above) and charge on which conviction was based, p. 101. Period July 1–Dec. 31, 1926. **171**

FELONIES *(continued)*

Source Number

11. Arrests, by disposition: (a) eliminated by police, in preliminary hearing, etc., by specific method of elimination (transferred to other jurisdictions; discharged; etc.); (b) number imprisoned or fined. Each county. 1925. p. 54. **172**

12. Arrests: (a) each offense; (b) per cent distribution, each offense, by disposition (eliminated by police; eliminated in preliminary hearing; etc.). 1925. p. 32. **172**

13. Cases held for grand Jury: (a) each charge; (b) per cent distribution by disposition (eliminated in grand jury; eliminated in County Court; etc.), each charge; (c) cases eliminated in grand jury, with median number of days (from arrest to final disposition, each county; from arrest to preliminary hearing, counties combined; from preliminary hearing to grand jury, each county). 1925. p. 33, 46. **172**

14. Cases disposed of in County Courts, by disposition (eliminated; imprisoned or fined; sentence suspended), with median number of days (as in 10), with the following intervals added: grand jury to arraignment, each county; arraignment to final disposition, each county. 1925. p. 46–47. **172**

15. Males presented for felonies: (a) by color (white; colored), each offense; (b) median age, by color, each offense. Each county. 1925. p. 14–15. **172**

16. Cases in County Courts: (a) by type of plea (guilty of offense charged; guilty of other offense; etc.), each county, p. 64–65; (b) per cent distribution, each type of plea, by disposition (acquitted; convicted of offense charged; etc.), each county, p. 64–65; (c) per cent distribution of total cases in County Courts, by certain types of disposition (disposition by jury, with subdivisions; disposition on plea of guilty, with subdivisions), p. 44. 1925. **172**

17. Cases in County Courts: (a) per cent which cases receiving suspended sentence were of cases in which **172**

FELONIES *(continued)*

Source Number

17. *(continued)*
guilt of a felony was established, by plea (guilty of offense charged; guilty of other offense; not guilty), each county, p. 41; (b) per cent distribution of cases in County Courts which were imprisoned or fined, by type of sentence (indeterminate; fixed and others), each county, p. 27; (c) cases in County Courts which received life sentence, each county, p. 30; (d) cases in County Courts which were imprisoned or fined, by type of plea (guilty of offense charged; guilty of other offense; etc.) and disposition (fined; imprisoned), each county, p. 70–71; (e) per cent distribution of cases imprisoned, each type of plea, by type of sentence (fixed term, by length of sentence; death; etc.), each county, p. 70–71; (f) per cent of the number imprisoned which received indeterminate sentences, by plea (as above), each county, p. 43. 1925.

18. Cases disposed of in County Courts: (a) by disposition (eliminated in County Court; imprisoned or fined), with median number of days from arrest to disposition, each plea (guilty of offense charged; guilty of other offense; etc.), each county, p. 74; (b) by disposition (as above), with median number of days from arrest to disposition, each offense, each county, p. 78–79; (c) by disposition (as above), distributed according to number of adjournments, with median number of days from arraignment to disposition, each county, p. 76. 1925. **172**

19. Arrests, on "fourth offender" charges: (a) by disposition (life imprisonment; guilty of felony as charged and placed under investigation; etc.); (b) "fourth offender" cases pleading guilty to or found guilty of lesser crimes, by crime with which originally charged and crime for which punished. Period Jan. 1, 1927–Jan. 12, 1928. p. 7–8. **171**

See also: *Arrests and summonses* 1, 4
Courts 12, 13, 15, 18, 21–23, 38, 44, 55–57, 80, 129
Truants 1

FERRIES

Source Number

1. Ferry traffic to and from New York City: (a) traffic (excluding interborough ferries), subdivided as to local and railroad passengers, by ferry and by terminal; (h) municipal ferry traffic (passengers; vehicles), by line. 1928. p. 5–6. **•210**

See also: *Transportation* 3

FINANCES, CITY

1. Amount of City budget. Each year, 1906–1929. p. 182. **•252**
2. City finances: (a) income by source; (b) outgo by purpose. Summary for 1927, 1928, and detailed accounts for 1928. **•120**
3. New York City budget: (a) money appropriated to City departments for salaries and running expenses; (b) appropriations made to charitable organizations, each organization. 1929. **•128**
4. Relative increase in population of New York City, total City budget, and budget of New York City Department of Health. Each year, 1911–1926. p. 10. Chart only. **215**
5. City finances: (a) revenue receipts from earnings of general departments, by principal divisions of the general departmental service (general government; protection to person and property; conservation of health; sanitation or promotion of cleanliness; highways; charities, hospitals, and corrections; schools; libraries; recreation; miscellaneous); (b) governmental-cost payments for operation and maintenance of general departments and payments for outlays, by principal divisions of the general departmental service (as above), and by subdivisions. 1926. p. 240, 264–368. **•283**

FINANCES, SOCIAL WORK

Source Number

1. Money spent on social work in New York City: (a) source; (b) expenditure. (Based on 474 organizations). 1923. **87**

See also: *Family service* 2
Legal aid 1
Outdoor relief 1
Settlements 3, 4

FIRES

1. Number of fire alarms (total; false); number of fires (buildings; vessels; miscellaneous). Each borough. 1928. p. 18. **130**
2. Fires: (a) per 100 edifices; (b) per 1000 inhabitants; (c) per cent confined to point of origin; (d) loss per capita. 1928. p. 16. **130**
3. Buildings in which fires occurred, by type: asylums; homes; churches; service stations; etc. By borough groups: (a) Manhattan, Bronx, Richmond; (b) Brooklyn, Queens. 1928. p. 18. **130**
4. Structure of buildings in which fires occurred: brick; frame; etc. By borough groups: (a) Manhattan, Bronx, Richmond; (b) Brooklyn, Queens. 1928. p. 18. **130**
5. Origin of fires in housing buildings, and cause of fires. 1922, 1923. p. 35. **276** May, 1925
6. Number of fires in tenements and per cent of fires to total buildings by origin of fire. By borough groups: (a) Manhattan, Bronx, Richmond; (b) Brooklyn, Queens. 1924. p. 16. **276** Apr., 1926
7. Fires in tenement houses by type of tenement (old-law; new-law): (a) place of origin (cellar; roof; etc.); (b) nature of occupancy (bedroom; elevator; etc.); (c) manner of extension (stairway; dumbwaiter; etc.). By borough groups: (a) Manhattan, Bronx, Richmond; (b) Brooklyn, Queens. 1928. p. 18. **130**
8. Number of fires, serious fires, deaths by fire, in (a) old-law, (b) new-law tenements. Manhattan. Each year, 1920–1925. p. 18. **276** Apr., 1926

FIRES, *(continued)*

Source Number

9. Deaths and injuries at fires; classes of buildings where deaths occurred (dwelling; factory; etc.); causes of fires causing deaths (electrical origin; gas stove; etc.); ages of persons meeting death, by sex; classification of business fires by kind of business; causes of fires; extent of fire losses by month; insured and uninsured losses. By borough groups: (a) Manhattan, Bronx, Richmond; (b) Brooklyn, Queens. 1928. p. 47–62. **130**

10. Deaths from fires in tenements by type of tenement (old-law; new-law): (a) all deaths from fires; (b) deaths by fire due to conflagration of building. Each borough. 1928. **152**

Allied topics: *Arson*
Burns

FOOD, COST OF

1. Average retail prices of each of the principal articles of food. Current month, corresponding month of preceding year, and preceding month of current year. **314**

2. Per cent changes in the retail cost of food in the current month, compared with the cost in the corresponding month of the preceding year, the preceding month of the current year, and with the average cost in 1913. **314**

3. Index numbers of cost of food (Jan., 1915 = 100): (a) yearly average, each year, 1917–1927; (b) average for each month, Oct., Nov., Dec., 1927, and Jan. through Aug., 1928. Published occasionally. p. 377. **188 Sept., 1928**

4. Average and relative retail prices of specified food articles. Each month, 1926, 1927. p. 120–121, 186. **311**

5. Changes in the retail cost of food, shown by index numbers. Each year, 1913–1925, and each month, 1926, 1927. p. 35. **311**

6. Cost of food (index numbers). New York City, Rochester, Buffalo. Each month. 1916–1925. Part II, p. 208. **41**

FOOD, COST OF *(continued)*

Source Number

7. Relative family expenditure for 22 articles of food in specified cities. Each month and each year, 1913–1920. (Index numbers, based on 1913). p. 42–45. **306**

8. Average retail price of specified food articles. 1913, and by month, 1920. p. 121. **306**

9. Minimum requirements and average minimum cost of food for one week for a family of 4 adults and 1 child, living at a fair American standard of living, by item of food. Each borough. 1926. p. 48–49. **102**

10. Minimum requirements and average minimum cost of food for one week, based on the needs of the family of an industrial worker, his wife, and 2 children under 14, living at a fair American standard in New York City. Each article of food. 1926. p. 16–17. **103**

See also: *Cost of living* 1, 3, 4

FOOD HANDLERS

See: *Physical examinations* 11, 12

FOOD INSPECTIONS

1. Food inspections (retail; wholesale) by the New York City Department of Health; violations (sanitary; food). Each borough. Current monthly through Dec., 1924. **132**

2. Samples examined and amount of adulteration of the 12 most important articles of food, 1922, 1923. Also total for all food stuffs combined, 1922, 1923. p. 136. **133** June, 1924

3. Examinations of food handlers by private physician: examinations; cases excluded by reason. Each borough. 1920. p. 218. **133** Sept., 1921

4. Important arrests and prosecutions for violation of the sanitary code, by type of violation (unclean premises; adulterated milk; etc.). Current monthly through Dec., 1924. **132**

See also: *Courts* 59

FOOD PRODUCTS INDUSTRY

Source Number

1. Food manufacturing industries in New York and its environs: (a) maps showing location of food plants having 20 or more employees, in New York and its environs, by branch of industry, 1900, 1912, 1917, 1922; (b) plants and employees, Brooklyn and Queens combined, 1900, 1912, 1917, 1922; (c) slaughtering and meat and fish packing establishments (combined) in New York City, classified by number of employees, 1900, 1912, 1917, 1922; (d) bakeries in New York City by number of employees, 1900, 1912, 1917, 1922; (e) bakeries and employees, Manhattan south of 59th Street, 1922; (f) confectionery establishments and employees, New York City, 1900, 1912, 1917, 1922; (g) confectionery establishments and employees by size of establishment, Manhattan below 59th Street, Manhattan above 59th Street, Bronx, Queens, Kings, Richmond, 1922; (h) cocoa and chocolate manufacturing establishments, wage earners, and value of products, New York City, 1899, 1904, 1909, 1914, 1919, 1921; (i) plants and percentage of employees in coffee, tea, and spice industry, Manhattan below 59th Street, 1900, 1917, 1922. Corresponding data for many other food manufacturing industries. "The Food Manufacturing Industry." p. 13–60. **258**
2. Location of small plants (less than 20 employees) in food industries. Manhattan and a part of the Bronx, Brooklyn, Queens. 1922. p. 68. Map only. **256**

See also: *Employment* 1–5, 7, 8, 10, 14
Manufactures 1, 3, 4, 11
Occupations, Children engaged in 3
Occupations, Persons engaged in 3, 10
Salaries and wages 1–7
Workmen's compensation (entire)

FORGERY

See: *Arrests and summonses* 1
Correction 20, 83, 84
Felonies 2–5, 7, 10, 12, 13, 15, 18

FREEZING

Source Number

See: *Accidents* 1
Deaths and death rate 38, 60, 61

FUNERAL COSTS

1. Funeral costs of 1840 estates, by value of estate: (a) number of estates, average amount of funeral and burial expenses, per cent of net estate, and per cent of gross estate, each county, New York County and Kings County; (b) extra charges in various estates (974) by type (monuments and mausoleums; cemetery plots and perpetual care; flowers), New York County; (c) average burial expense, average extra charge, per cent which net funeral bill was of net estate and of gross estate, for 974 estates, New York County. Period from latter part of 1926 through early part of 1927. p. 74, 77, 79, 83. **73**

2. Average cost of burial of 883 residents of New York City over 12 years of age who were holders of industrial policies of the Metropolitan Life Insurance Company which were paid during period Apr. 15–June 30, 1927; average amount of insurance carried. p. 275. **73**

3. Funeral costs of husbands of 319 widows receiving allowances from the New York City Board of Child Welfare: (a) average funeral expenditure; (b) average burial expenses for estates under $1,000, by borough, Manhattan and Brooklyn; (c) average funeral expenditures and per cent of net assets, by racial origin of families. [1927]. p. 118–121. **73**

GARMENT INDUSTRY

1. Shops and workers of (a) cloak, suit, and skirt industry, and (b) dress and waist industry: number of union and non-union shops; number of establishments; union and non-union workers by sex; workers by craft; location of shops; sanitary defects; etc. End of 1925. p. 56–60. **86**

GARMENT INDUSTRY *(continued)*

Source Number

2. Wages in the cloak, suit, and skirt industry: (a) average weekly wage rates by occupation (cutters; pressers; etc.) and kind of shop (American Association; Industrial Council; independent), 1925; (b) number of workers by occupation, 1925; (c) per cent of workers receiving each classified weekly wage rate (under $30; $30–40; etc.), by kind of shop, 1925; (d) average weekly wage rates by occupation, 1924, 1925; (e) average weekly hours and earnings, equivalent full time weeks per year per worker, and average earnings per year, by kind of shop, 1925; (f) average full time weeks of employment and annual earnings in inside shops, and in sub-manufacturing shops, 1924, 1925. p. 66–68. **314 June, 1926**

3. Men's clothing workers: union members by sex; average wage of union members by sex; housing activities; unemployment insurance. Compiled annually. **1**

4. Men's clothing industry: employees, average earnings, average hours, actual earnings, etc., by type of position held and sex; also number of establishments. 1926. **308**

5. Men's clothing industry: number of establishments; employees by sex; average hours worked by sex; earnings by sex. Each occupation. 1926. p. 762. **309**

6. Women's clothing industry by branch of industry: establishments; proprietors and firm members; average number of wage earners; wages; cost of materials; value of product. 1921. p. 515. **89**

7. Average number of workers per establishment in the women's clothing industry. Each year, 1899, 1904, 1909, 1914, 1919, 1921. p. 521. **89**

See also: *Employment* 1–5, 7, 8, 10, 14
Homework (entire)
Homework of children (entire)
Manufactures 1, 3, 4, 11
Occupations, Children engaged in 3

GARMENT INDUSTRY *(continued)*

Source Number

See also: *(continued)*
Occupations, Persons engaged in 3, 10
Salaries and wages 1–7, 12
Textile industry (entire)
Trade unions 2
Workmen's compensation (entire)

GUARDIANS

1. Guardians appointed and number of guardians' bonds. Supreme Court of the State of New York, First Judicial Department. New York County (Special Term, Part II); Bronx County (Special Term, Ex Parte Applications). 1928. p. 14–15, 36. ***207**

HANDICAPPED PERSONS

1. Characteristics of applicants to 12 placement agencies for the handicapped; number of applicants; sex; residence; age; marital condition; religion; ability to speak English; extent of education; dominant handicap; etc. Each agency. Period Oct. 19 to Nov. 14, 1925. **320**

Allied topic: *Defectives*

HEALTH AREAS

1. Number of health areas. Each borough. 1928. **321**

See also: *Population and population estimates, not including 1930 and later* 6
Vital statistics Note

HEALTH SERVICE

1. Organized health activities in settlements (sample, 30 settlements) by type of activity: medical examinations; clinics, by type; nutrition work; health education. Winter 1927/28. **334**

HEART DISEASE

Source Number

1. Deaths. Current month. **179**
2. Deaths and death rate from all heart diseases. Each year, 1900–1925. p. 5–6. **237**
3. Deaths from heart disease: pericarditis; angina pectoris; acute endocarditis; other diseases of the heart. Each year, 1901–1925, and by borough (including death rate), 1925. p. 1–2. **237**
4. Deaths from heart disease by sex and age groups (5-year periods). 1910, 1920, 1925, and period 1915–1924. p. 3, 8–9. **237**
5. Death rate from heart disease by age groups (5-year periods) and sex. Period 1915–1925. p. 1039. **71**
6. Clinic reports of the Committee on Cardiac Clinics of the Heart Committee of the New York Tuberculosis and Health Association: (a) composition of case load (old; new; readmissions) by age (adults; children); (b) disposition of case load, by age (adults; children); (c) clinic sessions, hours, visits; (d) personnel; (e) home visits; (f) disposition of closed cases; (g) etiological types; (h) comparative condition of closed cases on admission, on discharge. For (a) each clinic, by age of patients admitted (adults only; children only; adults and children), (b) by borough, (c) entire city. 1927, 1928. ***239**
7. Work of the cardiac clinics reporting to the Committee on Cardiac Clinics of the Heart Committee of the New York Tuberculosis and Health Association: composition of case loads by functional classification; per cent of new admissions; cases closed by reason; clinic visits per patient; patients per physician; patients per social worker; home visits per patient; etc. Each clinic. 1928. **238**
8. Cases of heart disease in hospitals reporting: total patients, bed days, and deaths, compared with same for heart patients; heart cases by sex; number of cases under 12 years of age by sex; etiology of heart deaths; cost of heart patients. Kings County and New York County, combined. 1927. p. 104–107. **90**

HEART DISEASE *(continued)*

Source Number

9. Heart patients in ten large general hospitals: per cent of total patients that were heart patients; patients by age groups; patients by sex; condition at discharge; length of stay and cost in hospital; diagnosis; occupation of patient. Each hospital. 1920 or 1921. p. 387–389. **70**

10. Special dispensary heart classes (43) for adults and children: number of patients; visits; doctors; clinic hours; etc. Each supervising organization. 1921. p. 390. **70**

11. Work of the Cardiac Vocational Guidance Committee of the Public Education Association: number of children (13 to 17 years old) referred to the Cardiac Committee by source of referral; number of children examined, reexamined; home visits paid; consultations held; cases closed by reason for closing; cardiac trade classes. 1925. **250**

12. Per cent of cardiac disease found among public school children examined by the Bureau of Child Hygiene of the New York City Department of Health. Period 1918–1922. p. 14. **4**

13. Children in public schools examined by a committee of the American Heart Association: (a) per cent of children examined who had organic heart disease, and per cent of each class of defect; (b) attendance rate of children in cardiac classes, 1921/22; (c) per cent of children with organic heart disease who had specified disease (chorea; diphtheria; scarlet fever; rheumatism; tonsilitis). [1923]. p. 13–18. **4**

14. Convalescent homes in or near New York City accepting patients convalescing from an acute cardiac disease: (a) bed capacity (total; heart patients); (b) age, sex, and color of patients accepted; (c) total days care of heart patients; (d) average cost per patient and total cost for year. Each home. [1921]. p. 389. **70**

HEART DISEASE *(continued)*

Source Number

See also: *Bellevue-Yorkville district* 6–10, 14
Bronx, Borough of 1
Clinics 1, 12, Note
Deaths and death rate 1, 3–7, 38, 39, 41, 44–48, 50–52, 54, 60–63, 65, 72–75
East Harlem 6–11
Education 38, 39
Health service (entire)
Negroes 8

HIGH SCHOOLS

See: *Education*

HIGHWAY LAW, VIOLATION OF

See: *Arrests and summonses* 1
Correction 20, 50, 54
Courts 12, 13, 17, 18, 21, 22, 24, 25, 28, 30, 32, 38, 55–58, 84, 91–93, 96, 97, 100, 105, 108

Other allied topic: *Traffic regulations, Violation of*

HOMELESS PERSONS

1. Agencies caring for the homeless which report monthly data to the Research Bureau of the Welfare Council of New York City (for men; for women and children): (a) bed capacity of agencies operating lodging houses; (b) nights' lodgings provided each night of the month; (c) different persons provided with lodgings. Each agency. Compiled monthly. **322**

   NOTE: The group reporting does not include all agencies eligible for reporting but includes a large proportion of such agencies.

2. Municipal Lodging House: (a) average daily census by month, 1897–1928; (b) detailed statistical analysis of average daily census by month, 1918–1928. p. 182–190. Charts only. **269**

HOMELESS PERSONS *(continued)*

Source Number

3. Municipal Lodging House: (a) nights' lodgings used by resident men and by non-resident men, each month, 1922–1928; (b) detailed study of a sample (3000 non-resident men and 3000 resident men), each month, Jan., 1927–Jan., 1928. **328**

4. Lodgers at the Municipal Lodging House by sex, with number of those who were children: (a) admissions by type (first admissions; readmissions); (b) age; (c) time in the United States; (d) time in New York City; (e) disposition of case (assigned to work by kind of work; dismissed); (f) nativity; (g) month of admittance; (h) number of positions filled by employment clearing bureau, by month. 1926. p. 298–302. **148**

5. Non-resident lodgers admitted to the Municipal Lodging House. Each month, 1926. p. 302. **148**

6. Lodgers at the Municipal Lodging House: (a) total; (b) daily average. Each year, 1914–1926. p. 301. **148**

7. Estimated number of homeless Jewish men who received shelter. 1927. p. 4. **29**

8. Age distribution of homeless Jewish men cared for by (a) Jewish Social Service Association, 1926, (b) Hebrew Immigrant Aid Society, 1927. p. 4–5. **29**
   NOTE: Also data on nativity, occupation, length of stay, etc., for one or the other of the above agencies.

See also: *Family service* 2
Public charges 4

HOMES, OWNERSHIP OF

See: *Ownership of homes*

HOMEWORK

1. Trend in homework industries in New York City district (5 boroughs): number of employers and number of homeworkers, by kind of work done (bags; boxes; buttons; etc.). Year ending June 30, each year, 1924–1927. p. 277. **188** **June, 1928**

HOMEWORK (*continued*)

Source Number

2. Homework in the men's clothing industry in New York City: number of workers included in study, by type of firm; number of firms employing homeworkers by type of firm; operations performed by homeworkers; number of firms and workers in the industry; size of firm; location of manufacturers; grade of garment made; trend of employment (graphs); etc. [1926]. **196**

3. Number of New York City firms distributing homework, and of homeworkers supplied with work. By kind of goods given out. [Jan., 1925]. p. 96. **188** **Jan., 1925**

4. Number and per cent of firms giving homework to contractors exclusively, by kind of goods given out. [Jan., 1925]. p. 96. **188** **Jan., 1925**

5. Number of firms giving work direct to homeworkers, number of homeworkers, and average number of homeworkers per firm. By kind of goods given out. [Jan., 1925]. p. 97. **188** **Jan., 1925**

6. Number and per cent of firms sending work outside the State by State to which sent, and by kind of goods given out. [Jan., 1925]. p. 97. **188** **Jan., 1925**

   NOTE: Items 3, 4, 5, and 6. Data based on 2004 firms registered with the Division of Homework Inspection of the State Department of Labor.

7. Adult homeworkers in homes which were investigated for tenement homework: (a) foreign-born homeworking mothers by nationality; (b) kind of work of adult homeworkers; (c) hours of work of adult homeworkers; (d) hourly earnings of adult homeworkers; (e) number of homeworking families by annual earnings of father; (f) total income from homework; (g) number of persons in the home; (h) rooms occupied; (i) rent paid. Manhattan, Bronx, Brooklyn (combined). 1923. p. 66–76. **159**

8. Women homeworkers in New York City, by industry. Year ending June 30, 1924, and year ending Dec. 31, 1928. p. 69. **314** **Aug., 1929**

HOMEWORK *(continued)*

Source Number

NOTE: The Bureau of Women in Industry of the New York State Department of Labor has some statistics compiled annually on employers and homeworkers, which may be seen at the office of the Bureau.

See also: *Textile industry* (entire)

HOMEWORK OF CHILDREN

1. Investigation of child homeworkers in 359 families: (a) number of child homeworkers by kind of work; (b) age; (c) time of work; (d) hours of work; (e) days absent from school; (f) scholarship; (g) retardation; (h) violation of labor law. Summer and fall, 1923. p. 53–65. **159**

HOMICIDE

1. Cases of murder and manslaughter, combined, reported to the Police Department: (a) by motive; (b) crimes committed inside of building and crimes committed outside of building; (c) by status of case (conviction obtained; case unsolved; etc.). Jan.–June, each year, 1928, 1929. p. 41. **146**
2. Cases charged with homicide: (a) arraignments by sex, each type of homicide (accident, motor vehicle; accident, other than motor vehicle; other than accidental); (b) cases disposed of, by sex and general disposition (discharged; held, each type of homicide (as above); (c) cases held to answer, by sex and security (bailed; bail not given; without bail), each type of homicide (as above). By court: Homicide Court, Manhattan; Homicide Court, Bronx. 1927. p. 122, 127–128. ***117**
3. Arraignments for homicide. Homicide Court, Manhattan. Period Jan. 1–Dec. 11, 1928. p. 129. **162**
4. Convictions for homicide by type of offense: murder, first degree; murder, second degree; manslaughter, first degree; manslaughter, second degree. County Court, New York County. Each year, 1900–1927. p. 508. ***244**

HOMICIDE *(continued)*

Source Number

5. Homicides: (a) total, each borough; (b) by negroes; (c) by relatives (husband; wife; child); (d) by method (accident; assault; etc.). Each year, 1921–1927. p. 508. **•244**
6. Homicides: (a) by method used; (b) by color (black; yellow). Each borough. 1928. p. 3. **114**

See also: *Arrests and summonses* 1, 3
Bronx, Borough of 1
Correction 20, 54, 83, 84
Courts 12, 13, 15, 16, 18, 21–23, 38, 54–57
Deaths and death rate 38–41, 44, 46, 60–63, 65, 73–75
Felonies 1–5, 7, 10, 12, 13, 15, 18
Violence, Crimes of 1, 2

HOSPITALS

1. Total hospital beds and number per 1000 total population. Each borough. 1928. p. 21. **30**
2. Comparison of hospital beds in New York City and total population, by per cent. Each borough. [1924]. p. 36. **216**
3. Estimated per cent of all hospital beds in the United States that are in New York City. [1922]. p. 45. **56**
4. Number of beds in general hospitals by type of hospital: (a) voluntary, subdivided as to Jewish and non-Jewish; (b) municipal; (c) proprietary. 1923; also by borough, 1928. p. 19–20. **30**
5. Hospitals in New York City (not including proprietary hospitals, hospitals for the insane or mentally defective, and United States Government hospitals), classified as (a) municipal hospitals by type (general; women's and children's; chronic and convalescent; special), further subdivided as to whether or not a member of the United Hospital Fund, and (b) municipal hospitals, each hospital: number of hospitals; beds; beds used; patients; days of treatment; days' stay. 1927. p. 36–37. **•272**

HOSPITALS *(continued)*

Source Number

6. Work done by hospitals belonging to the United Hospital Fund: (a) hospital days; (b) estimated free days; (c) cost per patient per day; (d) Out-Patient Department (total visits; free visits; cost per visit); (e) number of hospital patients classified by economic status (private; ward; free; public charge); (f) average length of stay; (g) number of beds; (h) employees; (i) nurses; (j) ambulance calls; (k) income; (l) expenditure; etc. Each hospital by type of hospital (general; women's and children's; special; chronic and convalescent). 1927. Supplementary statistical sheet. ***272**

7. Number and per cent of general hospital patients (Jewish; non-Jewish), by type of hospital: (a) voluntary, subdivided as to Jewish and non-Jewish; (b) municipal (hospitals of the New York City Department of Public Welfare; Bellevue and Allied Hospitals); (c) estimated patients at proprietary hospitals. 1925. p. 23–25. **30**

8. Hospitals of all types: (a) beds; (b) class of patients received (all races; white only; negro only); (c) patients treated; (d) days' treatment (pay; part pay; free); (e) medical staff (salaried physicians; internes); (f) nurses (graduate; pupil; special; attendant); (g) training schools for nurses; (h) social service departments, and number of paid workers. Each borough. 1922. p. 29, 31. **289**

9. General hospitals: beds; patients; days' treatment. Each borough. 1922. p. 30. **289**

10. Distribution of hospitals (general; special): (a) by number of hospital beds, each borough; (b) by number of hospitals by bed capacity (under 50; 50 to 100; etc.). [1924]. p. 39, 41. **216**

11. Distribution of bed capacity (based on 182 hospitals) by type of service given, and by kind of hospital: municipal; private general; private special; proprietary. [1924]. p. 75. **216**

HOSPITALS *(continued)*

Source Number

12. Per cent distribution of bed accommodation (private; semi-private; ward) in non-municipal general and non-municipal special hospitals. Each borough. [1924]. p. 43, 44. **216**

13. Number of hospital beds, and number of attending physicians. Each borough. [1924]. p. 46. **216**

14. Hospitals by ownership (public; semi-public; private): (a) number of hospitals; (b) bed capacity. Each borough. Dec., 1922. p. 4–5. **133** **Jan., 1923**

15. Bed capacity, average daily census, number of employees, number of nurses: (a) in general hospitals by bed capacity (under 100; 100–300; 300 and over); (b) in special hospitals by bed capacity. Each hospital. 1921, 1922. p. 132, 133. **216**

16. Per cent utilization of hospitals (days estimated capacity; days actually used), by type of ownership (private; municipal). Each borough. 1920. p. 65–66. **216**

17. Bed capacity of 182 hospitals in greater New York according to service and use (medical; surgical; cancer; etc.), and by type of hospital (municipal; private general; private special; proprietary). 1920. p. 45–46. **56**

18. Hospitals classified as public, community, and chronic: (a) number of hospitals; (b) beds (subdivided as to private; semi-private; charity); (c) patient days; (d) per cent of bed utilization; (e) operating cost. Brooklyn. 1925. p. 6. **19**

19. Nurses, attendants, doctors, source of revenue. Brooklyn hospitals. 1925. p. 6. **19**

20. Bed capacity of special hospitals (cancer; orthopedic; incurable and chronic cases; etc.). Dec., 1922. p. 6. **133** **Jan., 1923**

21. Public hospitals in New York City (Bellevue and Allied Hospitals; hospitals of the New York City Department of Health; hospitals of the New York City Department of Public Welfare): (a) number of hospitals; **157**

HOSPITALS *(continued)*

Source Number

21. *(continued)*
(b) number of patients (adults; children; infants born in hospitals); (c) economic status of patient (free; pay); (d) discharges; (e) deaths (adults; children; infants born in hospitals); (f) total remaining at close of year by sex; (g) number of days' treatment (free; pay); (h) average daily census; (i) bed capacity; (j) social service visits outside hospital. Each hospital. Year ending June 30, 1928. p. 181, 189, 197.

22. Total beds and average number of beds in use, in municipally owned and operated hospitals (total). 1926. **266**

23. Hospitals of the New York City Department of Public Welfare: (a) bed capacity; (b) initial census; (c) admissions; (d) births; (e) deaths; (f) discharges; (g) end census. Each hospital, and total. 1926. p. 31. **148**

24. Contagious disease hospitals maintained by the New York City Department of Health: (a) average daily census; (b) bed capacity; (c) per cent of beds occupied. Each hospital. 1928. p. 92. **131**

25. Contagious disease hospitals maintained by the New York City Department of Health: (a) patients treated; (b) patient days. Each year, 1926–1928. p. 92. **131**

26. General and special Roman Catholic hospitals: bed capacity, patients treated, free patients, sisters, each hospital; patients, sisters, free visits, prescriptions, free prescriptions, each out-patient department, each hospital. Manhattan; Bronx. 1928. p. 50, 54. ***40**

27. Jewish patients in Jewish, non-Jewish, and public hospitals. Manhattan; Bronx; Brooklyn; Richmond and Queens. 1925. p. 28. **30**

28. Ratio of Jewish hospital beds per 1000 Jewish population. Each borough. 1920, 1928, and estimate for 1930. p. 7, 12–13. **30**

HOSPITALS *(continued)*

Source Number

29. Number and per cent of Jewish and non-Jewish patients in Jewish hospitals. Each hospital, each borough. 1925. p. 26. **30**

30. Hospitals under Jewish auspices: (a) total beds; (b) beds for adults and children; (c) baby beds. Each hospital, each borough. 1928, and total beds, 1920. p. 7, 11. **30**

31. Degree of use in Jewish hospitals of (a) private, (b) semi-private, (c) ward beds. Each hospital, each borough. 1925. p. 33. **30**

32. Per cent of days' care to patients in Jewish hospitals by economic groups: private; semi-private; ward pay; public charge; free. Each hospital, each borough. 1925. p. 34. **30**

33. Residence by borough (Manhattan; Brooklyn; Bronx; Queens and Richmond) of patients admitted to Jewish hospitals. Each hospital, each borough. 1925. p. 37. **30**

34. Per cent of Jewish hospital service that is given to non-Jews. [1928]. p. 1. **30**

35. Average per capita daily cost of maintaining patients in private general hospitals. 1926, 1927. p. 32. **157**

36. Maintenance expenses, by principal items of budget and by type of hospital (voluntary; municipal), of all municipal hospitals and private hospitals receiving public funds. Each year, 1919–1922. p. 106–107. **216**

37. Charges made to patients in the various types of accommodations (private; ward; etc.), and number of beds available at the different prices. Manhattan; Brooklyn. 1920. p. 76–84. **216**

NOTE: On February 1, 1929, the public hospitals in New York City were combined into one group to form the newly organized Department of Hospitals. Previously,

HOSPITALS *(continued)*

NOTE: *(continued)*

the hospitals had been divided into three groups, as follows:

(a) Department of Public Welfare, which had jurisdiction over:

The City Hospital (and Children's Clearing Bureau); the Metropolitan Hospital; the New York Cancer Institute; the Children's Hospital on Randall's Island; the Central and Neurological Hospital; the Home for Dependents, Welfare Island; the Lincoln Hospital; the Kings County Hospital; the Bradford Street Hospital; the Cumberland Street Hospital; the Greenpoint Hospital; the Coney Island Hospital; the Sea View Hospital; the Farm Colony.

(b) Department of Health, which had jurisdiction over:

The Willard Parker Hospital; the Riverside Hospital; the Queens Borough Hospital; the Kingston Avenue Hospital; the Staten Island contagious disease hospital at Sea View; the Otisville Sanitarium.

(c) Bellevue and Allied Hospitals, which had jurisdiction over:

The Bellevue Hospital; the Fordham Hospital; the Gouverneur Hospital; the Harlem Hospital; the Neponsit Beach Hospital.

Statistical information was given separately for each hospital in annual reports of the Department of Public Welfare, the Department of Health, and Bellevue and Allied Hospitals.

See also: *Buildings* 2, 9, 13, 16, 17
Chronically ill persons 2, 3
Clinics 2, 4, 5, 7, 10, 11-13
Cripples 4
Fires 3, 9
Heart disease 8, 9
Hospital social service (entire)

HOSPITALS *(continued)*

Source Number

See also: *(continued)*
Mental disease 3, 8
Nurses 2
Physicians 1, 2, 4
Physiotherapy (entire)
Public charges 1–3
Sanitary districts 2
Tonsillectomies (entire)
Tuberculosis 18, 19, 26, 34, 35
Venereal disease 11

Other allied topic: *Ambulances*

HOSPITAL SOCIAL SERVICE

1. Jewish hospitals which do social service work; social service staff (social workers; clerks; student nurses; volunteer nurses). Each hospital. By borough: Manhattan; Brooklyn; Bronx. 1927. p. 2–4. **33**

See also: *Hospitals* 8, 21

HOTELS

1. Hotels in New York City (Manhattan) and capacity. Each hotel. [1928]. **229**

See also: *Building* 2, 4, 6, 9, 11, 13, 16, 17
Business (entire)
Deaths and death rate 18–20
Employment 4
Fires 3, 9

HOURS OF WORK

1. Standard weekly hours of shopworkers in representative factories in New York City: per cent working certain specified hours per week, by sex. Each industry. [1924]. p. 104. **314** May, 1924

HOURS OF WORK *(continued)*

Source Number

2. Hours and earnings of women in 5 industries (confectionery; paper box; shirts and collars; tobacco; mercantile): (a) establishments studied and women employed; (b) weekly hours; (c) earnings; (d) full-time, part-time, and over-time employees; (e) correlation between hours worked and earnings. By industry. Mar.–Apr., 1923. **191**

See also: *Candy industry* 1
Courts 59
Employment 12
Employment of children 2
Employment practice 1, 2
Garment industry 2, 4, 5
Homework 7
Homework of children (entire)
Laundries (entire)
Paper box industry (entire)
Stores 6

HOUSEWORK

1. Women 16 years of age and over engaged in housework at home: (a) by age (16–17; 18–19; 20–24; 25–34; 35–44; 45–54, 55–64; 65 and over; age unknown) and color (white; colored); (b) white women by age and nativity; (c) total by age, each borough section. Richmond County. 1925. p. 34. **206**

HOUSING

1. Suites by type of dwelling (old-law tenement; new-law tenement; etc.), Oct. 1, each year, 1920, 1926, 1927, 1928; net increase in number of suites by type of dwelling, Oct. 1, each year, 1920–1928. p. 57–58. **186**
2. Total persons and total number of suites in all types of dwellings. Each year, 1913–1928. p. 59. **186**
3. Suites by type of dwelling: old-law tenement; new-law tenement; converted dwelling; one-family house; two-family house. Each borough. Each year, 1925–1927. p. 14. **185**

HOUSING *(continued)*

Source Number

4. Total estimated population; total suites. Each year, 1913–1927. p. 15. **185**

5. Increase in suites since 1920, by type of dwelling. Each year, 1921–1927. p. 13. **185**

6. Suites in New York City by type of dwelling. Each borough. Oct. 1, 1926. p. 17. Chart only. **184**

7. Suites in various types of dwellings (5 types). Each borough. Sept. 30, 1925, 1926. p. 20–21. **184**

8. Suites in various types of dwellings in New York City, by type of dwelling: old-law tenement; new-law tenement; converted dwelling; one-family house; two-family house. Oct. 1, 1920 and 1926. p. 16. **184**

9. Suites in New York City, by type of residence: old-law tenement; new-law tenement; converted dwelling; one-family house; two-family house. Jan. 1, 1925. p. 12. **180**

10. Increase in number of suites in (a) tenements, (b) one-family dwellings, (c) two-family dwellings, and (d) suites in dwellings, between Jan. 1, 1920, and June 30, 1923, each borough; and same for boroughs combined, between July 1 and Sept. 30, 1923. p. 29. **181**

11. Residential buildings by type: one-family houses; two-family houses; tenements without elevators; hotels and apartments with elevators. Mar. 31, each year, 1915–1928. p. 33. ***17**

12. Total and per capita expenditures for new buildings and repairs; number of families provided for, and ratio per 10,000 population. 1928. p. 154–155. **314 May, 1929**

13. Per cent of families provided for by the different types of dwellings: one-family houses; two-family houses; multi-family houses. Each borough. 1921, 1926, 1927. p. 24. **312**

14. Families provided for: (a) per cent of families provided for by one-family, two-family, and multi-family dwellings; (b) total families provided for. Each borough. 1921, 1926, 1927. p. 61. Same: 1921, 1925, 1926, June, 1927. p. 4. **314 June, 1928**

HOUSING *(continued)*

Source Number

15. Residences by kind of housing: one-family houses; two-family houses; tenements without elevators; hotels and elevator apartments. Each borough. Each year, 1918–1926. p. 20–21. **102**

16. Families provided with dwellings in new buildings, 1924, 1925; number of these families per 10,000 population as of 1920 census and estimated population, 1924, 1925. p. 123. **314** June, 1926

17. Tax exempt dwellings, by type of dwelling: one-family; two-family; multi-family. Each borough. [Dec., 1922]. **314** Dec., 1922

See also: *Bronx, Borough of* 4
Building 1–6, 8–11, 13–17
Dwellings (entire)
Garment industry 3

Other allied topics: *Apartments*
Boarding homes for business women
Housing construction
Housing surveys
Ownership of homes
Rent
Room registries
Tenements

HOUSING CONSTRUCTION

1. Plans for residential buildings exclusive of hotels and clubs, approved by the Building Department: number of buildings; number of families accommodated; total valuation. 1927, 1928, and Dec., 1927, Nov., 1928, and Dec., 1928. p. 501. **188** Jan., 1929

2. Plans filed, number of families to be accommodated, estimated cost: (a) dwellings; (b) tenements. Each borough. Each year, 1920–1923. p. 10. **182**

3. New buildings providing housing and estimated cost: (a) dwellings; (b) tenements; (c) other residence buildings. Manhattan. Each year, 1918–1928. p. 99. **111**

HOUSING CONSTRUCTION *(continued)*

Source Number

4. All new dwellings (one-family; two-family; multi-family): (a) families provided for; (b) average cost per family. Each borough. Period Jan.–June, 1927. p. 95. **314 Nov., 1927**

See also: *Buildings* 2–6, 8–11, 13–17

Other allied topics: *Apartments*
Housing
Housing surveys
Tenements

HOUSING SURVEYS

1. Housing situation in New York City: new residences (tenements; one-family; two-family; etc.); number of apartments; buildings demolished; old-law tenements; new-law tenements; comparison of housing increase with population; average families per apartment; average persons per room; monthly rent; vacant apartments; size of apartments; tenant turnover. Each borough. Between 1920 and 1923. **254**

2. Housing survey conducted in representative neighborhoods: number of premises visited; lodgers; families; persons; rooms; amount of overcrowding; etc. Manhattan; Brooklyn; Bronx. Spring and Fall, 1920. p. 27–34. **133 Feb., 1921**

   NOTE: See also items 8 and 9.

3. Survey of housing conditions based on a canvass of houses in certain designated, representative sections of the given boroughs: houses investigated, lodgers, houses containing lodgers, houses overcrowded, families occupying houses, persons occupying houses, average families per house, average persons per house, Spring, 1920, Fall, 1920, 1923; also number of vacant apartments, rooms vacant, average rental of vacant apartments, average number of rooms in vacant apartments, 1923. Manhattan; Bronx; Brooklyn. p. 409–416. **136 Dec. 29, 1923**

4. Nine representative tenement blocks in Manhattan and Brooklyn: number of tenements; apartments; rooms; **138**

HOUSING SURVEYS *(continued)*

Source Number

4. *(continued)*
   size of families; average rent; income of family; vacant apartments; sanitary conditions. Each block. Jan., 1924. p. 7–12.
5. Housing survey of 8 selected city blocks in Manhattan and Brooklyn: vacancies; turnover; overcrowding; average rents; rents by length of tenancy. Each block. Feb., 1909; Apr., 1919; Oct., 1923; Sept., 1925; Jan., 1927. (Dates vary for different items). p. 38–46, 50, 57–61. **184**
6. Housing situation in 8 selected blocks (varies slightly from blocks studied in item 5): length of tenancy; vacant apartments; rents paid; overcrowding. Comparison of specified years, 1909–1928. p. 55–74. **185**
7. Housing survey of 2 sections (one in Harlem; one on the lower East Side): (a) buildings by type (tenement; factory; etc.), type of construction, apartments, vacancies, rooms, toilets, heat and hot water furnished, etc., for each street in each section; (b) analysis of bedrooms available and their adult and child occupants, for each section. 1927. p. 121–122. **136** **July 23, 1927**
8. Housing conditions in two tenement blocks in Manhattan (East 112th Street to East 113th Street, 1st Avenue to 2nd Avenue; Rivington Street to Stanton Street, Columbia Street to Sheriff Street): number of houses; families; persons; rooms; rents; etc. [1921]. p. 158. **133** **July, 1922**
   NOTE: See also items 2 and 9.
9. Result of a survey of two city blocks (as in 8): houses; families; persons; rooms; and averages. 1920. p. 78. **133** **Apr., 1921**
   NOTE: See also items 2 and 8.

Allied topics: *Housing*
Housing construction

ILLEGITIMACY

1. Illegitimate births. Each month, 1928. p. 155. **131**
2. Illegitimate births per 1000 total births. Each year, 1916–1926. p. XIV. ***176**

ILLEGITIMACY *(continued)*

Source Number

3. Women and illegitimate babies under care of Jewish Board of Guardians: (a) number under care during year; (b) number received during year by nativity and by age-range; (c) cases closed during year. Manhattan and Bronx, combined. 1928. p. 36. **80**
4. Paternity proceedings in the Court of Special Sessions: (a) warrants issued; (b) warrants executed; (c) cases pending disposition at beginning of year; (d) issues joined during the year; (e) issues disposed of during the year, by disposition (orders of filiation granted; proceedings dismissed; etc.); (f) cases pending disposition at end of year. Each county. 1928. p. 23–33. **122**
5. Paternity cases referred to the New York City Department of Public Welfare, by disposition: temporarily adjudicated or settled in the office; referred to the court. Manhattan, Bronx, and Richmond, combined; and Brooklyn and Queens, combined. 1926. p. 27. **148**

See also: *Births and birth rate* 10, 11
Correction 20
Courts 105, 106
Negroes 18

ILLITERACY

1. Illiterate persons: (a) by color (white; Negro) and age (10 years and over; 21 years and over); (b) illiterate whites by age, nativity, and parentage (native; foreign or mixed). Each borough, 1920; and per cent of illiterate persons in each group, by sex, 1900, 1910, 1920. p. 1182–1185. **285**
2. Illiterate persons: (a) by color (white; Negro), age (10–14; ten-year periods to 65 and over; 21 and over), and sex; (b) illiterate whites by age, nativity, and parentage. Each borough. 1920. p. 1198–1200. **285**
3. Illiterate persons ten years of age and over by degree of illiteracy (can neither read nor write, can read but not write) and sex, 1920; also per cent of illiterates ten years of age and over, who can read but not write, by sex, 1900, 1910. Each borough. p. 1232. **285**

ILLITERACY *(continued)*

Source Number

4. Illiterate persons: (a) number 10 years and over, for total, for white persons, and for Negroes; (b) white persons 10 years and over by nativity; (c) number of all illiterate persons, 16–20 years; (d) number 21 years and over by sex, for total, for white persons, and for Negroes; (e) white persons 21 years and over by sex and nativity. Each assembly district and each borough. 1920. p. 63–68. **288**

5. Illiterate persons by age (10–15; 16–20; 21 and over), sex, and color (white; Negro; other). Each tabulation tract (one or more sanitary districts containing total population of 1000 or more persons). 1920. p. 2–819. **51**

6. White illiterates by age (10–15; 16–20; 21 and over), sex, nativity, and parentage. Each tabulation tract (one or more sanitary districts containing a total population of 1000 or more persons). 1920. p. 2–819. **51**

See also: *East Harlem* 4

IMMIGRANT HOMES

1. Roman Catholic homes for immigrants: capacity; rates. Each home in Manhattan and Bronx. 1928. p. 87. ***40**

See also: *Lodging houses* (entire)

IMMIGRATION

1. Foreign-born persons enumerated in 1920, by year of immigration (1900 or earlier; 1901–1905; 1906–1910; 1911–1913; 1914; 1915; 1916; 1917; 1918; 1919; year not reported). Each borough. p. 788. **285**

2. Foreign-born persons enumerated in 1920, by year of immigration (1900 or earlier; 1901–1905; 1906–1910; 1911–1915; 1916–1917; 1918–1919; year not reported), and sex. Each borough. p. 791–792. **285**

3. Foreign-born white persons enumerated in 1920, by year of immigration (1900 or earlier; 1901–1910; 1911–1919; year not reported). Each borough. p. 790. **285**

IMMIGRATION *(continued)*

Source Number

4. Foreign-born Negroes, Chinese, Japanese, enumerated in 1920, each group separately, by year of immigration (1900 or earlier; 1901–1905; 1906–1910; 1911–1913; 1914; 1915; 1916; 1917; 1918; 1919; year not reported). p. 795. **285**

5. Foreign-born white persons enumerated in 1910, by year of immigration (1890 or earlier; 1891–1895; 1896–1900; 1901–1904; 1905–1910; year not reported) Each borough section, each borough. p. XXXIII. **51**

See also: *Richmond, Borough of* 7

Other allied topics: *Americanization*
Naturalization

INCOME

1. Number of Federal income tax returns. Each county. 1926. p. 258. ***305**

2. Persons paying Federal income tax, and population per income tax return, each borough, also number reporting $5,000, $5,000–$10,000, and $10,000 and over. 1922. **228**

See also: *Housing surveys* 4
Standard of living 1–3, 5–8

INFANT DEATHS AND DEATH RATE

1. Infant death rate. Each week, last thirteen weeks, and average for corresponding week, 1923–1928. Published weekly. **136**

2. Deaths and death rate of infants: total deaths and death rate; deaths and death rate from selected causes (contagious diseases; respiratory diseases; congenital diseases; diarrheal diseases). Each borough. 1928. p. 31. **131**

3. Death rate of infants, based on births and deaths distributed to borough residence of mother. Each borough. 1927, 1928. p. 31. **131**

INFANT DEATHS AND DEATH RATE *(continued)*

Source Number

4. Births, deaths of infants, and infant death rate. Each year, 1907–1928. p. 32. **131**

5. Infant deaths and death rate. Each year, 1910–1928. p. 162–164. **131**

6. Infant mortality rate. Each borough. Average, 1916–1920; average, 1921–1925; and each year, 1923–1928. p. 22. **3**

7. Deaths of infants per 1000 live births, by age: under one month; 1–2 months; 3–11 months. Each year, 1915–1928. p. XXI. ***176**

8. Deaths of infants by age (under 1 month; 1 to 2 months; 2 to 3 months; 3 to 6 months; 6 to 9 months; 9 to 12 months; under 1 year): (a) all causes; (b) diarrheal diseases. Each week, 1928. p. 140. **131**

9. Deaths of infants, by age (under 1 day; 1 day; 2 days; 3 to 6 days; 1 week; 2 weeks; 3 weeks; under 1 month; 1–11 months, each month), color (white; colored), and cause of death: measles; scarlet fever; whooping-cough; diphtheria; influenza; dysentery; erysipelas; meningococcus meningitis; tetanus; tuberculosis of the respiratory system; tuberculosis of the meninges, etc.; other forms of tuberculosis; syphilis; convulsions; bronchitis; bronchopneumonia; pneumonia; diseases of the stomach; diarrhea and enteritis; congenital malformations; congenital debility; premature birth; injury at birth; other diseases of early infancy; external causes; unknown or ill-defined diseases; all other causes. 1926. p. 226–227. ***279**

10. Infant mortality rate by color (white; colored). 1926. p. 1782. **317**

11. Deaths and death rate of infants, by "nativity" (country of birth) of both parents, selected countries. 1928. p. 141. **131**

INFANT DEATHS AND DEATH RATE *(continued)*

Source Number

12. Death rate of infants, by cause: communicable diseases; respiratory diseases; gastro-intestinal diseases; congenital malformations; congenital debility; premature birth; injury at birth; other causes. Each year, 1917–1926. p. XXII. Same by sex, 1926. p. XXIII. ***176**

13. Deaths and death rate of infants by type of disease: (a) contagious; (b) respiratory; (c) congenital; (d) diarrheal; (e) other causes. Each borough. 1924. p. 116. Published occasionally. **133** Oct., 1925

14. Infant death rate from congenital diseases. Each borough. Each year, 1916–1920. p. 232. **133** Oct., 1921

15. Deaths and death rate under one month from selected diseases: syphilis; convulsions; pneumonia and acute bronchitis; diarrhea and enteritis; congenital malformations; premature birth; congenital debility; injuries at birth. 1920. p. 8. **96**

16. Deaths of infants: (a) by age groups (under 1 day; 1 to 7 days; 1 to 2 weeks; 2 to 3 weeks; 3 to 4 weeks; under 1 year) and sex; (b) by age groups (up to 1 year) and by general cause (causes peculiar to newly born; infectious diseases; all other causes); (c) deaths under one year and deaths under one day by nationality of mother. Manhattan. 1927. p. 56–57. **136** June 23, 1928

See also: *Baby health stations* 1
Bellevue-Yorkville district 15–17
Bronx, Borough of 1, 2
Deaths and death rate 22–29, 33, 38, 55–58, 65, 67–69, 74, 76, 77
East Harlem 6, 7
Sanitary districts 2
Tuberculosis 20, 21, 25
Vital statistics 3, 4, 7, 8, 10, 12, Note

INFANTICIDE

See: *Deaths* 38, 60, 61
Homicide 5, 6

INFANTILE PARALYSIS

Source Number

See: *Poliomyelitis*

INFLUENZA

1. Cases and deaths. Current week. **317**
2. Deaths. Current month. **179**
3. Cases and deaths, case rate and death rate, fatality rate. 1927. p. 8. **317 Supp. # 70**
4. Cases and deaths. Each week, Jan. 1, 1921–Dec. 22, 1928. p. 242. **136 Dec. 1, 1928**
5. Cases and deaths. Each week, Sept.–May, during period Sept., 1918–May, 1922. p. 106. **136 Apr. 8, 1922**

See also: *Bellevue-Yorkville district* 15
Bronx, Borough of 1, 3
Deaths and death rate 3, 6, 38–46, 50, 54, 60–63, 65, 72–74
Diseases, Transmissible 1, 3–5, 7, 9
East Harlem 6–8, 10, 11
Infant deaths and death rate 9
Pneumonia 8
Serums (entire)
Vital statistics Note

INSURANCE

See: *Fires* 9
Funeral costs 2

INTERMENTS

1. Interments in New York City, by cemetery. Each borough. 1928. p. 157. **131**

Allied topics: *Funeral costs*
Mortuary, City

INTOXICATED DRIVER

See: *Highway law, Violation of*

INTOXICATION

Source Number

See: *Alcoholism*
Drunkenness

JAILS

See: *Correction*

JEWISH POPULATION

1. Estimated Jewish child population, aged 5–14, and estimated total Jewish population of all ages. Each district of Jewish Education Association; each borough. 1928. ***83**

2. Estimates of the Jewish population in New York City: (a) based on school registration; (b) based on method used by Dr. Laidlaw; (c) based on study of Jewish deaths. End of year 1927. p. 170. ***5**

3. Estimated Jewish population in New York City: total population and Jewish population, each borough; Jewish population by borough sections and per cent of total borough population, Manhattan, Bronx, Brooklyn. 1916, 1925. p. 2–9. **25**

4. Density of Jewish population showing ratio of Jews to the total population. By borough sections. 1925. p. 10. **25**

5. Jewish children 7–13 years of age: (a) number, 1916, 1927; (b) per cent which Jewish children 7–13 years of age were of all children of those ages, 1916, 1923, 1927; (c) increase or decrease of Jewish children, each borough, and city as a whole, for period 1925–1927 and period 1916–1927. p. 1–2. **36**

6. Estimated number of Sephardic Jews in New York City. 1926. p. 34. **78**

See also: *Deaths and death rate* 2–7

JEWISH RELIGIOUS SCHOOLS

See: *Education* 26–29

JUNIOR HIGH SCHOOLS

Source Number

See: *Education*

JUVENILE DELINQUENTS

See: *Delinquents, Juvenile*

KINDERGARTENS

See: *Education*

LANGUAGE

1. Foreign-born white persons unable to speak English, by age (10 years and over; 21 years and over) and sex. Each borough. 1910, 1920. p. 1258. **285**
2. Foreign-born white persons unable to speak English, by age (10–14; 15–19; 20–24; 10-year periods to 65 and over) and sex. Each borough. 1920. p. 1261. **285**
3. Foreign white stock by mother tongue. Each borough. 1910, 1920. p. 1006–1009. **285**
4. Foreign white stock by mother tongue, nativity, and parentage. Each borough. 1920. p. 1021–1022. **285**
5. Foreign-born white persons by race, stock, country of birth, and mother tongue spoken in country of birth. 1920. p. XXIV–XXV. **51**
6. Foreign-born white persons by country of birth and leading mother tongue spoken in New York. Each borough. 1920. p. XXIV. **51**
7. Foreign-born white persons by leading mother tongue spoken in New York. Each borough section, each borough. 1920. p. XXXI–XXXIII. **51**
8. Estimated distribution, by mother tongue, of persons having Russia as country of origin. Each borough. 1920. **50**

See also: *Religion of population* 1
Standard of living 8

LARCENY

Source Number

1. Cases of grand larceny reported to the Police Department, by type: store, residence, etc.; automobile; pickpocket. 1927, 1928. p. 41. ***144**

See also: *Arrests and summonses* 1, 3
Correction 20, 50, 54, 83, 84
Courts 12, 13, 15, 16, 18, 21–23, 38, 55–57, 67–71, 74, 77, 79, 91–93, 96, 97, 100, 105, 108
Delinquents, Juvenile 3
Felonies 1–5, 7, 12, 13, 15, 18, 19

Other allied topics: *Burglary*
Robbery

LAUNDRIES

1. Women workers in power laundries (34 laundries): (a) number of women, by type of laundry and type of operation; (b) laundries classified by weekly hours scheduled; (c) hours worked in one week; (d) hours worked compared with hours scheduled; (e) workers by hours scheduled and type of laundry; (f) workers by basis of pay and operation; (g) weekly rate of pay by scheduled weekly hours; (h) week's earnings by operation; (i) week's earnings by basis of pay; (j) week's earnings by hours worked; (k) year's earnings by operation; (l) year's earnings by weeks worked; (m) actual earnings compared with expected earnings. Year ending Apr. 15, 1926. **197**

See also: *Employment* 4, 5
Occupations, Children engaged in (entire)
Occupations, Persons engaged in 3, 10

LEGAL AID

1. Finances of legal aid societies: (a) current expenditures of 7 agencies for organized legal aid; (b) income of 5 agencies; (c) value of property owned by 7 agencies. Each year, 1910–1926. **331**

LEGAL AID *(continued)*

Source Number

2. Legal aid cases received; amount of money collected for clients; operating expenses. Each organization reporting: New York Legal Aid Society; New York Educational Alliance; New York National Desertion Bureau; New York Voluntary Defenders Committee. Prior to 1905, and each year, 1905–1923. p. 119–121. **307**

LEPROSY

1. New cases, and deaths. 1928. p. 53. **131**

2. Leprosy cases on active list. Jan. 1 and Dec. 31, 1928. p. 53. **131**

See also: *Deaths and death rate* 38, 60, 61
Diseases, Transmissible 3, 7, 9

LIBRARIES

1. Volumes in free libraries and volumes per capita; circulation of free libraries and circulation per capita. Each county. 1927. p. 238–239. **173**

2. Libraries in public schools by type (teacher training; high; junior-senior high; junior high; elementary school; elementary class; elementary reference): (a) libraries; (b) books; (c) aggregate circulation. 1926/27, 1927/28. p. 726. **124**

LICENSES

1. Licenses issued, each year, 1924–1927; fees charged for licenses, 1927; revenue from licenses, each year, 1924–1927. By type of license: amusement; bathing establishment; public dance hall; etc. p. 29–31. ***142**

LODGING HOUSES

1. Lodging houses for the general public, under permit from the New York City Department of Health; lodging houses for sailors and immigrants, under permit from the State Industrial commission. 1928. p. 108. **131**

LODGING HOUSES *(continued)*

Source Number

2. Lodging houses supervised by the New York City Department of Health (lodging; sailor boarding; immigrant lodging). Each borough. [1924]. p. 372. **136 Nov. 29, 1924**

See also: *Building* 4, 6
Homeless persons 1–6
Fires 3, 9

MALARIA

1. Cases and deaths, case rate and death rate, fatality rate. 1927. p. 11. **317 Supp. # 70**

See also: *Deaths and death rate* 3, 38, 39, 41, 44, 46, 60, 61, 72, 73, 75
Diseases, Transmissible 2, 3, 7, 9

MALNUTRITION

1. Children in public and parochial schools who were graded by the medical inspectors of the New York City Department of Health as to nutrition, and per cent found undernourished. Each year, 1914–1920. p. 109. **133 May, 1921**

MANSLAUGHTER

See: *Homicide*

MANUFACTURES

1. Manufacturing establishments; average number of wage earners; wages; cost of materials; value of products. Each manufacturing industry, each borough, 1927; and industries combined, each borough, 1925. p. 49–59. **278**

2. Manufacturing establishments; wage earners; amount of wages; value of products. Brooklyn. Twelve specified years, 1850–1927. p. 21. ***17**

3. Number of employees of inspected factories, classified by industry: chemical; men's clothing; women's clothing; metal; printing; food; textile; wood; tobacco; all other. Manhattan south of 59th Street. Each year, 1900, 1912, 1917, 1922. p. 34. **256**

MANUFACTURES *(continued)*

Source Number

4. Employees of inspected factories by branches of industry (industrial sub-groups). Manhattan south of 59th Street. 1900, 1922. p. 35. **256**

5. Manufacturing establishments; employees (shop; office) by sex. Staten Island. Fiscal year 1921. p. 22. **93**

6. Number of industrial establishments employing five or more persons per plant; number of employees (shop; office). By type of industry. Staten Island. Fiscal year 1921. p. 23. **93**

7. Average number of wage earners in manufacturing industries, by sex and age (16 and over; under 16). Each borough. 1909, 1914, 1919. p. 975. **287**

8. Number of manufacturing establishments reporting; average number of wage earners; wages; rent and taxes; cost of materials; value of products; value added by manufacture. Each county. 1919. p. 971. **287**

9. Establishments distributed by ownership (individuals; corporations; all others); average number of wage earners by ownership of establishments; value of products by ownership of establishment. Each borough. 1914, 1919. p. 998. **287**

10. Establishments; average number of wage earners; wages; cost of materials; value of products. Each selected industry. Each borough. 1909, 1914, 1919. p. 1026–1034. **287**

11. Establishments; persons engaged in the industry (proprietors and firm members; salaried officers, superintendents, and managers; clerks, etc., by sex; average number of wage earners); number of wage earners on fifteenth day of maximum month; number on fifteenth day of minimum month; wage earners on Dec. 15, by sex and age (16 and over; under 16). All industries combined and each specified industry. Each borough. 1919. p. 1058–1087. **287**

See also: *Building* 1, 2, 4, 6, 9–11, 13, 15–17
Business (entire)

Source Number

MANUFACTURES *(continued)*

See also: *(continued)*
Candy industry (entire)
Chemical industry (entire)
Employment 1–3, 7–9, 11–13
Employment of children 1, 2
Fires 3, 9
Garment industry (entire)
Hours of work 1
Occupations, Children engaged in (entire)
Occupations, Persons engaged in 1–3, 10
Paper box industry (entire)
Painting industry (entire)
Salaries and wages 1–6, 8
Textile industry (entire)
Tobacco products industry (entire)
Wood industry (entire)
Workmen's compensation (entire)

MARITAL CONDITION OF POPULATION

1. Persons by marital condition, sex, age (15–19; 20–24; 25–34; 35–44; 45–54; 55–64; 65 and over), and color (white; Negro). Each borough. 1920. p. 501–506. **285**

2. White persons by marital condition, sex, age (as in 1), nativity, and parentage. Each borough. 1920. p. 501–506. **285**

3. Colored persons (other than Negro) 15 years of age and over, by marital condition, sex, and color (Indian; Chinese; Japanese; other). Each borough. 1920. p. 501–506. **285**

4. Persons 15 years of age and over, by marital condition, sex, and color (white; Negro; Indian; Chinese; Japanese; other). Each borough. 1900, 1910. p. 501–506. **285**

5. White persons 15 years of age and over, by marital condition, sex, nativity, and parentage (native; foreign or mixed). Each borough. 1900, 1910. p. 501–506. **285**

See also: *Marriages and marriage rate* 4
Occupations, Persons engaged in 8–10

MARRIAGES AND MARRIAGE RATE

Source Number

1. Marriages and marriage rate: (a) each year, 1898–1928; (b) each borough, 1928. p. 133–134. **131**
2. Marriages and marriage rate. Each borough. Current monthly through Dec., 1927. **133**
3. Persons married: (a) by color (white; Negro; Chinese; Japanese); (b) by marital condition; (c) by nativity; (d) by type of marriage (religious; civil), further subdivided by Catholic, Protestant, Jewish, Ethical Culture, Judicial, and City Clerk. Each month. 1928. p. 155. **131**
4. Girls involved in (a) child marriages (14–16 years), and (b) youthful marriages (16–18 years): girls by age; by nativity; cases of falsification of age; number of annulments granted; cause of annulments. New York County. 1925, 1926. **336**

See also: *Bronx, Borough of* 1
Divorce 1
Vital statistics 1, 2, 5, 6, 8

Other allied topics: *Divorce*
Marital condition of population

MATERNAL MORTALITY

See: *Puerperal diseases and conditions*

MATERNITY CLINICS

See: *Clinics, Prenatal*

MATRIMONIAL CAUSES

See: *Divorce*

MEASLES

1. Cases reported. Current week. **317**
2. Cases and deaths. Current month. **179**

MEASLES *(continued)*

Source Number

3. Cases and deaths; case rate and death rate; case fatality; place of treatment (home; hospital). Each borough. Current quarter year and corresponding quarter of preceding year. **136**

4. Cases and deaths. Each month, 1927, 1928. p. 176. **131**

5. Cases and deaths. Each week, Jan. 1, 1921–Nov. 10, 1928. p. 218. **136 Nov. 10, 1928**

6. Deaths and death rate. Each year, 1868–1928. p. 177. **131**

7. Cases and deaths, case rate and death rate, fatality rate, estimated expectancy. 1927. p. 13. **317 Supp. # 70**

8. Cases and deaths, case rate and death rate, case fatality. Each borough. Each year, 1916–1925. **72**

9. Deaths of children under 5 years. Each year, 1910–1925. p. 79. **136 May 15, 1926**

10. Measles in relation to season: case rate; death rate. Each month, average, 1910–1923. p. 9. **95 Oct., 1924**

See also: *Bellevue-Yorkville district* 6–8, 10, 15
Bronx, Borough of 1, 3
Deaths and death rate 3, 38, 39, 41, 44–46, 49, 50, 54, 60–62, 64, 65, 72–75
Diseases, Transmissible 1–12
East Harlem 6–11
Infant deaths and death rate 9
Nursing service 1
Vital statistics 12, Note

MENDICANTS

1. Persons arrested by the mendicant squad of the police, each offense: corporation ordinance, violation of (peddling without a license, etc.); disorderly conduct (beggars); pullers-in ordinance, violation of; vagrancy (beggars); miscellaneous. Jan.–June, each year, 1928, 1929. p. 75. **146**

MENINGITIS

	Source Number
1. Meningococcus meningitis: cases and deaths. Current week.	**317**
2. Cerebrospinal meningitis: cases and deaths. Each week, Jan. 1, 1922–Nov. 3, 1928. p. 209.	**136** Nov. 3, 1928
3. Cerebrospinal meningitis: cases and deaths. Each month, 1927, 1928. p. 185.	**131**
4. Deaths and death rate from epidemic meningitis, each year, 1877–1928; cases and deaths, each quarter year, 1923–1928. p. 81–82.	**136** Mar. 16, 1929
5. Cerebrospinal meningitis: cases, case rate, and case fatality; deaths and death rate by age (all ages combined; under 10; under 2). Each year, 1912–1927. p. 35.	**136** Feb. 2, 1929
6. Meningococcus meningitis: cases and deaths; case rate and death rate; fatality rate; estimated expectancy. 1927. p. 14.	**317** Supp. # 70
7. Meningococcus meningitis: cases and deaths; case rate and death rate; case fatality. Each borough. 1923, 1924. p. 205.	**136** Sept. 26, 1925
8. Meningococcus meningitis: cases and deaths by age groups (each year, 1–15; 5-year groups to 70 and over) and sex. Each borough. 1921. p. 185.	**133** Aug., 1922
9. Cases of meningococcus meningitis confirmed by examination of fluids. Each borough. 1921. p. 184.	**133** Aug., 1922

See also: *Bellevue-Yorkville district* 15
Deaths and death rate 3, 38–41, 44–46, 50, 54, 60–63, 65, 72–74
Diseases, Transmissible 1–5, 7, 9, 10
Infant deaths and death rate 9
Nursing service 1
Serums (entire)
Vital statistics 12, Note

MENTAL DEFECTIVES

See: *Defectives, Mental*

MENTAL DISEASE

Source Number

1. State hospitals for the insane: (a) patients admitted (first admissions) by sex, and rate per 100,000 population, year ending June 30, 1928; (b) total population under treatment by sex, and rate per 100,000 population, June 30, 1928. From each county. p. 260. **200**

2. First admissions from New York City to the civil State hospitals by sex and psychosis. Period 1915–1920. p. 47. **248**

3. Beds for psychopathic patients in public hospitals; number of patients admitted. 1921. p. 626. **263**

4. Commitments granted for insanity, by the Supreme Court of the State of New York, First Judicial Department. New York County (Special Term, Part II); Bronx County (Special Term, Ex Parte Applications). 1928. p. 14–15, 36. ***207**

5. Prisoners in New York County Penitentiary, Workhouse, and Reformatory (each institution), found insane by examiners in lunacy, classified by State hospital to which transferred: Matteawan State Hospital; Dannemora State Hospital. 1928. p. 82. **121**

6. State hospitals for mental disease in New York City: (a) patients on books at beginning of year (in hospitals; on parole or otherwise absent); (b) patients on books at end of year (as above); (c) patients admitted during the year (first admissions; readmissions; transfers); (d) patients withdrawn during the year (discharges; transfers; death). Each public institution. 1922. p. 100, 108. **294**

7. State hospitals for mental disease in New York City: (a) physicians; (b) other officers and employees (resident dentists; occupational therapists; social workers; graduate nurses; other nurses and attendants; all others); (c) patients during year; (d) average daily patient population. Each hospital. 1922. p. 242, 254. **294**

MENTAL DISEASE *(continued)*

Source Number

8. Psychopathic wards of general hospitals: (a) patients on books at beginning of year; (b) patients admitted during year; (c) patients withdrawn during year (discharges; deaths); (d) patients on books at end of year. Each institution. 1922. p. 238. **294**

See also: *Clinics* 1, Note
Correction 77–79
Courts 39–41, 67, 74
Deaths and death rate 38, 60, 61
Hospitals 17

MENTAL HEALTH

1. Mental health survey of Staten Island, based on four groups: (a) 44 inmates of Richmond County Jail; (b) 100 Children's Court cases; (c) 158 children of preschool age; (d) 3042 public school children. Period Jan.–Apr., 1924. **101**

See also: *Clinics* 1, Note
Health service (entire)

METAL INDUSTRY

1. Metal industry in New York and its environs: (a) number of plants and number of employees, Manhattan south of 59th Street; Manhattan north of 59th Street, and the Bronx; Brooklyn; Queens; 1900, 1922; (b) value of land occupied by metal plants by number of employees and by branch of industry, Manhattan, 1922; (c) maps showing location of metal plants (with 20 or more employees) in New York and its environs, 1900, 1922; (d) number of plants by number of employees and by type of industry, Manhattan south of 59th Street; Manhattan north of 59th Street, and the Bronx; Brooklyn; Queens; each year, 1900, 1912, 1917, 1922. "The Metal Industries." p. 11–49. **257**

See also: *Employment* 1–3, 7, 8, 10
Manufactures 1, 3, 4, 11

METAL INDUSTRY *(continued)*

Source Number

See also: *(continued)*
Occupations, Children engaged in (entire)
Occupations, Persons engaged in 3, 10
Salaries and wages 1–6
Workmen's compensation (entire)

MIDWIVES

1. Registered midwives; births attended; per cent of total births. Each year, 1909, 1914, 1919, 1924, 1928. p. 34. **131**

2. Midwives registered, births reported by midwives, and per cent of total births. Each year, 1909, 1914, 1919, 1924, 1927. p. 17. **136** **May 19, 1928**

3. Midwives registered, number of births attended, per cent of total births. Each year, 1909–1926. p. 205–206. **136** **Dec. 17, 1927**

See also: *Births and birth rate* 5, 10, 11, 14
Occupations, Persons engaged in 3, 10

MISDEMEANORS

1. Cases of misdemeanors reported. Period Jan.–June, each year, 1928, 1929. p. 43. **146**

2. Cases of misdemeanors reported, by disposition: arrest; pending; other. Each county. Period Jan.–June, each year, 1928, 1929. p. 44–49. **146**

See also: *Arrests and summonses* 4
Courts 12, 13, 15, 18, 21–23, 38, 44, 55–57, 80, 91–93, 96, 97, 100
Truants 1

MISSING PERSONS

1. Missing persons reported to the police by sex: (a) missing persons during reporting period; (b) missing persons during reporting period who were found during reporting period; (c) missing persons during preceding year who were found during reporting period. Each county. Jan.–June, each year, 1928, 1929. p. 44–49. **146**

MORTUARY, CITY

Source Number

1. Unidentified dead persons reported to the police, by sex: (a) number reported (identified; pending), period Jan.–June, each year, 1928, 1929; (b) number reported during 1928 who were identified, period Jan.–June, 1929. p. 50. **146**

2. Bodies received, and disposition of these bodies (buried in City Cemetery; taken out by undertakers; sent to colleges), (a) adults and (b) infants. 1926. p. 307–308. **148**

3. Unidentified dead, and autopsies. 1926. p. 308. **148**

Allied topics: *Funeral costs*
Interments

MOTOR VEHICLES

1. Motor vehicles and motorcycles registered by type of license: passenger; dealer; trailer; etc. Each county. 1927. p. 133. ***208**

2. Motor vehicles registered by type: passenger cars; buses and taxis; trucks; motorcycles; dealers and trailers. Each year, 1919–1926. p. 123. **53**

3. Population, motor vehicles registered, and persons per motor vehicle. Each year, 1916–1926, with estimates for 1930 and 1935. p. 49, 51. **260**

4. Motor vehicles registered by type: passenger cars; omnibuses; trucks; motorcycles. Each borough. Each year, 1919–1926. p. 41. **260**

5. Passenger cars per hundred families. Each borough. 1922. p. 31. **221**

See also: *Standard of living* 5–7

Other allied topic: *Traffic regulations, Violation of*

MOVEMENT OF POPULATION

Source Number

1. Geographic shifting of population: (a) total population; (b) boys 9–18 years old. Each borough. 1920, 1926. Opposite p. 10. **88**

2. Tabulation tracts of 1910 classified according to amount of gain or loss in population. Period 1910–1920. p. IV. Map only. **51**

See also: *Density of population* 4–7

MUMPS

1. Cases. Current week. **317**

2. Cases and deaths, case rate and death rate, fatality rate. 1927. p. 16. **317 Supp. # 70**

See also: *Bronx, Borough of* 3
Deaths and death rate 38, 60, 61
Diseases, Transmissible 2, 3, 7, 9, 11, 12

MUNICIPAL LODGING HOUSE

See: *Homeless persons* 1–6
Public charges 4

MURDER

See: *Homicide*

NATIVITY OF POPULATION

1. Total persons by nativity. Each borough. 1900, 1910, 1920. p. 47, 55, 76. **285**

2. White persons by nativity and parentage. Each borough. 1900, 1910, 1920. p. 47, 55. **285**

3. White persons by nativity and parentage. Each borough section, each borough. 1910, 1920. p. XXXI–XXXIII. **51**

4. White persons by nativity. By district, each borough. 1920. Separate sheet for each district. **241**

NATIVITY OF POPULATION *(continued)*

Source Number

5. White persons 21 years of age and over by nativity, sex, and parentage (native; foreign or mixed). Each assembly district and each borough. 1920. p. 63–68. **288**

6. White persons 10 years of age and over by nativity. Each assembly district and each borough. 1920. p. 63–68. **288**

See also: *Age of population* 6–8
Birthplace of population (entire)
Boy population (entire)
Citizenship of population 2–6
Color of population 3
Country of origin of population 1–3, 5–9
Density of population 8
East Harlem 4
Education 1–3, 5
Illiteracy 1, 2, 4, 6
Immigration (entire)
Language 1–7
Marital condition of population 2, 5
Marriages and marriage rate 4
Occupations, Children engaged in 2
Occupations, Persons engaged in 5–9
Ownership of homes 1
Population and population estimates, not including 1930 and later 1
Richmond, Borough of 1–3, 5–11
Sex of population 3, 4

NATURALIZATION

1. Naturalization cases: (a) cases on calendar; (b) applications granted; (c) applications denied; (d) applications adjourned; (e) orders signed during year; (f) orders signed during preceding year. Supreme Court of the State of New York, First Judicial Department, Special Term Ex Parte applications, Bronx County. 1928. p. 36. ***207**

NATURALIZATION *(continued)*

Source Number

2. Total applications for naturalization received; persons filing first papers, by sex; persons to whom final naturalization papers were issued, (a) by sex, (b) by "country of allegiance" (nationality), and (c) by country of birth. Each borough. Available annually for year ending June 30. **315**

See also: *Citizenship of population* 2–6

NEGROES

1. Negroes (black; mulatto), 1910, 1920; and total Negroes, 1890. p. 35. **285**
2. Approximate distribution of Negroes. Each borough; also Manhattan by districts: Harlem; Columbus Hill; etc. 1927. p. 5. **242**
3. Principal locations of Negroes in New York City. [1928]. p. 49. Map only. **338**
4. Distribution of Negro population in Harlem. Jan., 1928. p. 6. Map only. **242**
5. Distribution of Negroes in Harlem. 1913, 1920, 1926. Map only. **243**
6. Growth of Negro area in Upper Manhattan. 1910 to 1920, and 1920 to 1925. p. 48. Map only. **338**
7. Negro children arraigned before the Children's Court: (a) by sex and cause (delinquent; neglected; material witnesses; others), each borough, 1925; (b) white and Negro children arraigned, by color; each year, 1919–1925, and period Jan.–June, 1926; (c) Negro children arraigned, by sex, age (under 7; 7 to 10; 10 to 13; 13 to 16), and specific cause, 1925, and Jan.–June, 1926; (d) white children arraigned by sex and cause, 1925; (e) cases of Negro children disposed of, by sex, each specific charge, and disposition (petitions dismissed; discharged from probation; etc.), 1925, and period Jan.–June, 1926; (f) Negro children committed to institutions, by sex, each institution, 1925; (g) Negro **107**

NEGROES *(continued)*

Source Number

7. *(continued)*
children committed to institutions who were placed in the care of the New York and Brooklyn Societies for the Prevention of Cruelty to Children, with average number of days under care, each society, and for each institution, 1925, and period Jan.–June, 1926; (h) Protestant Negro children committed to Catholic institutions, by sex, each institution, 1925, and period Jan.–June, 1926. p. 13, 17, 19–20, 22, 27–28, 48–49.

8. Deaths and death rate among Negroes from selected causes: pulmonary tuberculosis; cancer; heart disease; pneumonias; Bright's disease and nephritis; violence. 1900, 1925. p. 94. **136 June 12, 1926**

9. Tuberculosis death rate of Negroes as compared with that of white persons. Each year, 1910–1924. p. 11. **242**

10. Deaths and death rate of Negro population from tuberculosis (pulmonary; other forms). Brooklyn. Each year, 1913–1922. **230 July-Oct., 1923**

11. Colored convalescent patients: (a) number of colored patients at homes which accommodate Negroes; (b) number of patient days (white; colored). Each home, classified as for children, adults, or both. 1925. p. 106. **275**

12. Negro population of Columbus Hill (Sanitary Areas # 147 and 151): (a) death rate from selected causes, each cause (tuberculosis; heart disease; pneumonia) and infant death rate from selected causes, each cause (congenital debility; respiratory diseases; diarrhea), each year, 1916–1920; (b) Negroes in gainful occupations, by occupation and sex, 1922. **79**

13. Negro population of Columbus Hill (Sanitary Areas # 147 and 151) and vicinity: (a) population distributed as living in families and as living separately, 1922; (b) population by sex and age (men; women; **79**

NEGROES *(continued)*

Source Number

13. *(continued)*
children), 1922; (c) "social state" (marital condition), 1922; (d) persons per apartment and persons per room in 100 apartments in model houses and in 100 apartments in older houses, 1922; (e) estimated number of arrests of Negroes, by offense, 1921; (f) persons 6–20 years of age in school or out of school, by age (6–14; 15–20) and "nativity" (foreign white; native white; Negro; other colored), 1910, 1920.

14. Negro population of (a) Columbus Hill (Sanitary Areas # 147 and 151) and (b) Columbus Hill and vicinity: (a) total population by "racial class" (native white; white of foreign descent; foreign-born white; Negro; other colored), 1910, 1920; (b) Negroes by "nativity" (native; West Indian; other foreign; unknown), 1922; (c) density of population, 1910, 1920, 1922; (d) death rate for all ages and infant death rate, each year, 1916–1920; (e) school attendance by "nativity," 1910, 1920, and estimated number of Negroes, 1922; (f) classification of school marks of Negro pupils in three schools, 1921/22. **79**

15. Health work for mothers and children in a colored community (8 blocks, west of Columbus Circle): births according to place and means of delivery; duration of prenatal care; deaths of mothers; results of birth; infant mortality; Wasserman findings; end results of pregnancies of syphilitic mothers. Period Apr., 1917–Apr., 1923. **217**

16. Negro population in Flushing, Long Island (study based on 317 persons, comprising 79 families selected as a random sample of Negro neighborhoods in Flushing): age distribution by sex; birthplace; standard of living; rent paid by number of rooms; occupants by sex; wages by sex; recreation opportunities. 1921. **106**

17. Per cent of Negro families with lodgers. [1928]. p. 87. **338**

18. Illegitimate births to Negro mothers (study based on 500 selected case records from several social agencies): **255**

NEGROES *(continued)*

Source Number

18. *(continued)*
place of birth of mothers; age; education; religion by birthplace; occupation; reason for applying to social agency; mode of living (with parents; furnished room; etc.); relationship with father of child; moral character; marital condition of father; number of illegitimate children; disposition of children (home; relatives; etc.). [1922 and 1923].

See also: *Population and population estimates, 1930 and later* 3

NEWSBOYS

1. One thousand newsboys: nationality; age; hours of work; earnings; disposition of earnings; physical condition. 1925. **236**

See also: *Employment certificates* 4

NEW YORK HARBOR

See: *Port of New York*
Waterfront

NON-SUPPORT OR NEGLECT OF FAMILY

1. Cases of Jewish desertions reported to the National Desertion Bureau from New York City (exclusive of Brooklyn): (a) number, each month, 1912–1921; (b) per cent distribution by source of report (United Hebrew Charities; other agencies; direct), each year, 1912–1923. p. 32–34. **76**

See also: *Arrest and summonses* 1
Correction 20, 54
Courts 12, 13, 17, 18, 21, 22, 24, 25, 28, 32, 34, 35, 38, 48, 49, 52, 53, 101, 105, 106, 108

NURSES

1. Number of candidates examined for licenses, and number failing. Each year, 1917–1922. p. 203. **216**

NURSES *(continued)*

Source Number

2. Number of nurses, and relative proportion of graduate and pupil nurses in 53 hospitals. Each hospital. 1920. p. 212. **216**

3. Public health nurses of the New York City Department of Health distributed by field position: school work; baby health stations; etc. 1928. p. 64. **131**

See also: *Hospitals* 6, 8, 15, 19
Occupations, Persons engaged in 3, 10

NURSING SERVICE

1. Visits made by nurses of the New York City Department of Health, classified by disease: diphtheria; scarlet fever; poliomyelitis; meningococcus meningitis; typhoid fever; measles; whooping-cough; tuberculosis. Each borough. 1921. p. 236. **133** **Oct., 1922**

2. Visits made by nurses of the New York City Department of Health engaged in school follow-up work, by cause of visit: physical defects; contagious diseases; etc. Each borough. 1928. p. 66. **131**

3. Visits of nurses from the baby health stations of the New York City Department of Health. Each borough. 1928. p. 67. **131**

4. Nursing visits made by Roman Catholic Sisters: cases; hours' nursing; financial relief to the poor. Each house of Sisters, each order. Manhattan; Bronx. 1928. p. 55. ***40**

See also: *Baby health stations* 7
Family service 2

OCCUPATIONS, CHILDREN ENGAGED IN

1. Children 10–15 years of age engaged in gainful occupations by sex. Each borough. 1910, 1920. p. 597. **286**

2. Children 10–17 years of age engaged in gainful occupations, by age (10–13; 14; 15; 16; 17): (a) by sex and **286**

OCCUPATIONS, CHILDREN ENGAGED IN (continued)

Source Number

2. *(continued)*
   color (white; Negro; other); (b) white children by nativity, sex, and parentage (native; foreign or mixed). Each borough. 1920. p. 600.

3. Children engaged in gainful occupations, by age (10–13; 14; 15; 16; 17), and sex, each selected occupation. Each borough. 1920. p. 639–648. **286**

See also: *Boy population* (entire)
Housework (entire)
Occupations, Persons engaged in 4, 6, 7
Richmond, Borough of 10

Other allied topics: *Employment bureaus*
Employment certificates

OCCUPATIONS, PERSONS ENGAGED IN

1. Estimated number of persons gainfully employed in New York City distributed by occupation (manufacturing; trade; clerical; professional; domestic; transportation) and sex. 1928. Part III. ***227**

2. Persons 10 years of age and over engaged in gainful occupations, by sex; per cent, by sex, each general division of occupations. Each borough. 1920. p. 129–130. **286**

3. Persons 10 years of age and over engaged in gainful occupations, by sex, each specified occupation. Each borough. 1920. p. 186–203. **286**

4. Number and proportion of persons 10 years of age and over engaged in gainful occupations, by age (10–13; 14; 15; 16; 17; 18; 19; 20–24; 25–44; 45–64; 65 and over; age unknown) and sex. Each borough. 1920. p. 452–455. **286**

5. Persons 10 years of age and over engaged in gainful occupations: (a) total by sex and color (white; **286**

OCCUPATIONS, PERSONS ENGAGED IN (*continued*)

Source Number

5. (*continued*)
Negro; Indian; Chinese; Japanese; other); (b) white persons by nativity, sex, and parentage (native; foreign or mixed). Each borough. 1920. p. 368.

6. Persons 10 years of age and over engaged in gainful occupations, by age (10–17; 18–19; 20–24; 25–44, including age unknown; 45–64; 65 and over): (a) by sex and color (white; Negro; Indian; Chinese; Japanese; other); (b) white persons by nativity, sex, and parentage (native; foreign or mixed). Each borough. 1920. p. 462. **286**

7. Persons 10 years of age and over engaged in gainful occupations: (a) total by sex and color (white; Negro; other); (b) white persons by nativity, sex, and parentage (native; foreign or mixed); (c) total by sex and age (10–17; 18–19; 20–24; 25–44, including age unknown; 45–64; 65 and over). Each selected occupation. Each borough. 1920. p. 1157–1179. **286**

8. Women 15 years of age and over engaged in gainful occupations, by marital condition (married; single, widowed, divorced, and unknown): (a) by color (white; Negro; Indian; other); (b) white women by nativity and parentage (native; foreign or mixed). Each borough. 1920. p. 805. **286**

9. Married women 15 years of age and over engaged in gainful occupations, by age (15–19; 20–24; 25–34; 35–44; 45 and over, including age unknown: (a) by color (white; Negro; Indian; other); (b) white women by nativity and parentage (native; foreign or mixed). Each borough. 1920. p. 805. **286**

10. Women 15 years of age and over engaged in gainful occupations: (a) by marital condition (married; single, widowed, divorced, and unknown); (b) married women by age (15–19; 20–24; 25–34; 35–44; 45 and over, including age unknown). Each selected occupation. Each borough. 1920. p. 840–847. **286**

OCCUPATIONS, PERSONS ENGAGED IN (*continued*)

See also: *Agriculture* 4
Housework (entire)
Occupations, Children engaged in (entire)
Richmond, Borough of 10
Trade unions (entire)
Unemployment (entire)

Other allied topics: *Candy industry*
Chemical industry
Employment
Employment bureaus
Employment by the City of New York
Employment certificates
Employment of children
Food products industry
Garment industry
Homework
Homework of children
Hours of work
Laundries
Manufactures
Metal industry
Paper box industry
Printing industry
Stores
Textile industry
Tobacco products industry
Wood industry

OLD AGE

See: *Age of population*
Dependents, Aged

OPEN AIR CLASSES

See: *Education* 44–47

OUTDOOR RELIEF

Source Number

1. Financial trends of agencies engaged in giving outdoor relief (15 family service agencies; 23 relief societies; 3 public departments): (a) gross income of public agencies by source (dividends, interest, and contributions; receipts from city funds; receipts from State funds) and of private agencies by source (earnings; dividends, interest, and rent; contributions); (b) current expenditures of agencies (public; private) by purpose (relief; service and administration) and the same in terms of constant purchasing power; (c) current expenditures of agencies (public; private) per inhabitant, by purpose (relief; service and administration) in terms of constant purchasing power; (d) expenditures of public agencies by beneficiary (widows with children, Board of Child Welfare; veterans and their families, Department of Public Welfare; poor adult blind, Department of Public Welfare; transportation of paupers, Department of Public Welfare; volunteer firemen and their families, Exempt Firemen's Benevolent Fund; administration and investigation); (e) gross amounts received from all sources of income by private agencies by type (gross earnings, with subdivisions; dividends, interest, and rent; contributions, with subdivisions); (f) functional expenditures of private agencies by function (relief; administration and service; shelter for the homeless and employment for the indigent; shelter for dependent children; day nurseries and kindergartens; summer camps; protective and correctional work; health work; wages, etc., for the handicapped; religious work; all other) and the same in terms of constant purchasing power; (g) functional expenditures of private agencies (family service agencies; relief agencies) in terms of constant purchasing power; (h) functional expenditures of all private agencies and of family service agencies per inhabitant in terms of constant purchasing power; (i) value of property owned by private social agencies (family service agencies; relief agencies) by type of property (real estate; securities; current funds). Each year, 1910–1926. **330**

OUTDOOR RELIEF *(continued)*

Source Number

2. Private social agencies engaged in giving outdoor relief, by type (family service; other relief). Each year, 1910–1926. **330**

See also: *Dependents, Aged* 5
Family service 1
Settlements 3–5

OUT-PATIENT DEPARTMENT

See: *Clinics*

OVERCROWDING

1. Per cent of patients admitted to contagious disease hospitals in New York City who came from overcrowded rooms. Each borough. [1926]. p. 22. **183**

See also: *Homework* 7
Housing surveys (entire)

OWNERSHIP OF HOMES

1. Home owners: (a) total by sex and color (white; Negro; other); (b) white home owners by sex, nativity, and parentage. Each tabulation tract (one or more sanitary districts having a total population of 1000 or more). 1920. p. 2–819. **51**

2. Number of homes by proprietorship (owned; rented; unknown), and owned homes subdivided as to encumbrance (free; encumbered; unknown). Each borough, 1900, 1910, 1920; each assembly district, each borough, 1920. p. 1286–1296. **285**

See also: *Standard of living* 3

PAPER BOX INDUSTRY

1. Paper box industry in New York City, a study based on 85 shops and 1921 workers: number of plants and workers by district; plants, by number of workers; **198**

PAPER BOX INDUSTRY *(continued)*

Source Number

1. *(continued)*
plants (union; non-union) and workers (union; non-union) by hours of labor; plants by hours of labor and district; plants by hours of labor and number of workers; workers by sex and amount of undertime and overtime; wages by sex and type of operative; earnings by sex, type of operative, and status with union. Spring, 1927.

See also: *Employment* 2, 4, 5, 7, 8
Hours of work 2
Manufactures 1, 11
Occupations, Children engaged in (entire)
Occupations, Persons engaged in 3, 10
Salaries and wages 1–6

PARENTAGE OF POPULATION

See: *Age of population* 6–8
Country of origin of population (entire)
Education 1–3, 5
Illiteracy 1, 2, 6
Language, 3, 4
Marital condition of population 2, 5
Nativity 2, 3, 5
Occupations, Children engaged in 2
Occupations, Persons engaged in 5–9
Ownership of homes 1
Religion of population 1
Sex of population 3, 4

PARKS

1. Total land area, park area, and per cent park to total. Each borough. [1928]. p. 180. ***252**

2. Open spaces in New York and its environs: total area in acres; park area; population per park area; cemeteries; municipal water shed properties. Each county. 1921, 1927. p. 54, 237–238. **262**

PARKS *(continued)*

Source Number

3. Municipally owned parks and park spaces: (a) number; (b) area in acres. Each year, 1890, 1905, 1916, 1926. p. 31. **310**
4. Park area, population, and persons per acre of park. Each borough. Each year, 1900, 1910, 1920, 1925. p. 39. **262**
5. Public parks, playgrounds, and parkways: area of each group in acres, 1922, 1925; number in each group, [1925]. Each borough. Part II, p. 257. **41**
6. Public parks (June, 1924) compared with golf and country clubs (July, 1923): (a) number of parks or clubs; (b) members; (c) acreage; (d) acreage per member for clubs compared with population per acre for parks. p. 240. **262**
7. Parks and total park area; number of playgrounds and total playground area; number of combination parks and playgrounds and total combination area; number of parks. Brooklyn. [1927]. p. 40. ***17**
8. Municipally supported parks: number of parks; acreage; area of largest park; cost of maintenance; park revenue; number of pools, beaches, baseball fields, etc. By borough: Queens; Richmond. 1924. **223, 224**

See also: *Bronx, Borough of* 4
Playgrounds 2–6
Recreation 3

PAROCHIAL SCHOOLS

See: *Education*

PAROLE

1. Parole cases under Division of Protective Care, Catholic Charities, by sex: (a) cases on hand at beginning of year; (b) cases received during year; (c) cases withdrawn during year, by cause (expiration of sentence or transfer to other agencies; discharged; violation of parole); (d) cases on hand at end of year. Manhattan and Bronx, combined. 1928. p. 60. ***40**

PAROLE *(continued)*

Source Number

2. Cases received during year by Division of Protective Care of Catholic Charities: (a) by sex and institution from which released; (b) by sex and age. Manhattan and Bronx, combined. 1928. p. 64. ***40**

3. Parole cases under Division of Protective Care, Catholic Charities: offenses committed in violation of parole, by sex, and the length of time of the parole period before violation, each offense. Manhattan and Bronx, combined. 1928. p. 70, 72. ***40**

4. Persons on parole to Catholic Charities, Division of Protective Care, by sex and principal occupational groups. Manhattan and Bronx, combined. 1928. p. 74, 76. ***40**

5. Jewish women on parole to the Jewish Board of Guardians: (a) supervised during year; (b) number paroled during year; (c) reported with "condition satisfactory"; (d) number discharged from parole. 1928. p. 34. **80**

6. Jewish men paroled to the Jewish Board of Guardians from State penal and correctional institutions: (a) under supervision; (b) paroled during year; (c) discharged from parole, by result (rearrested; absconded; parole complete). 1928. p. 35. **80**

See also: *Correction* 25–29, 43, 50–52, 54
Courts 20, 76, 78, 108, 118
Sex offenses (entire)
Truants 3

PELLAGRA

1. Cases and deaths. Current week. **317**

2. Cases and deaths, case rate and death rate, fatality rate. 1927. p. 17. **317 Supp. # 70**

See also: *Deaths and death rate* 38, 60, 61
Diseases, Transmissible 3, 7, 9

PENSIONS

Source Number

1. New York City Employees Retirement System: (a) number and salaries of active members, by group (laborers; mechanics; clerks), sex, and age; (b) number and salaries of active members, by group (as above), sex, and length of service; (c) number and retirement allowance of pensioners (disability; service), by sex, age, and group (as above); (d) number and retirement allowances of beneficiaries of members killed in active service in the actual performance of duty, by sex, age, and group (as above); (e) separations from active service during year, by age, sex, and group (as above); (f) deaths among pensioners (disability; service). Year ending June 30, 1926. p. 29–109. **129**

2. Street Cleaning Department Relief and Pension Fund: (a) receipts and disbursements on pension account; (b) employees pensioned during year; (c) pensioners deceased during year, by length of service, age at retirement, and time for which pensioned. 1927. p. 27–30. ***149**

3. New York Fire Department Relief Fund: (a) pensioners on roll during year, added during year, deducted during year; (b) receipts; (c) disbursements; (d) receipts and disbursements of the relief fund; (e) receipts and disbursements of the New York Fire Department Life Insurance Fund. 1928. p. 26–30. **130**

4. Employees of the New York City Department of Health who were members of the New York City Employees Retirement System: (a) members accepted; (b) retired on pension; (c) other separations from active membership. Period 1920–1927 and 1928. p. 124. **131**

5. Pension fund of the New York City Department of Health: members at beginning of year; members withdrawn (retired; resigned; joined the New York City Employees Retirement System; died); members at end of year. 1928. p. 124. **131**

6. Police Pension Fund and Relief Bureau: (a) pensions approved; (b) men killed on duty; (c) widows receiving **146**

PENSIONS *(continued)*

Source Number

6. *(continued)*
pensions; guardians receiving pensions; (d) members died (active; retired); (e) relief cases approved. Jan.–June, each year, 1928, 1929. p. 63.

7. Police Pension Fund: (a) receipts, 1928; (b) disbursements to each person, 1928; (c) pensions granted and terminated, 1927, 1928; (d) number of pensioners, active members of force, amount of pensions paid, and active pay-roll, each year, 1918–1928; (e) age of members retired, by cause (disability; service), and length of service of members retired, by cause, 1926, 1927. ***145**

8. Hunter College Teachers Retirement System: (a) receipts; (b) disbursements; (c) balance; (d) members by sex, age, and salary; (e) by sex, salary, and years of service; (f) pensioners by sex, age, and amount received. 1927. ***139**

9. Teachers Retirement System of the City of New York: members and beneficiaries at beginning of year; registered during year; withdrawn during year; remaining at end of year; teachers examined for retirement; recommended for retirement; receipts; disbursements; received. 1927. ***151**

10. Board of Education Retirement System: membership; pensioners; pay-roll of pensioners; lump-sum payments; assets. June 30, 1928. p. 336. **124**
NOTE: System covers all employees who are not members of the Teachers' Retirement System.

PERSONNEL OF SOCIAL AGENCIES

1. Personnel of reporting organizations affiliated with the Federation for the Support of Jewish Philanthropic Societies in New York City: sex; religion (Jewish; non-Jewish) by groups of institutions (correctional; care of the aged; etc.); nativity; age by groups of institutions; educational training; occupation; previous experience classified by groups of institutions; length of service by occupation; salaries. 1926. **23**

PERTUSSIS

Source Number

See: *Whooping-cough.*

PHYSICAL EXAMINATIONS

1. Physical examination of children in first, third, and sixth grades, combined, in public and parochial schools: number of children examined; defects found, each defect; number of school medical inspectors. 1927, 1928. p. 40–41. **131**

2. Medical inspection of pupils in grades 3B and 6B of day elementary schools: (a) pupils by sex; (b) number of physical examinations given, by sex of pupils. Two schools in each school district of Manhattan. 1926. p. 5. **126**

3. Findings in 3331 physical examinations of children 16 years of age and under, who were examined in several settlements in New York City. [1926]. p. 492–494. **75**

4. School medical inspection by the Bureau of Child Hygiene: number and registration of schools; number of inspectors; number of nurses; etc. Each borough. 1924. p. 121. **133** **Oct., 1925**

5. School children examined by medical inspectors of the New York City Department of Health during 1923, by type of defect found. p. 273. Same by borough for 1921/22, in issue of June, 1923. p. 131. **133** **Dec., 1924**

6. Physical defects of school children, by type of defect; treatments obtained; defects terminated. 1923. p. 274. **133** **Dec., 1924**

7. Per cent of children in public and parochial schools found defective by medical inspectors of the Bureau of Child Hygiene, by type of defect, each year, 1915–1920; per cent of children having defects by type of defect and by borough. 1920. p. 104. **133** **May, 1921**

8. Number of physical examinations in public and parochial schools; number of pupils with general defects; with defective teeth only; per cent of those examined needing treatment. Each year, 1915–1920. p. 105. **133** **May, 1921**

PHYSICAL EXAMINATIONS *(continued)*

Source Number

9. Physical examinations of school children made by (a) family physicians, (b) school medical inspectors: total examinations made; number of defects found, by type of defect. 1915/16, 1918/19, 1920. p. 106. **133** **May, 1921**

10. Preschool age children examined at baby health stations of the New York City Department of Health, by findings. Manhattan. 1922. p. 127–128. **133** **June, 1923**

11. Examination of food handlers by (a) private physicians and (b) occupational clinics of the Department of Health: cases examined; cases of suspected communicable diseases; positive cases. 1928. p. 55. **131**

12. Examination of food handlers, bakers, and massage operators, by private physicians and clinics, with results. Each borough. Period May 19–Dec. 31, 1923. p. 172–173. **136** **June 7, 1924**

13. Physical examinations, made by the New York City Department of Health, for employment certificates (regular; vacation): number of examinations made; total certifications of physical fitness; rejections (temporary; permanent) by defect. 1928. p. 45. **131**

See also: *Bellevue-Yorkville district* 21
Clinics 1, 12, Note
Diseases, Transmissible 13
East Harlem 12
Employment certificates 11
Food inspection 3
Health service (entire)
Heart disease 12, 13
Malnutrition (entire)
Truants 4
Venereal disease 7–10

PHYSICIANS

1. Licensed physicians; estimated number of these physicians who were Jewish; and the per cent of Jewish licensed physicians who had a hospital affiliation. 1927. p. 5–6. **35**

PHYSICIANS *(continued)*

Source Number

2. Jewish physicians affiliated with non-Jewish hospitals. 1927. p. 7. **35**
3. Physicians registered. Each borough. [1923]. p. 1. **136 Jan. 5, 1924**
4. Physicians registered, and physicians having affiliations with hospitals (exclusive of consultants). 1921. p. 45. **216**

See also: *Births and birth rate* 5, 10, 11, 14
Hospitals 8, 13, 19
Physical examinations 9, 11
Tuberculosis 4, 19

PHYSIOTHERAPY

1. Facilities for physiotherapy, by kind of therapy available. By hospital. [1924]. p. 158–159. **216**

See also: *Clinics* 1

PLAYGROUNDS

1. Municipal playgrounds and athletic space. Each borough. 1926. p. 64–69. Maps. **262**
2. Acres of play space (a) parks, (b) schools. Each borough. [1928]. p. 157. **262**
3. Park playgrounds, area in acres, and average area per playground; school playgrounds, area in acres, and average area per playground. Each borough. [1928]. p. 157–158. **262**
4. Area of park playgrounds, area of school playgrounds, number of children 5 to 15 years (1920 census), required area for adequacy, per cent of adequacy, maps showing degree of adequacy. Manhattan, Bronx, Brooklyn, subdivided into "Play districts." [1928]. p. 159–166. **262**
5. Paid workers by sex; workers employed all year; volunteer workers; total average daily attendance of participants; expenditures for all play area. For each of the following: Manhattan; Bronx; Brooklyn, Parks and Playgrounds Association; Parks and Playgrounds Committee (Brooklyn); Board of Education. 1925. **267**

PLAYGROUNDS *(continued)*

Source Number

6. Playgrounds, community centers, and other areas under leadership. By managing authority: Bureau of Recreation, Manhattan; Department of Parks, Bronx; Department of Parks, Brooklyn; Division of Extension Activities, Board of Education; Parks and Playgrounds Association; Parks and Playgrounds Committee (Brooklyn). 1925. **267**
7. After-school athletic centers at public schools, by sex of persons attending: (a) centers; (b) sessions; (c) aggregate attendance; (d) average attendance. Each borough. 1926/27, 1927/28. p. 712. **124**
8. Afternoon playgrounds, conducted by the Division of Extension Activities of public schools, in settlement houses and other institutions other than schools: (a) centers; (b) sessions; (c) aggregate attendance; (d) average attendance. Each borough. 1926/27, 1927/28. p. 714. **124**
9. Vacation playgrounds conducted by the Division of Extension Activities of public schools, by type of center (regular; mothers' and babies'; open air; all-day care; evening; annexes; institutional; save-a-life): (a) centers; (b) sessions; (c) aggregate attendance. 1927, 1928. p. 725. **124**

See also: *Community centers* 1
Parks 5, 7
Recreation 3, 5

PLURAL BIRTHS

See: *Births and birth rate* 12, 13

PNEUMONIA

1. Deaths. Current week. **317**
2. Cases and deaths from pneumonia (all forms). Current month. **179**

PNEUMONIA *(continued)*

Source Number

3. Death rate from pneumonia (all forms) and acute bronchitis, combined. Each year, 1868–1928. p. 179. **131**

4. Cases and deaths, case rate and death rate, fatality rate. 1927. p. 19. **317** Supp. # 70

5. Deaths from (a) bronchopneumonia, and (b) lobar pneumonia. Each week, Jan. 9 to Apr. 3, 1921–1926. p. 49–50. **136** Mar. 27, 1926

6. Deaths of children under 5 years from (a) bronchopneumonia and (b) lobar pneumonia. Each year, 1920–1925. p. 79. **136** May 15, 1926

7. Cases and deaths. Each week, Sept.–May, during period Sept., 1918–May, 1922. p. 107. **136** Apr. 8, 1922

8. Case rate and death rate of influenza and pneumonia, combined. By week of year, average 1921–1925. **136** Dec. 11, 1926

See also: *Bellevue-Yorkville district* 6–10, 15, 16
Bronx, Borough of 1, 3
Deaths and death rate 1, 3, 4–7, 38–50, 54, 60, 61–63, 65, 72–75.
Diseases, Transmissible 1–5, 7, 9
East Harlem 6–11
Infant deaths and death rate 9
Negroes 8
Serums (entire)
Vital statistics 6, 12, Note

POISON

1. Deaths from poison, by kind of poison taken. Each borough. 1928. p. 10–11. **114**

See also: *Accidents* 1, 2
Deaths and death rate 38, 60, 61
Diseases, Occupational 1, 2
Homicide 5
Suicide 1–3
Workmen's compensation (entire)

POLICE DETENTION

Source Number

1. Prisoners detained by police, by sex. Each specified precinct. For a period from Jan. 1 to a date after July 1, 1928. p. 149–174. **162**
2. Prisoners: (a) total, Mar. 3, 1928; (b) male prisoners, 1927. Bellevue Hospital Prison Ward. p. 127. **162**

POLICE WELFARE DIVISION (OF THE POLICE DEPARTMENT)

1. Cases handled by the Welfare Division of the Police Department by type: destitution, temporary aid, etc.; distress relieved; employment obtained; follow-up cases; investigations of police candidates; juvenile delinquents; subpoenas served; truants; miscellaneous. Period Jan.–June, each year, 1928, 1929. p. 77. **146**
2. Cases received by the Police Welfare Division, from a selected area in Brooklyn: (a) number of children received, by disposition (referred to Children's Court; remaining under supervision); (b) by offense, one precinct in the selected area. 1926. p. 17, 48. **167**

See also: *Delinquents, Juvenile* 7

POLIOMYELITIS

1. Cases and deaths, estimated expectancy of cases. Current week. **317**
2. Cases and deaths. Each week, Jan. 1, 1921–Aug. 25, 1928. p. 127. **136** Aug. 25, 1928
3. Cases and deaths. Each month, 1927, 1928. p. 184. **131**
4. Deaths from acute anterior poliomyelitis. Each year, 1918–1928. p. 193. **136** June 22, 1929
5. Cases and deaths, case rate and death rate, fatality rate, estimated expectancy. 1927. p. 20. **317** Supp. #70
6. Cases and deaths: (a) each week, Jan.–Sept., 1923; (b) each month, average, 1921–1923. p. 330–331. **136** Oct. 20, 1923

POLIOMYELITIS *(continued)*

Source Number

7. Cases (519): age; sex; nationality; color; extent and type of paralysis; contagion; multiple cases; mortality; etc. 1921. p. 186–187. **133 Aug., 1922**

See also: *Cripples* 2
Deaths and death rate 38, 39, 41, 44, 46, 54, 60–63, 65, 75
Diseases, Transmissible 1–5, 7–9
Nursing service 1

POPULATION, AGE OF

See: *Age of population*

POPULATION AND POPULATION ESTIMATES, NOT INCLUDING 1930 AND LATER

1. Estimated mid-year population. Each borough. Published weekly for current year. **136**
2. Estimated mid-year population. Each borough. Each year, 1920–1928. **282**
3. Estimated mid-year population. Each year, 1898–1928; each borough, 1928. p. 133–134. **131**
4. Population estimate. Each tuberculosis clinic district and each borough. Jan. and July, 1929. **232 Jan. 1, 1928**
5. Total population, citizens and aliens. Each borough; each assembly district; each election district; each election district block. June 1, 1925. p. 12–16, 38–46, 56–65, 77–80, 82–83, 122–276. **205**
6. Population by "health area." 1925. **321**
7. Population of New York City; per cent of total population of State found in New York City. Each decade, 1830–1920. p. 13. **206**
8. Estimated population. Each borough. Each year, 1898–1925. **119**

POPULATION AND POPULATION ESTIMATES, NOT INCLUDING 1930 AND LATER *(continued)*

Source Number

9. Estimated population of Queensboro (based on U.S. Census reports, new buildings erected 1921–1926, installation of new gas and electric meters, and the increase in postal delivery service). By wards (subdivided into communities). Jan. 1, 1920, and Jan. 1, 1927 (estimated). p. 39. **251 Jan., 1927**
10. Day population (estimated) of Manhattan south of 59th Street on a typical business day. By origin, and means of transportation. 1924. p. 62. **260**
11. Population of each borough as at present constituted. Each decade, 1790–1920. p. 78. **284**
12. Population for total area and for each county as constituted at each Federal census. 1850–1920. p. 80–81, 119–120. **284**
13. Population of area of city as it existed at the time of each Federal census, 1790–1920. p. 8. **288**
14. Population of each assembly district. 1920. p. 264. **284**
15. Population by district. 1920. Separate sheet for each district. **241**
16. Population of each sanitary district. Each borough. 1920. p. 2–819, 830–833. **51**
17. Population in 1910 of each tabulation tract of 1920 (one or more sanitary districts having a total population of 1000 or more). p. 2–819. **51**

See also: *Age of population* 1–5
Agriculture 5
Bellevue-Yorkville district 1, 2
Birthplace of population 2
Bronx, Borough of 1, 3, 4
Density of population 4–7
East Harlem 1, 6
Finances, City 4
Sanitary districts 2
Vital statistics 8, 11

POPULATION, COLOR OF

Source Number

See: *Color of population*

POPULATION, COUNTRY OF ORIGIN OF

See: *Country of origin of population*

POPULATION, DENSITY OF

See: *Density of population*

POPULATION ESTIMATES, 1930 AND LATER

1. Foreign-born population in New York City. 1850–1920, and prediction to the year 2250. p. 33, 40. **246**
2. Predicted population of New York City. 1950, 2000, 2050, 2100. p. 28. **246**
3. Negro population of New York City. 1850 to 1920, and prediction to the year 2100. p. 32, 40. **246**
4. Predicted age distribution of New York City population (under 5 years; 5–9; 10–14; 15–19; 20–44; 45 and over). 1920–2100 (10-year periods). p. 39. **246**
5. Population. Each borough, and environs of New York City, each year, 1790–1920, and estimated population to the year 1965. p. 86. Chart only. **259**
6. Predicted population of New York City: (a) by Lewis; (b) by Pearl and Reed. 1930, 1940, 1950, 1960, 1965. p. 118. Also estimates of Lewis for each county, 1940, 1960, 1965. p. 119. **259**
7. Population. Each borough. 1920, and estimated 1930, 1940. p. 590–592. **253 Nov., 1928**

POPULATION, JEWISH

See: *Jewish population*

POPULATION, MARITAL CONDITION OF

Source Number

See: *Marital condition of population*

POPULATION, MOVEMENT OF

See: *Movement of population*

POPULATION, NATIVITY OF

See: *Nativity of population*

POPULATION, RELIGION OF

See: *Religion of population*

POPULATION, SEX OF

See: *Sex of population*

PORT OF NEW YORK

NOTE: A bibliography of the statistical data on the Port of New York district for the years 1920–1928, which are available in the publications and unpublished reports of the Port of New York Authority, has been compiled by M. E. Pellet, librarian. A copy may be seen at the office of the Welfare Council.

PRINTING INDUSTRY

1. The printing industry in New York and its environs: (a) plants and employees, Manhattan south of 59th Street, 1900, 1912, 1917, 1922; (b) value of products, 1899, 1904, 1909, 1914, 1919, 1921; (c) maps showing location of printing plants with 30 or more employees in New York and its environs, 1900, 1912, 1917, 1922; (d) plants and employees of all classes of plants and of all classes of plants excluding newspapers and plants with less than 20 employees, in Manhattan south of 14th Street, 14th to 42nd Streets, 42nd to 59th Streets, 1922; (e) employees in plants with 20 or more employees, by borough, Brooklyn, **257**

PRINTING INDUSTRY *(continued)*

1. *(continued)*
Queens, Bronx, 1900, 1912, 1917, 1922; (f) employees in plants with 20 or more employees, in sections of Manhattan, south of 14th Street, 14th to 42nd Streets, 42nd to 59th Streets, 1900, 1912, 1917, 1922; (g) front-foot values of land occupied by establishments with 30 or more employees (by type of industry; by size of plant), 1922; (h) plants and employees by size of plant, Manhattan south of 59th Street, 1900, 1912, 1917, 1922; (i) plants and employees by size of plant and by branch of industry, in sections of Manhattan, south of 14th Street, 14th to 42nd Streets, 42nd to 59th Streets, 1900, 1912, 1917, 1922. "The Printing Industry." p. 11–53.

See also: *Employment* 1–5, 10, 14
Manufactures 1, 3, 4, 11
Occupations, Children engaged in (entire)
Occupations, Persons engaged in 3, 10
Salaries and wages 1–7, 10
Trade unions 2
Workmen's compensation (entire)

PRISONERS

See: *Correction*

PRIVATE SCHOOLS

See: *Education*

PROBATION

See: *Courts* 24, 25, 33–36, 53, 58, 63, 64, 76, 81–83, 97, 105–107, 118–120, 127–129
Delinquents, Juvenile 3, 7
Prostitution 2
Sex offenses (entire)
Wayward minors (entire)
Women's Bureau, Police Department (entire)

PROSTITUTION

Source Number

1. Arrests for prostitution: (a) each year, 1922–1927; (b) per cent distribution by district, 1927; (c) cases under Police Department and Ninth (Women's) Court, Manhattan and Bronx, in which bail was forfeited, each year, 1922–1927; (d) amount of bail fixed, with authority by which fixed (regularly assigned magistrates; station house; others), 1927. Manhattan and Bronx, combined. p. 36–37, 41. ***54**
2. Arraignments for prostitution, in Ninth (Women's) Court, Manhattan and Bronx: (a) by specified charge (aiding and abetting prostitution; knowingly residing in a disorderly house; etc.), each year, 1926, 1927, p. 35; (b) cases charged with prostitution, by disposition (discharged; convicted; etc.), 1927, p. 38; (c) cases determined, each month, 1927, p. 31; (d) cases convicted of prostitution, by sentence (New York City Workhouse; State Reformatory for Women, Bedford Hills; House of the Good Shepherd; other institutions; probation; etc.), 1927, p. 39; (e) persons convicted of prostitution in 1927, by number of times convicted within calendar year, and number of persons whose latest previous conviction was within twelve months, p. 40; (f) persons convicted of prostitution who were without previous record, each year, 1926, 1927, p. 41. ***54**

See also: *Arrests and summonses* 1
Correction 20, 40, 43
Courts 12, 13, 17, 18, 21, 22, 24–28, 32, 34, 37, 38, 67–71, 73, 74, 77, 81, 82, 101, 102, 104, 133
Sex offenses (entire)
Venereal disease 8, 10

PUBLIC CHARGES

1. Public charges of the City admitted to (a) public hospitals, and (b) public homes. 1926. p. 22. **148**
2. Cases submitted by private hospitals to the New York City Department of Public Welfare for acceptance as charges upon the City, and number approved and rejected. 1926. p. 22. **148**

PUBLIC CHARGES *(continued)*

Source Number

3. Institutional care for the dependent sick, as provided by the New York City Department of Public Welfare: average daily census (patients; staff and officers; etc.); average cost per day (food; nursing; etc.); itemized expenses. Total institutions and each institution: City Hospital; Metropolitan Hospital; Children's Hospital; King's County Hospital; Cumberland Hospital; Bradford Street Hospital; Coney Island Hospital; Greenpoint Hospital; Sea View Hospital; Lincoln Hospital; Cancer Clinic. 1926. p. 14–15. **148**

4. Institutional care for the dependent poor, provided by the New York City Department of Public Welfare: average daily census (inmates; officers and staff; nurses; other paid employees); itemized expenses; average cost per day for food; etc. Home for Dependents, Welfare Island; Municipal Lodging House; City Farm Colony, Staten Island. 1926. p. 12–13. **148**

5. New admissions to the Home for Dependents, and per cent over and under 60 years of age. Each year, 1909–1926. p. 297. **148**

NOTE: Additional statistics about the inmates of the New York City Home for Aged and Infirm and the New York City Farm Colony (sex; nativity; age; religion; etc.) will be found in the annual report of the State Board of Charities, year ending June 30, 1928, p. 220–233, and in the annual report of the New York City Department of Public Welfare for 1926, p. 290–296.

See also: *Blind persons* 2
Children, Dependent or neglected 5–16, 19, 20, 22, 23
Chronically ill persons 2, 3
Courts 24
Dependents, Aged 1
Hospitals 6, 21, 23, 32
Tuberculosis 26, 27

Other allied topic: *Child Welfare, Board of*

PUBLIC SCHOOLS

Source Number

See: *Education*

PUERPERAL DISEASES AND CONDITIONS

1. Deaths from puerperal septicemia. Current month. **179**

2. Deaths and death rate from puerperal causes, by color (white; Negro; other). 1925. p. 110. **136** July 10, 1926

3. Deaths from puerperal causes by age groups (5-year periods) and disease. 1925. p. 109. **136** July 10, 1926

4. Death rate per 1000 live births from (a) puerperal septicemia, (b) all puerperal causes. 1920, 1924, 1925. p. 127. ***292**

See also: *Bellevue-Yorkville district* 6–8, 10, 18
Bronx, Borough of 1
Deaths and death rate 1, 3, 6, 7, 38, 39, 41, 44–46, 50, 54, 60–63, 72–75
Diseases, Transmissible 2
East Harlem 6–8, 10
Vital statistics Note

PUSH CART MARKETS

1. Push cart markets (based on questionnaire sent to 744 peddlers): peddlers (marital condition; race; citizenship; etc.); commodities sold; prices; clientele; etc. [1925]. **277**

QUEENS, BOROUGH OF

Note 1: The Queensboro Chamber of Commerce has available at its office statistical information relative to the growth and development of the borough of Queens.

Note 2: See all items in the Guide which are given for each borough.

RABIES

Source Number

1. Deaths from rabies. 1928. p. 53. **131**
2. Dog bites reported; cases of rabies found in animals. 1928. p. 62. **131**
3. Rabies: (a) in animals, cases reported; (b) in man, deaths. 1927. p. 21–22. **317 Supp. # 70**
4. Persons bitten by rabid dogs, and persons treated with vaccine. Each borough. 1925 and period Jan.–Oct., 1926. p. 193. **136 Dec. 4, 1926**
5. Dog bites, each year, 1921–1925; rabid dogs, 1920, 1925. p. 17. **136**
6. Patients receiving rabies vaccine from the New York City Department of Health: patients treated; cases in which biting animal proved rabid; deaths of patients treated. 1927, 1928. p. 78. **131**
7. Patients receiving rabies vaccine from the New York City Department of Health: patients treated; per cent bitten by animals proved to be rabid; total deaths among patients treated; per cent of deaths in cases in which biting animal was rabid; deaths after 15 days or more of treatment. Each year, 1917–1922. p. 87. **133 Apr., 1923**
8. Number of persons bitten by rabid dogs, and number of request for vaccine. Each borough. 1919, 1920, 1921. p. 266. **133 Nov., 1922**

See also: *Accidents* 1
Clinics 1
Deaths and death rate 38, 60, 61
Diseases, Transmissible 2, 3, 7, 9

RAILROADS

1. Trains entering New York City daily from points 80 miles or more distant. Each railroad. [1928]. p. 7. **229**
2. Passenger traffic on trunk line railroads to and from New York, each railroad, 1927, 1928; passengers subdivided as to (a) commuters, (b) others, each railroad and terminal. 1928. p. 3–4. ***210**

RAILROADS *(continued)*

Source Number

3. Traffic at New York City railroad terminals. Each terminal. 1927, 1928. p. 7. ***210**

See also: *Suicides* 1
Trade unions 2
Transportation 1, 3

RAPE

See: *Arrests and summonses* 1
Correction 20, 50, 54
Courts 12, 13, 18, 21, 22, 38
Felonies 2, 3

RATS

1. Rat-flea survey: total rats caught; number having fleas; total fleas taken by kind of flea; average fleas per rat. Each month, Apr., 1923, to Feb., 1925. p. 1917–1918. **317 Sept. 11, 1925**

RECREATION

1. Licensed amusement houses and number of seats: (a) theatres; (b) motion picture places, by type (common show motion picture; motion picture theatre; open-air motion picture); (c) concert halls. Each borough. 1927. p. 11, 12. ***142**

2. Average admission prices for moving picture theatres, for (a) adults, (b) children. Data collected Aug.-Oct., 1927. p. 45. **103**

3. Playground and community recreation activities: number of paid workers and number of volunteers by sex; expenditures; recreation facilities provided and attendance (tennis courts; swimming pools; etc.). By managing authority. 1928. p. 108–109. ***247**

4. Jewish recreational facilities in New York City by type of organization (a) Y.M.H.A.'s and Y.W.H.A.'s, (b) settlement houses, (c) synagogue centers; and in many cases, by individual organizations: number of **37**

RECREATION *(continued)*

Source Number

4. *(continued)*
organizations; median age of persons served; median length of stay in present quarters; recreation facilities available; number of persons served; incomes and expenditures of organizations; organized classes by subject taught. End of 1928.

5. Children served by recreational agencies: (a) by age; (b) by type of agency (churches; community centers; schools having playgrounds); (c) per cent of child population served computed on 1920 population data. Selected area of Brooklyn. 1926. p. 25. **167**

6. Juvenile delinquency cases, by play districts: (a) child population 7–15 years of age; (b) arrests among that population. Each play district in Manhattan. 1920. p. 139, 145. **270**

7. Arrests of children 7–15 years of age: (a) total; (b) number of arrests for more serious offenses; (c) per cent of arrests that were for more serious offenses and per cent that were for less serious offenses. Each play district in Manhattan. 1920. p. 163. **270**

8. Play space adequacy by play districts in Manhattan: (a) child population 7–15 years of age; (b) play space needed; (c) play space in use; (d) index of adequacy. Each play district in Manhattan. 1920. p. 143, 145. **270**

9. Number of children 7–15 years of age per acre in each play district in Manhattan. 1920. p. 148. **270**

10. School baths and swimming pools, in public schools, by sessions (day; evening): (a) number of centers; (b) sessions; (c) aggregate attendance; (d) average attendance. Each borough. 1927/28; summer, 1928. p. 710. **124**

11. Settlements (sample, 33 settlements) having athletics for boys (major activity; minor activity), by type of athletics (basketball; tennis; etc.). Period Mar.–May, 1928. **333**

RECREATION *(continued)*

Source Number

See also: *Bathing establishments* (entire)
Beaches, Bathing (entire)
Building 2, 4, 6, 9–11, 13, 15, 16
Business 1
Camps (entire)
Community centers (entire)
Cost of living 4, 15
Dance halls (entire)
Finances, City 5
Libraries (entire)
Licenses (entire)
Parks (entire)
Playgrounds (entire)
Settlements 4, 5
Theatres (entire)
Trade unions 2
Vacation homes (entire)

REFORMATORIES

See: *Correction*

RELIGION OF POPULATION

1. Persons estimated, by religion (Roman Catholic; Protestant; Greek Catholic; Jewish): (a) total by color (white; Negro; other); (b) white by native parentage and foreign parentage; (c) foreign-parentage whites by leading mother-tongue spoken in New York. Each borough. 1920, and gain, 1910–1920. p. 826. **51**
2. Persons, estimated, by religion (as in 1). Each borough section, each borough. 1920, and per cent, 1900, 1910. p. 828. **51**
3. Persons, estimated, by religion (Roman Catholic; Protestant and Greek Catholic; Jewish) and age (under 7; 7–13; 14 and 15; 16 and 17; 18–20; 21 and over). Each borough. 1920. p. 839. **51**

See also: *Boy population* (entire)
Churches 1, 2

RENT

Source Number

1. Changes of rents in New York City. Each year or half year, 1914–1926. Index numbers, based on 1914. p. 48–49. **184**

2. Representative minimum range of rent per room per month, and representative average minimum rent per room per month. By type of housing. Each borough. 1926. p. 34. **102**

3. Changes of rents in New York City. By year, half year, or quarter year, Dec., 1914–Dec., 1924. Index numbers. p. 14–15. **180**

4. Rents paid for apartments, and building costs. Each year, 1914–1922. Index numbers. p. 184. **100**

5. Per cent increase in rents from Dec., 1914, to Dec., 1917, Dec., 1918, June, 1919, Dec., 1919, June, 1920, and Dec., 1920. p. 459. **253 June., 1921**

6. Representative average minimum rents per month in 3 and 4 room flats, with and without bath. Data collected Aug.-Oct., 1927. p. 30. **103**

7. Variations in rent of 4 room apartments by period of tenancy. Oct., 1923. p. 22. **180**

8. Rents in tenements constructed in 1924: number and per cent of rooms by rent paid. By borough: Manhattan; Bronx; Brooklyn; Queens. p. 29. **183**

9. Rents per room per month paid by tenants entering 3 room and 4 room apartments. Six selected blocks in Manhattan. Period 1923–1925. p. 46. **183**

10. Average monthly rent. Selected blocks in New York City. 1920, 1923. p. 13. **181**

See also: *Apartments* 6–15
Cost of living 1, 3, 4, 6
Homework 7
Housing surveys 1, 3–6
Standard of living 4
Tenements 5

RICHMOND, BOROUGH OF

Source Number

1. Population: (a) by sex; (b) by color (white; colored); (c) white population by nativity. Each borough section (two). 1920, 1925. p. 31. **206**

2. Population: (a) total by sex; (b) by color (white; Negro; other); (c) white population, by nativity; (d) foreign-born white population by citizenship (citizens; aliens). Each assembly district divided into groups of sanitary districts. 1925. p. 39. **206**

3. Population: (a) total by age (under 5; 5-year groups to 100 and over; unknown; under one year; each year, 1–24), sex, and color (white; Negro; other); (b) white population by age, sex, and nativity. 1925. p. 32. **206**

4. Population by age (under 5; 5-year groups to 85 and over; age unknown) and sex. Each borough section (two). 1925. p. 32. **206**

5. Foreign-born white persons, by country of birth, age (under 5; 5–14; 15–20; 21–24; 25–34; 35–44; 45–54; 55–64; 65 and over; age unknown) and sex. 1925. p. 37. **206**

6. Foreign-born white persons: (a) by country of birth, sex, and citizenship (citizens; aliens), each borough section, 1925; (b) by country of birth, entire county, 1920. p. 34. **206**

7. Foreign-born white persons: (a) by country of birth and length of residence in the United States; (b) number who are citizens, by country of birth and length of residence in the United States. 1925. p. 36. **206**

8. Population 7–20 years of age, and number of those persons attending school: (a) by age (7–13; 14–15; 16–17; 18–20) and sex, each borough section; (b) by age and color (white; colored); (c) white population by age and nativity. 1925. p. 33. **206**

9. Total population and persons attending school: (a) by age (under 5; each year, 5–20; 21 years and over) and sex; (b) by age and color (white; colored); (c) white persons by age and nativity. 1925. p. 33. **206**

RICHMOND, BOROUGH OF *(continued)*

Source Number

10. Persons 10 years of age and over engaged in gainful occupations: (a) by age (10–13; 14; 15; etc. . . . 20–24; 10-year periods to 65 and over; age unknown), sex, and color (white; colored); (b) by sex and color, each borough section; (c) white persons by sex, age, and nativity; (d) white persons by sex and nativity, each borough section. 1925. p. 33. **206**

11. Number of families, by number of persons in family: (a) by color (white; colored); (b) white families by nativity; (c) foreign-born white families by country of birth. 1925. p. 39. **206**

NOTE: See all items in the Guide which are given for each borough.

RINGWORM

1. Cases of ringworm found among school children. Each year, 1912–1922. p. 154. **136** May 19, 1923

ROBBERY

See: *Arrests and summonses* 1
Correction 20, 50, 54, 83, 84
Courts 12, 13, 15, 16, 18, 21–23, 38, 110, 115, 122
Delinquents, Juvenile 3, 5
Felonies 2–5, 7, 10, 12, 13, 15, 18

Other allied topics: *Burglary*
Larceny

ROMAN CATHOLIC SCHOOLS

See: *Education*

ROOM REGISTRIES

1. Room registries for women and girls which report monthly data to the Research Bureau of the Welfare Council of New York City: (a) applicants by age (under 35; 35 and over) classified as newly registered **326**

ROOM REGISTRIES *(continued)*

Source Number

1. *(continued)* and formerly registered; (b) placements by age; (c) individuals placed, by age; (d) homes on approved list (on first day of month; added during month; withdrawn during month; on last day of month); (e) homes not accepted (after investigation; without investigation). Each registry. Compiled monthly.

SALARIES AND WAGES

1. Average weekly earnings in representative factories, in 11 principal divisions of industry (stone, clay, and glass; metals and machinery; wood manufactures; fur, leather, and rubber goods; chemicals, oils, paints, etc.; pulp and paper; printing and paper goods; textiles; clothing and millinery; food and tobacco; water, light, and power), with subdivisions for (a) all employees, (b) shop workers only, by sex. Current month. **188**
2. Average weekly earnings of office workers in factories, by type of industry (11 principal divisions, with subdivisions, as in item 1) and sex. Oct., 1928. p. 434. **188** **Nov., 1928**
3. Changes in payrolls by industry (11 principal divisions, with subdivisions, as in item 1), by sex, from Jan., 1923, to Jan., 1924, and Jan., 1925. p. 166. **194**
4. Average weekly earnings of workers in factories by sex and industry (11 principal divisions, with subdivisions, as in item 1). June, 1923. p. 169–170, 175. **194**
5. Average weekly earnings of (a) all employees, (b) shop employees by sex, in representative factories, by kind of industry. Feb., 1926. Part II, p. 211–213. **41**
6. Average weekly earnings of factory employees, by industry. April, 1925. p. 87–88. Published occasionally. **314** **July, 1925**
7. Earnings in 10 specified industries: (a) average weekly and annual earnings by sex, year ending June 30, 1925; and (b) increase in weekly wages by sex, year ending June 30, 1915, and 1925. Each industry. p. 59–63. **160**

SALARIES AND WAGES *(continued)*

Source Number

8. Average weekly wages in the manufacturing industries. Semi-annually, 1914–1922. p. 37. **221**

9. Union scales of wages and hours of labor, in 20 specified occupations: bricklayers; plumbers; etc. 1913, and each year, 1918–1929. p. 145–166. **314 Sept., 1929**

10. Union scales of wages and hours of labor in specified trades (barbers; bus drivers; etc.) by type of work done. May 15, 1928. **313**

11. Wages in the building trades (old rate; new rate), by kind of work done. Spring, 1926. p. 242–243. **41**

12. Minimum union weekly wage rates in the New York cloak and suit trade, by type of work. 1910, and each year, 1913–1924. p. 531. **89**

13. Salaries of teaching and supervising personnel in public schools by type of work: (a) persons; (b) lowest schedule rate; (c) highest schedule rate; (d) average salary. Mar. 31, 1928. p. 738. **124**

14. Salaries of teachers in public schools (regular day schools): (a) average salary by sex and type of work, 1910, 1925; (b) salaries in 1925 by sex and type of work, also in terms of the purchasing power of 1900; (c) average number of years of training, by sex and type of work; (d) average number of years of training, by sex and "economic status" (married; unmarried, living at home; etc.); (e) years of teaching service, by sex, "economic status," and type of work; (f) women teachers by number of dependents, "economic status," and type of work; (g) teachers by sex, "economic status," length of teaching service, and number of dependents; (h) married men teachers by number of children and number of dependents; (i) earnings from outside sources, by sex, "economic status," and type of school work; (j) earnings from outside sources of married men teachers, classified by number of children and type **52**

SALARIES AND WAGES *(continued)*

Source Number

14. *(continued)*
of school work; (k) average rents paid and sub-rentals received, by sex, "economic status," and type of work; (l) average rents paid by married men teachers, by type of housing; (m) rentals paid by all teachers, by "economic status" and salary; (n) monthly expense for meals, by sex, "economic status," and type of work; (o) monthly expense of married men teachers for meals, by number of children and type of work. Items (c)–(o), May, 1926. p. 226–251.

15. Salaries of teachers in Jewish religious schools (Hebrew schools; parochial schools): (a) number of teachers by sex; (b) number of teaching hours per week, by sex; (c) total salaries, average salary, and median salary, by sex; (d) years of teaching experience and median salary; (e) weeks of vacation. 1926. ***84**

See also: *Candy industry* (entire)
Employment 1–3
Employment by the City of New York (entire)
Employment of children 4
Garment industry 2–6
Homework 7
Hours of work 2
Laundries (entire)
Manufactures 1, 2, 8, 10
Outdoor relief 1
Paper box industry (entire)
Stores 6

SALOONS

1. Decrease of saloons in Manhattan (per cents). Each year, 1916, 1918, 1920, 1921, 1922, 1924. p. 18. **342**

2. Saloons in New York City. Each year, 1910–1924. Chart only. p. 23. **342**

SANITARY DISTRICTS

Source Number

1. Number of sanitary districts, distributed as having population and not having population. Each borough. 1910, 1920. p. 844. **51**

2. House to house survey of sanitary district # 18, to determine medical needs of the district: analysis of mortality; births; infant mortality; population; hospital and dispensary service used, by distance traveled by patient. 1923. p. 225–232. **74**

SAVINGS BANKS

1. Condition of savings banks: total resources; liabilities; number of open accounts; number of accounts opened in preceding year; number of accounts closed in preceding year; amount deposited; amount withdrawn; etc. Each county and bank. Jan. 1, 1929. ***155**

2. Savings bank depositors; savings bank deposits. Brooklyn. Dec. 31, each year, 1915–1928. p. 35. ***17**

3. Savings banks: number of banks; deposits; depositors; average due each depositor; resources. By borough: Manhattan; Brooklyn. Each year, 1918–1926. Part, II, p. 124. **41**

4. Number of savings banks, depositors, amount of deposits, average deposit, increase in deposits, each borough; also per cent of total population who were depositors, and per cent who were 15 years of age and over. July 1, 1921. p. 26–29. **221**

5. Savings banks in public schools: (a) receipts, payments, cash balance at end of period, new accounts, new interest-bearing accounts, year ending Feb. 1, 1927 and 1928; (b) number of schools authorized to operate school savings banks, and schools operating such banks, May 1, 1928. p. 336–337. **124**

SCARLET FEVER

1. Cases and estimated expectancy of cases. Current week. **317**

2. Cases and deaths. Current week. **179**

SCARLET FEVER *(continued)*

Source Number

3. Cases and case rate, deaths and death rate, case fatality. Each borough. Current quarter year and corresponding quarter of preceding year. **136**
4. Cases and deaths. Each week, Jan. 1, 1921–Sept. 29, 1928. p. 169. **136 Sept. 29, 1928**
5. Cases and deaths. Each month, 1927, 1928. p. 174. **131**
6. Deaths and death rate. Each year, 1868–1928. p. 175. **131**
7. Cases and deaths, case rate and death rate, fatality rate, estimated expectancy. 1927. p. 23. **317 Supp. # 70**

SCHOOL ATTENDANCE

SCHOOL CHILDREN

SCHOOLS

SERUMS

1. Amount and value of biological products (diphtheria antitoxin; influenza serum; etc.) distributed by the New York City Department of Health during 1923. p. 203. **133 Sept., 1924**

SETTLEMENTS

Source Number

1. Membership of a sample group of settlements: (a) members of 18 settlements, by sex, each settlement; (b) members of 16 settlements, by sex and age, each settlement; (c) families and individuals in 18 settlements, each settlement; (d) families in 17 settlements classified by number of settlement members per family, each settlement; (e) family relationship of members of 16 settlements; (f) members of 8 settlements classified as to cultural background (Italian; Jewish; etc.), each settlement; (g) members of 12 settlements classified by distance between settlement and place of residence, each settlement; (h) members of 8 settlements classified as affiliated during current year and affiliated prior to current year, each settlement. Winter and Spring, 1928. **335**

2. Settlements and neighborhood houses operated. Manhattan; Brooklyn; Bronx. Each year, 1910–1926. **332**

3. Income by source and functional expenditures by purpose (general settlement activities; camps operated; religious activities; relief), of 118 settlements and neighborhood houses; value of property. Manhattan; Brooklyn; Bronx. Each year, 1910–1926. **332**

4. Functional expenditures of a sample group of 27 settlements, by type of service. Each year, 1910–1926. **332**

5. Activities of 18 settlements, by duration of activity during the period 1910–1926. **332**

6. Roman Catholic settlements: (a) staff (religious; lay); (b) number on register (boys; girls; adults); (c) children sent to summer homes; (d) classes (religious; lay); (e) clubs; (f) expenditures. Each settlement in Manhattan and Bronx. 1928. p. 97. ***40**

See also: *Physical examinations* 3
Recreation 4, 11

SEX OFFENSES

Source Number

1. Sex offenders arraigned before the Ninth (Women's) Court, Manhattan and Bronx: (a) by offense (incorrigibility; offering to secure a prostitute; etc.) and disposition (defaulted; discharged; etc.); (b) cases defaulted, by type of bail forfeited (cash; Liberty Bonds; etc.), each offense (as above); (c) cases committed to the workhouse, by length of sentence, each offense (as above). Period Jan. 1–June 30, 1920. p. 494–497. **344**

See also: *Arrests and summonses* 1
Correction 21, 50, 54, 83, 84
Courts 12, 13, 15, 17, 18, 21–28, 32, 38, 79, 91–93, 96, 97, 100, 105, 108, 129, 130
Felonies 2, 4, 5, 7, 10, 12, 13, 15, 18
Wayward minors (entire)

SEX OF POPULATION

1. Total persons, white persons, and Negroes, by sex. Each borough. 1910, 1920. p. 115. **285**
2. Total persons, white persons, and Negroes, by sex. Each assembly district and each borough. 1920. p. 63–68. **288**
3. Persons by sex: (a) total by color (white; Negro; other); (b) white persons by nativity and parentage. Each assembly district and each borough. 1920. p. 63–68. **288**
4. Ratio of males to females: (a) total by color (white; Negro; other); (b) white persons by nativity and parentage. Each borough. 1900, 1910. p. 128. **285**

See also: *Age of population* 2, 3, 5–7
Bellevue-Yorkville district 2
Birthplace of population 5, 12
Boy population (entire)
Bronx, Borough of 3
Citizenship of population 3, 5–7
Color of population 4
Country of origin of population 8
Education 2, 3, 5
Illiteracy 1–3, 5, 6

SEX OF POPULATION *(continued)*

Source Number

See also: *(continued)*
Language 1, 2
Marital condition of population (entire)
Nativity of population 5
Occupations, Children engaged in (entire)
Occupations, Persons engaged in (entire)
Ownership of homes 1
Richmond, Borough of 1–6, 9, 10

SHELTERED WORKSHOPS

1. Sheltered workshops which report monthly data to the Research Bureau of the Welfare Council of New York City: (a) persons enrolled by sex (on first day of reporting period; admitted during reporting period; persons withdrawing during the reporting period who were placed; other persons withdrawing; enrolled on last day of reporting period); (b) persons in shop; (c) capacity of shop on last day of reporting period; (d) vacancies on last day of reporting period; (e) total moneys paid; (f) basis of payment (piece work; hourly wage; etc.); (g) persons employed in the conduct of the shop who do not have a handicap of a type which the shop is fitted to serve (full-time; part-time); (h) hours worked during reporting period. Each shop. Compiled for four-week period or five-week period. **327**

NOTE: The group reporting does not include all shops eligible for reporting but includes a large proportion of such shops.

SILICOSIS

1. Findings in an examination for silicosis of 208 rock drillers, blasters, and excavators: results of X-ray examinations as to presence and degree of development of silicosis; nativity; age; marital condition; race; stages of silicosis in relation to age; length of exposure in relation to incidence and stages of silicosis; occupation and length of exposure in relation to incidence and stages of silicosis; previous respiratory diseases; heart disease; tuberculosis. [1928]. p. 44–57. **264**

SLEEPING SICKNESS

Source Number

See: *Encephalitis lethargica*

SMALLPOX

1. Cases and deaths; estimated expectancy of cases. Current week. **317**
2. Cases and deaths, case rate and death rate, fatality rate, estimated expectancy. 1927. p. 25. **317 Supp. # 70**
3. Cases and deaths. 1928. p. 53. **131**
4. Deaths and death rate. Each year, 1868–1928. p. 183. **131**

See also: *Deaths and death rate* 3, 38, 39, 41, 44, 46, 49, 60–62, 72, 73, 75
Diseases, Transmissible 2, 3, 7, 9

Other allied topic: *Serums*

SOLICITATION OF FUNDS

1. Requests made to the New York City Department of Public Welfare for permission to solicit funds, by number approved and disapproved. 1926. p. 28. **148**

SORE THROAT (SEPTIC)

1. Cases and deaths, case rate and death rate, fatality rate. 1927. p. 24. **317 Supp. # 70**

See also: *Diseases, Transmissible* 2

STANDARD OF LIVING

1. Families divided into expenditure groups (high; medium; low), with map showing distribution of these groups. 1926. p. 3. **240**
2. Geographical distribution of purchasing power of population. 1923. Separate map for each district. **241**
3. Ownership of homes (owned; rented) by size of income (high; medium; low). 1926. p. 24. **240**

STANDARD OF LIVING *(continued)*

Source Number

4. Rent-paying families by amount of rent paid (high; medium; low). 1926. p. 26. **240**

5. Per cent distribution of English-reading, automobile-owning families by income (high; medium; low). 1926. p. 28. **240**

6. Per cent of families in each income group (high; medium; low) who own automobiles. 1926. p. 28. **240**

7. Per cent of high-priced, medium-priced, and low-priced automobiles, distributed by income groups of families (high; medium; low). 1926. p. 31. **240**

8. Families classified by expenditure groups (high; medium; low) and language read (English; foreign). 1926. p. 16. **240**

STARVATION

See: *Deaths and death rate* 38, 60, 61

STILLBIRTHS AND STILLBIRTH RATE

1. Stillbirths and stillbirth rate: (a) each year, 1898–1928; (b) each borough, 1928. p. 133–134. **131**

2. Stillbirths: (a) by color (white; Negro; other) and sex; (b) by parentage (native; foreign; mixed; unknown) and sex; (c) by months of uterogestation. 1928. p. 135. **131**

3. Stillbirths by sex and month. 1926. p. 172. ***279**

4. Stillbirths: (a) by cause; (b) by period of uterogestation. 1926. p. 187. ***279**

See also: *Bellevue-Yorkville district* 4, 5
Births and birth rate 1, 4, 9
Bronx, Borough of 1
East Harlem 6, 7
Vital statistics 1, 5–8, 10

STORES

	Source Number
1. Retail stores by type: (a) grocery stores (delicatessen; independent, classified as A, B, and C; chain); (b) drug stores (A; B; C; chain); (c) hardware; (d) men's wear; (e) women's wear and dry goods; (f) shoe stores; (g) furniture stores; (h) radio stores. Each borough, and by sales division; and for (c)–(h) by block in Manhattan, Brooklyn, and Bronx. 1928.	**220**
2. Total retail stores, number of drug stores, number of grocery stores. By district. Each borough (except Manhattan). 1923.	**241**
3. Total retail stores, and number of grocery, drug, confectionery, tobacco, men's furnishings, women's furnishings, dry goods, shoes, furniture, electrical supplies, hardware, auto supplies, jewelry stores. Each borough, and by district, Manhattan and Queens. 1923.	**241**
4. Retail outlets by kind of store, and kinds of merchandise for which stores are outlets, for (a) independent, (b) chain stores. By borough: Manhattan; Queens; and total for New York City. 1923.	**241**
5. Stores (wholesale; retail; chain) by kind of store (drug; grocery; etc.), 1926; number of buyers 15 years of age and over, by sex, 1920, and estimates for 1927. Manhattan and Bronx; Queens; Brooklyn; Richmond. p. 202.	**245**
6. Persons employed in 5 and 10 cent stores by sex: (a) number of stores and workers studied (full-time; part-time); (b) period of service; (c) days absent; (d) weekly hours; (e) weekly wage rates; (f) commissions earned; (g) bonuses; (h) weekly wage in relation to length of service. Manhattan, Bronx, and Brooklyn, combined. Winter, 1921.	**189**

See also: *Building* 2, 9–11, 13–17
Employment 4
Employment of children 1, 2
Fires 3, 9
Occupation, Children engaged in (entire)
Occupations, Persons engaged in 3, 10

STREET RAILWAYS

Source Number

1. Number of passengers carried by street railways: (a) each line; (b) each borough. 1928. p. 39. Also published quarterly. **213**
2. Traffic on electric railways (surface; elevated and subway) as shown by miles of main travel; revenue passengers; passenger-car miles. 1912, 1917, 1922. p. 88. **280**
3. Number of passengers carried on (a) I.R.T. and (b) B.M.T. lines. Each year, 1918–1924. p. 25. **175**
4. Fares collected from passengers on the I.R.T. and B.M.T. lines. Each station and each borough. 1927, 1928. p. 46–50. **213**
5. Average amount expended by street railway companies in settlement of personal claims. Each year, 1914–1927. p. 129. ***211**

See also: *Salaries and wages* 10
Transportation 1, 2

Other allied topic: *Accidents, Street railway*

STRIKES

1. Number of strikes. Each year, 1916–1928. p. 135. **314** **July, 1929**
2. Number of strikes, employees involved, and days lost. Each year, 1910–1921, and Jan.–June, 1922. p. 132. **136** **Apr. 28, 1923**

SUBWAYS

See: *Street railways*
Transportation

SUICIDE

1. Deaths from suicide, by method used, country of birth, and sex. 1928. p. 139. **131**
2. Suicides: (a) by method used (poison by kind), (b) by color (black; yellow). Each borough. 1928. p. 4. **114**

SUICIDE *(continued)*

Source Number

3. Suicides, by method used and sex: (a) by marital state; (b) by age. 1928. p. 5. **114**

4. Mean monthly rate and corrected rate of suicides. Each year, 1910–1923. p. 1. **95 Aug., 1925**

5. Suicide rate, as compared with periods of economic depression. Each year, 1900–1925. p. 202. Chart only. **136 Dec. 18, 1926**

See also: *Asphyxiation* 2
Bronx, Borough of 1
Deaths and death rate 3, 6, 7, 38–41, 44, 46, 52, 60–63, 65, 72–75
Homicide 5

SUMMONSES, POLICE

See: *Arrests and summonses*

SUNDAY SCHOOL MEMBERS

See: *Churches* 1, 2

SUNSTROKE

1. Deaths and death rate from sunstroke during heat waves. Each year, 1872, 1892, 1896, 1901, 1911, 1917, 1925, 1928. p. 125. **136 Aug. 25, 1928**

See also: *Accidents* 1
Deaths and death rate 38, 39, 41, 44, 46, 60, 61

TAX EXEMPTION

1. Value of real estate exempt from general property tax: (a) by ownership (United States; county; etc.); (b) by use to which real estate is put (charitable; religious; educational; curative; etc.). Each county. 1927. p. 174–185. ***208**

2. Assessed value of tax-exempt real property, classified by use. 1925. p. 60, 62. **209**

TAX EXEMPTION *(continued)*

Source Number

3. Assessed value of real property: (a) tax exempt locally; (b) taxable locally; (c) ratio between (a) and (b). 1925. p. 46. **209**

4. Assessed value of tax-exempt real property classified by ownership (United States; State; county; city; private). 1925. p. 56, 58. **209**

TENEMENTS

1. Number of buildings and apartments: (a) old-law tenements; (b) new-law tenements; (c) converted dwellings. Each borough. Jan. 1, 1928; Dec. 31, 1928. **152**

2. New-law tenements, apartments, and rooms: (a) in each borough, 1927, 1928; (b) classified according to location, by district, each borough, 1928. **152**

3. New-law tenements by (a) height in stories, (b) number of apartments, (c) apartments per floor, (d) bath accommodations. Each borough. 1928. **152**

4. New tenement plans filed: number of buildings; apartments; rooms. Each borough. 1927, 1928. **152**

5. Tenements constructed: (a) number; (b) by size (apartments per tenement; rooms per apartment); (c) by cost (per apartment; per room). Each year, 1920–1928, and each borough. 1928. p. 64–65. **186**

6. Newly constructed tenements: tenements; apartments; rooms. Each year, 1920–1923. p. 2. **138**

See also: *Apartments* (entire)
Buildings 2, 4, 8–11, 13, 15–17
Deaths and death rate 18–20
Employment of children 3
Fires 3, 6–10
Homework 7
Housing construction 2, 3
Housing surveys 1, 4, 7, 8

Other allied topics: *Housing*
Rent

TETANUS

Source Number

1. Cases and deaths. 1928. p. 53. **131**
2. Deaths during year; cases in (a) June and (b) July. Each year, 1920–1925. p. 107. **136** **July 3, 1926**
3. Cases by cause. Each month, 1924. p. 155. **136** **June 27, 1925**

See also: *Accidents* 1
Deaths and death rate 38, 60, 61
Diseases, Transmissible 2, 3, 7, 9
Infant deaths and death rate 9
Serums (entire)

TEXTILE INDUSTRY

1. Textile industry in New York and its environs, subdivided into (a) men's clothing, (b) women's clothing, (c) textiles: location of plants by branch of industry (maps); number of plants and wage earners by size of plant and branch of industry; home workers; fluctuation of employment; location of homes of workers; etc. 1922 or earlier. "The Clothing and Textile Industries." p. 13–104. **258**

See also: *Employment* 2, 4, 7, 8, 10
Manufactures 1, 3, 4, 11
Occupations, Children engaged in (entire)
Occupations, Persons engaged in 3, 10
Salaries and wages 1–6
Trade unions 2
Workmen's compensation (entire)

THEATRES

1. Seating capacity of legitimate theatres and assessed value. Each theatre. [1928]. p. 11. **229**
2. Theatres by type of production (movie; vaudeville; burlesque; etc.). Each borough. Jan., 1921. p. IX. **68**

See also: *Building* 1
Fires 3, 9
Licenses (entire)
Recreation 1, 2

TOBACCO PRODUCTS INDUSTRY

Source Number

1. Tobacco products industry in New York and its environs: (a) cigar workers by sex, Manhattan south of 59th Street, Manhattan north of 59th Street, four boroughs combined (Bronx, Brooklyn, Richmond, Queens), each year, 1900–1922; (b) cigar factories with 50 or more employees, Manhattan south of 14th Street, 14th to 59th Streets, north of 59th Street, 1900, 1912, 1922; (c) cigar factories in Manhattan, classified by amount of output, 1912, 1917, 1921; (d) cigar factories with 20 or more employees by the front-foot value of the land occupied, and by employees, Manhattan south of 59th Street, Manhattan north of 59th Street, [1922]; (e) cigar factories and employees by number of employees per plant, Brooklyn and Queens, combined, Bronx, 1922; (f) maps showing the location of tobacco factories with 10 or more employees in New York and its environs, 1900, 1912, 1917, 1922; (g) chart showing cigarette production in the United States, in Manhattan, in New York and its environs, 1922; (h) cigarette factories and employees by size of factories, Manhattan, 1900, 1912, 1922; (i) tobacco product plants and number of employees in the tobacco products industry by size of plant, Manhattan south of 59th Street, 1900, 1912, 1917, 1922. "The Tobacco Products Industry." p. 13–58. **257**

See also: *Employment* 1–5, 7, 8, 10, 14
Hours of work 2
Manufactures 1, 3, 4, 11
Occupations, Children engaged in (entire)
Occupations, Persons engaged in 3, 10
Salaries and wages 1–7
Trade unions 2

TONSILLECTOMIES

1. Tonsil operations performed; capacity for operations per week and per year. Each hospital. Each borough. 1920. **45**

TRADE SCHOOLS

Source Number

See: *Education*

TRADE UNIONS

1. Women gainfully employed, and women in trade unions. 1920. p. 28. **190**

2. Women in trade unions by industries. 1914, 1920. p. 31. **190**

See also: *Garment industry* 1–3
Paper box industry (entire)

TRAFFIC REGULATIONS, VIOLATION OF

1. Arrests and summonses, each division (motorcycle; traffic; other), by disposition (fined or bond forfeited, with amount of fines; sent to jail, with number of days). 1928, divided as first 11 months, combined, and December. p. 28. ***144**

2. Persons in custody after conviction for traffic violations. Traffic Detention Pens, Manhattan. Jan. 1–Nov. 30, 1928. p. 129. **162**

3. Arraignments for traffic violations by sex, each offense: arraignments before magistrates as such (defacing identification marks; failing to keep to right; etc.); arraignments at Special Sessions held by magistrates (highway law, violation of; obstructing traffic and parking; etc.). By court: Traffic Court, Manhattan; Traffic Court, Bronx; Traffic Court, Brooklyn; also Special Sessions held by magistrates, each Traffic Court. 1927. p. 119, 125, 136. ***117**

4. Cases before the court for traffic violations, which were disposed of: (a) total, by sex and general disposition (discharged; convicted or held), each offense (as in item 3); (b) convictions by disposition (fined; workhouse; sentence suspended; probation; straight sentence; fine and imprisonment), each offense (as in item 3); (c) cases fined, by disposition (fines paid, by number paying specified amount; committed), each ***117**

TRAFFIC REGULATIONS, VIOLATION OF (*continued*)

Source Number

4. (*continued*)
offense (as in item 3). By court: Traffic Court, Manhattan; Traffic Court, Bronx; Traffic Court, Brooklyn; also Special Sessions held by magistrates, each Traffic Court. 1927, p. 120–121, 126–127, 137–138.

5. Arraignments for traffic violations: (a) number, Jan. 1–Dec. 11, 1928; (b) amount of fines collected, Jan. 1–Nov. 30, 1928, and year 1927. Traffic Court, Manhattan, and Special Sessions held by magistrates. p. 129. **162**

6. Arraignments for traffic violations and amount of fines collected. Traffic Court, Brooklyn, and Special Sessions held by magistrates. Period Jan. 1–Nov. 20, 1928. p. 136. **162**

7. Cases heard which were charged with traffic violations. City Magistrates' Courts, Richmond. Period Jan. 1–Nov. 24, 1928. p. 281. **162**

8. Taxicab drivers convicted. Traffic Court, Manhattan, and Special Sessions held by magistrates. 1927. p. 129. **162**

9. Motor vehicle licenses: (a) suspended; (b) revoked. Traffic Court, Manhattan; Traffic Court, Bronx; Traffic Court, Brooklyn; Homicide and Traffic Court (Part 3), Brooklyn; District Court, Queens; District Court, Richmond. Courts combined, each borough. 1927. p. 52. ***117**

See also: *Arrests and summonses* 1, 4
Correction 20
Courts 12, 13, 15, 17, 18, 21–25, 28, 32, 38, 55, 56, 58, 84, 101, 102, 104

Other allied topic: *Highway law, Violation of*

TRANSPORTATION

1. Transit and transportation problem in New York and its environs: riding habits of the population, by means of transportation (subway; elevated; etc.); movement **261**

TRANSPORTATION *(continued)*

Source Number

1. *(continued)* of population and area of greatest density (maps); number of commuters and their source; proposed additions to relieve the congestion (maps); estimates of future traffic; water front situation; etc. 1925.

2. Passengers carried on (a) rapid transit lines, (b) street surface lines, (c) Hudson and Manhattan Railroad, (d) bus lines. Each line. 1926, 1927, 1928. p. 63. *212

See also: *Bronx, Borough of* 4
Employment 9
Ferries (entire)
Occupations, Persons engaged in 1–3, 10
Population and population estimates, not including 1930 and later 10
Railroads (entire)
Street railways (entire)
Trade unions 2
Unemployment (entire)
Workmen's compensation (entire)

TRICHINOSIS

1. Cases and deaths. 1928. p. 53. 131

See also: *Diseases, Transmissible* 3, 7, 9

TRUANTS

1. Findings regarding 251 adolescents from Manhattan released from Truant School, June, 1920–Oct., 1922: offenders by type (truant; delinquent; misdemeanant; felon) and age (each year, 14–23); country of birth of parents; sex; color; arraignments; nativity; length of residence of foreign-born parents in United States; number of children in family; income per family and per person; occupation of mother; rooms in home; persons per room; cases known to social agencies; etc. 1927. 166

TRUANTS *(continued)*

Source Number

2. Children from Manhattan committed to the Truant School (random sample): (a) by weekly income of families, and contributions to family income by minors under 18; (b) by number of terms taken to reach grade in school and aggregate number of times retarded before compulsory action became necessary; (c) by home conditions (normal; both parents dead; father dead; etc.); (d) by occupation of living father (job requiring education; job not requiring education); (e) by cause of lack of parental control, estimated by officers of the Bureau of Attendance; (f) by occupation at which skillful; (g) by school work especially disliked; (h) by incident first causing truancy; (i) by diversions when truant. Manhattan. 1926. p. 8, 10–12, 15, 17–20. **169**

3. Children committed for truancy; also number committed for violation of parole. Each authority: City Magistrates' Court; Children's Court; Director of Bureau of Attendance. Each school year, 1914/15–1925/26, and period Sept., 1926–Feb. 7, 1927. p. 21. **169**

4. Medical examination of cases of truancy in Manhattan and Bronx in which hearings were held: (a) number of children found normal; (b) children found to have defects; (c) defects found, by type; (d) cases followed up, by result; (e) children referred for mental test, by result. Period Sept., 1921–June, 1922. p. 15–16. **126**

See also: *Arrests and summonses* 1
Corrections 20
Courts 85, 110, 115, 122, 129
Delinquents, Juvenile 3, 5
Education 9, 13, 16, 17, 36, 45
Negroes 7
Police welfare division (of Police department) 1

TRUANT SCHOOLS

See: *Education*

TUBERCULOSIS

	Source Number
1. Deaths. Current week.	**317**
2. Cases and deaths from (a) pulmonary and acute miliary tuberculosis, and (b) other forms. Current month.	**179**
3. Cases reported; deaths and death rate by type of case (pulmonary; other); cases under supervision of the New York City Department of Health. Each borough. Current quarter and corresponding quarter of preceding year.	**136**
4. Cases on register of the New York City Department of Health, by type of care: clinic care; private physician; etc. Mar. 31, 1925, 1927, 1929. p. 185.	**136** June 15, 1929
5. Cases and deaths, case rate and death rate, fatality rate: (a) all forms of tuberculosis; (b) tuberculosis of the respiratory system. 1927. p. 27, 29.	**317** Supp. # 70
6. Deaths from (a) pulmonary tuberculosis, (b) other forms of tuberculosis. Each year, 1898–1925. p. 1.	**230** Jan.-Feb., 1926
7. Deaths and death rate from (a) pulmonary tuberculosis, (b) other forms of tuberculosis. Each year, 1915–1924. p. 15.	**230** Jan.-Feb., 1925
8. Deaths and death rate from (a) pulmonary tuberculosis, (b) other forms of tuberculosis. Each year, 1898–1922. p. 4.	**230** Jan.-Feb., 1923
9. Deaths from pulmonary tuberculosis in (a) the combined Bellevue-Yorkville tuberculosis clinic districts, (b) Manhattan, (c) New York City. Each year, 1915–1922. Chart only.	**97** Oct., 1924
10. Distribution and location of deaths by sanitary area. Period 1915–1922. Manhattan, Vol. III, No. 2; Bronx, Vol. VI, No. 1; Brooklyn, Vol. V, No. 1. Maps only.	**230**
11. Non-pulmonary tuberculosis: cases and death rate. Each year, 1910–1925. p. 133.	**136** Aug. 21, 1926
12. Deaths and death rate from pulmonary tuberculosis. Each borough. Each year, 1915–1925. p. 11. For 1910–1922, see Jan.–Feb., 1923.	**230** Jan.-Feb., 1926

TUBERCULOSIS *(continued)*

	Source Number
13. Pulmonary tuberculosis: deaths and death rate; new cases and case rate; total cases registered at end of year and case rate. Each borough. 1925. p. 11.	**230** Jan.-Feb., 1926
14. Deaths and death rate from pulmonary tuberculosis. Each borough. 1924, 1925. p. 8. Published annually.	**230** Jan.-Feb., 1926
15. Deaths and death rate from pulmonary tuberculosis. Each year, 1868–1928. p. 182.	**131**
16. Pulmonary tuberculosis: deaths and death rate by color (white; Negro). Each year, 1910–1928. p. 100–101.	**136** Mar. 30, 1929
17. Deaths from pulmonary tuberculosis among leading racial groups, each group. Each year, 1918–1921. p. 3.	**230** May-June, 1923
18. Hospital beds occupied by tuberculous patients, and death rate from pulmonary tuberculosis. Each year, 1907–1921. p. 249.	**69**
19. Cases of tuberculosis by type of treatment: attending clinic; in hospital; private physician; etc. Each borough. Dec. 31, 1923. p. 10.	**230** Jan.-Feb., 1924
20. Death rate from tuberculosis (all forms) by sex and age: under 1; 1–4; 5–9; 10–14; 15–19; 20–24; by 10-year age groups to 75 and over. 1917, 1926. p. xxxviii.	***176**
21. Deaths and death rate, by type of tuberculosis (pulmonary; meningitis; abdominal; other): (a) children under 15; (b) infants. Each year, 1898–1923. p. 294, 296.	**59**
22. Death rate of children from tuberculosis (all forms), by age groups (under 5; 5–9; 10–14) and sex. Each year. 1898–1923. p. 299.	**59**
23. Death rate by age groups (5-year periods) and sex. 1910, 1920. p. 18.	**230** May-June, 1923
24. Deaths and death rate from tuberculosis by sex. Each year, 1910–1921. p. 1.	**230** Sept.-Oct., 1922
25. Tuberculosis in infants (4000 infants under 2 years), in New York Nursery and Child's Hospital, and Babies'	**6**

TUBERCULOSIS *(continued)*

Source Number

25. *(continued)*
Hospital: results of tuberculin skin tests, by color (white; colored); skin tests by nationality; etc. Period 1920–1926. p. 359–378.

26. Tuberculosis patients who were public charges of the New York City Department of Public Welfare in (a) public hospitals, (b) private hospitals, (c) sanatoria, (d) preventoria: number of patients at beginning of year; number admitted, discharged, died, during year; number remaining at end of year. Each institution and each group of institutions. 1926. p. 23. **148**

27. Persons making application to the New York City Department of Public Welfare for care in a sanatarium, hospital, or preventorium, by kind of agency through which application was made (New York City Department of Health clinic; Associated Clinics; etc.). 1926. p. 24. **148**

28. Tuberculosis clinics of the New York City Department of Health, and persons for whom they provide. Each borough. 1920. p. 223. **133 Oct., 1923**

29. Work of clinics belonging to the Association of Tuberculosis Clinics of the City of New York: patients receiving treatment (on hand at beginning of quarter; new admissions; readmissions), patients discharged (tuberculous; non-tuberculous; suspects), and patients remaining (tuberculous; non-tuberculous; suspects), for clinics treating (a) adults and children, and (b) children; reasons for discharging patients; condition of discharged cases (arrested, quiescent, or improved; unimproved; died); visits to clinics (children; total); tuberculosis cases registered by source of report (private physician; city institution; etc.); clinic sessions; clinic hours; physicians; nurses; nurses' visits. For (a) each clinic (or clinic district), (b) each borough, (c) clinics divided as clinics of Bellevue and **9**

TUBERCULOSIS *(continued)*

Source Number

29. *(continued)* Allied Hospitals, private clinics, and clinics of the New York City Department of Health. Current quarter year.

30. Work of clinics belonging to the Association of Tuberculosis Clinics: number of cases under observation, Jan. 1; new cases; readmissions; total cases treated (children; adults and children); visits to clinics (children; adults and children); nurses' visits; discontinued cases by cause. For (a) each clinic (or clinic district), and (b) each borough. 1927, 1928. Tables II–IV. **8**

31. Total cases (tuberculous; non-tuberculous; suspects) treated in clinics belonging to the Association of Tuberculosis Clinics: (a) each clinic (or clinic district); (b) each borough. 1928. Table II. **8**

32. Condition on admission and at discharge of cases terminated at clinics belonging to the Association of Tuberculosis Clinics. 1928. Table V-b. **8**

33. Cases terminated at the clinics belonging to the Association of Tuberculosis Clinics, by diagnosis (pulmonary tuberculosis; other tuberculosis; non-tuberculous; doubtful). 1927, 1928. Table V-a. **8**

34. Work of organizations belonging to the Tuberculosis Sanatorium Conference of Metropolitan New York: patients on Jan. 1; admissions and readmissions; deaths; patients discharged; patients remaining Dec. 31; patient days; capacity, Dec. 31; vacancies, Dec. 31. For (a) children, (b) men, (c) women, (d) total. Each hospital, sanitarium, or special institution. 1928. Supplementary statistical sheet. ***271**

35. New York City hospitals and sanatoria for the tuberculous: number of patients treated; average daily census; bed capacity at end of year; patients remaining at end of year. Each hospital or sanatorium. 1927, 1928. p. 5. ***271**

TUBERCULOSIS *(continued)*

Source Number

See also: *Bellevue-Yorkville district* 6–10, 15, 16
Bronx, Borough of 1, 3
Clinics 1, 12, Note
Cripples 2
Deaths and death rate 1, 3, 4–7, 38–50, 52, 54, 60–64, 72–75
Diseases, Transmissible 1–5, 7, 9
East Harlem 6–11
Education 44, 45
Health service (entire)
Hospitals 17, 20
Infant deaths and death rate 9
Negroes 8–10
Nurses 3
Nursing service 1
Population and population estimates, not including 1930 and later 4
Serums (entire)
Vital statistics 6, 12, Note

TULAREMIA

1. Cases and deaths. 1927. p. 30. **317 Supp. # 70**

TWINS

See: *Births and birth rate* 12, 13

TYPHOID FEVER

1. Cases and deaths, estimated expectancy of cases. Current week. **317**
2. Cases and deaths. Current month. **179**
3. Cases reported (correct; erroneous); deaths; case fatality; per cent of cases in which possible mode of infection was traced. Subdivided as (a) residents contracting disease in New York City, (b) residents contracting disease out of town, and (c) non-residents. Each borough. Current quarter year. **136**

TYPHOID FEVER *(continued)*

Source Number

4. Cases (reported; confirmed); deaths; case fatality. Each borough. Third quarter, 1927, 1928 (with 1928 data further subdivided as to residence). p. 226. **136** Nov. 17, 1928
5. Cases and deaths. Each week, 1921–1928. p. 258. **136** Dec. 15, 1928
6. Cases and deaths. Each month, 1927, 1928. p. 180. **131** 1928
7. Deaths and death rate. Each year, 1868–1928. p. 181. **131** 1928
8. Cases reported by mode of infection. Each year, 1922–1928. p. 91. **136** Mar. 23, 1929
9. Deaths and death rate. Each year, 1868–1927. p. 165. **136** Sept. 29, 1928
10. Cases and deaths, case rate and death rate, fatality rate, estimated expectancy. 1927. p. 31. **317** Supp. # 70
11. Cases and deaths, case rate and death rate. Each year, 1898–1924. p. 19. **133** Apr., 1925
12. Typhoid fever cases by season. Each year, 1912–1924. p. 20. **133** Apr., 1925
13. Typhoid fever carriers on active list. 1928. p. 54. **131**

See also: *Bellevue-Yorkville district* 6–8, 10
Bronx, Borough of 1
Deaths and death rate 1, 3, 38, 39, 41, 44–46, 49, 50, 52, 60–62, 64, 72–75
Diseases, Transmissible 1–5, 7–10
East Harlem 6–10
Nursing service 1
Serums (entire)
Vital statistics 12, Note

TYPHUS

1. Cases and deaths. 1927. p. 32. **317** Supp. # 70
2. Cases and deaths. 1928. p. 53. **131**
3. Cases of endemic typhus. New York City; Brooklyn (Jewish Hospital). Each year, 1915–1927. p. 3086. **317** Nov. 23, 1928

See also: *Deaths and death rate* 3, 38, 44, 61
Diseases, Transmissible 2, 3, 7, 9
Vital statistics 12

UNDULANT FEVER

Source Number

1. Cases; deaths. 1928. p. 54. **131**

UNEMPLOYMENT

1. Persons in New York City with gainful occupations, Jan., 1920; persons unemployed as of (a) Oct. 17, 1921, (b) Dec. 15, 1921, (c) Mar. 15, 1922, (d) June 15, 1922, (e) Oct. 17, 1922. By type of industry. **91 Mar. 27, 1922, p. 11 Oct. 30, 1922, p. 2**

VACANT LAND

1. Total parcels of land; vacant parcels; per cent of land vacant. Each section or ward, each borough. [1928]. p. 40, 44, 48, 52, 56. ***150**

See also: *Area* 8, 9
Parks 2
Sanitary districts (entire)

VACATION HOMES

1. Roman Catholic vacation homes: children attending by sex; age range; staff (religious; lay). Each home in Manhattan and Bronx. 1928. p. 38. ***40**

See also: *Settlements* 6

Other allied topic: *Camps*

VACATION SCHOOLS

See: *Education*

VAGRANCY

See: *Arrests and summonses* 1, 4
Correction 3, 20, 43, 50, 58
Courts 12, 13, 15, 17, 18, 21–28, 32, 34, 37, 38–41, 70, 74, 77, 82, 101, 102, 104
Mendicants (entire)

VENEREAL DISEASE

Source Number

1. Cases of venereal disease (syphilis; gonorrhea) reported to the New York City Department of Health: (a) by source of report; (b) by borough. For current quarter year, and corresponding quarter of preceding year. **136**

2. Persons with (a) syphilis, and (b) gonorrhea, by sex and stage of infection (acute; chronic) and by source of report (physician; hospital or out-patient department). Each borough. Specified day, 1928. **21**

3. Cases and case rate: (a) syphilis; (b) gonorrhea. 1927. p. 193. ***177**

4. Syphilis and gonorrhea cases, 1925, 1926; syphilis cases (a) by source of reports and (b) by borough, 1926. p. 193–194. **136** **Nov. 26, 1927**

5. Cases (a) syphilis, (b) gonorrhea, reported to the New York City Department of Health by source of report: own laboratory; institution; physician. Each borough. 1920, 1921. p. 210–211. **133** **Sept., 1922**

6. Cases of gonorrhea in children reported to the New York City Department of Health: (a) by age, sex, and reporting agency; (b) by type of disease and sex. 1925, 1926. p. 10–11. **136** **Jan. 15, 1927**

7. "Court work" cases: cases examined by sex; cases found to be diseased, by disease. 1928. p. 62. **131**

8. Cases convicted of prostitution in the Ninth (Women's) Court, Manhattan and Bronx, who were reported by the New York City Department of Health as suffering from venereal disease in communicable stage: (a) per cent of all cases convicted of prostitution; (b) per cent among recidivists; (c) per cent among those without previous record; (d) average length of stay in hospital of persons released in custody of the New York City Department of Health. Each year, 1926, 1927. p. 40. ***54**

9. Venereal disease cases among prisoners in custody in the New York County Penitentiary and the New York City Workhouse, by disease (gonorrhea; syphilis); number **121**

VENEREAL DISEASE *(continued)*

Source Number

9. *(continued)*
of cases treated: cases cured; cases incomplete, due to expiration of sentence; cases still under treatment. Also number of Wasserman tests made, by result. Each institution. 1927. p. 80.

10. Women convicted in the Ninth (Women's) Court, Manhattan and Bronx, and examined for venereal disease, by condition and offense; also by age and number of previous convictions. Period Jan. 1–June 30, 1920. **344**

11. Hospital provision for the treatment of venereal disease in New York City: number of hospitals visited; total beds; free beds; private beds; clinics; cases of gonorrhea (acute; chronic); cases of syphilis (acute; chronic); Wasserman tests given. [Fall 1921]. p. 3–4. **178 Jan., 1922**

See also: *Bellevue-Yorkville district* 15, 16
Bronx, Borough of 3
Clinics 1, 12, Note
Cripples 2
Deaths and death rate 7, 38, 60, 61, 65
Diseases, Transmissible 1–5, 7, 9
Hospitals 17
Infant deaths and death rate 9, 15
Serums (entire)

VIOLENCE, CRIMES OF

1. Arrests for crimes of violence by age (under 16; 16–20; 21–25; 26–30; 31–35; 36–40; 41–50; 51–60; over 60), each crime. Period Jan.–June, each year, 1928, 1929. p. 43. **146**

2. Cases of crimes of violence reported to the police, each selected offense. 1927, 1928. p. 41. ***144**

3. Persons in custody because of crimes of violence. Bronx County Jail and Bronx County Jail Annex, combined. Year ending June 30, 1928. p. 201. **162**

See also: *Arrests and summonses* 1
Assault and robbery (entire)
Burglary (entire)
Homicide (entire)

VITAL STATISTICS

	Source Number
1. Deaths and death rate, deaths corrected by borough residence and corrected death rate, births, marriages, stillbirths. Each borough. Current week.	**136**
2. Marriages and marriage rate, births and birth rate, deaths and death rate (including corrected death rate. Each borough. Current quarter year.	**136**
3. Total deaths, death rate, deaths under 1 year, deaths at 65 years and over, births, birth rate. Each borough. Each month, Oct., 1927–Sept., 1928. p. 406.	**20**
4. Births, deaths (all ages; under 1 year), 1927; and birth, death, and infant mortality rates, 1926, 1927. p. 1905.	**317** July 20, 1928
5. Births and birth rate, marriages and marriage rate, deaths and death rate, stillbirths and stillbirth rate. Each year, 1910–1927. p. 507.	***244**
6. Births, still births, and marriages, total deaths, and deaths from selected causes, each cause: tuberculosis; pneumonia; kidney disease; cancer; nervous diseases. Brooklyn. Each year, 1910–1927. p. 507.	***244**
7. Births and birth rate, deaths and death rate, infant deaths and infant death rate, stillbirths and stillbirth rate. By color (white; colored). 1926. p. 18.	***279**
8. Estimated mid-year population; births and birth rate; deaths and death rate; marriages and marriage rate; stillbirths and rate per 1000 total births; deaths of infants under one year, and death rate; deaths of children under 5 years, and death rate. Each year, 1898–1926. p. 4–5.	***176**
9. Difference between the birth and death rates. 1914 and each year, 1919–1926. p. XII.	***176**
10. Births and birth rate; deaths and death rate; infant deaths and death rate; stillbirths. Each month, 1926. p. 20.	***176**
11. Population; births and birth rate; deaths and death rate. Each clinic district. Manhattan. 1921. p. 4–5.	**230** July-Oct., 1923

VITAL STATISTICS *(continued)*

Source Number

12. Births and birth rate; infant mortality rate; total deaths and death rate; death rate from selected causes, each cause: typhoid fever; typhus; measles; scarlet fever; whooping-cough; diphtheria and croup; pulmonary tuberculosis; other forms of tuberculosis; cancer and sarcoma; epidemic cerebrospinal meningitis; broncho and lobar pneumonia. 1921. p. 331. **136 Oct. 21, 1922**

NOTE: A summary of vital statistics in each of the 270 health areas in New York City is being compiled monthly by the New York City Department of Health. At the end of the year, a fuller report is planned.

See also: *Births and birth rate* (entire)
Deaths and death rate (entire)
Infant deaths and death rate (entire)
Marriages and marriage rate (entire)
Stillbirths and stillbirth rate (entire)

VOCATIONAL GUIDANCE

1. Full time elementary, junior high, prevocational, vocational, and high schools, with and without vocational guidance. [1922/23]. p. 49–50. **49**

VOCATIONAL SCHOOLS

See: *Education*

VOTERS

1. Total registration, and enrollment by party, of voters by sex. By assembly district, each county. 1928. p. 28–35. ***127**

WATERFRONT

1. Uses of the waterfront. Each borough. [1928]. p. 178. Map only. **262**

WAYWARD MINORS

Source Number

1. Arraignments under the Wayward Minor Act: (a) total number of arraignments and per cent of persons arraigned charged with immoral relations, each year, 1926, 1927; (b) arraignments by determination (discharged; found guilty as charged; cases pending), 1927; (c) cases convicted by disposition (committed to reformatory institutions; placed on probation; disposition postponed, pending discharge from hospital; other), 1927. Ninth (Women's) Court, Manhattan and Bronx. p. 42. ***54**

See also: *Correction* 20, 50
Courts 69, 70, 110, 115, 122
Delinquents, Juvenile 3, 5

Other allied topic: *Adolescent offenders*

WHOLESALE ESTABLISHMENTS

1. Location of principal concentrated wholesale markets. Manhattan south of 59th Street, 1922. (Frontispiece). Map only. **258**

2. Location of various wholesale establishments by kind of establishment. Manhattan south of 59th Street. 1900, 1922 (varies). "The Wholesale Market." p. 11–59. Maps only. **258**

3. Location of (a) wholesale grocery establishments, and (b) wholesale fur establishments. Manhattan south of 59th Street. 1900, 1922. p. 98–99. Maps only. **256**

See also: *Stores* 5

WHOOPING-COUGH

1. Cases. Current week. **317**

2. Cases and deaths. Current month. **179**

3. Cases and deaths. Each week, Jan. 1, 1921–Nov. 24, 1928. p. 231. **136 Nov. 24, 1928**

WHOOPING-COUGH *(continued)*

Source Number

4. Cases and deaths, case rate and death rate, fatality rate. 1927. p. 33. **317 Supp. # 70**

5. Deaths and death rate. Each year, 1868–1928. p. 178. **131**

See also: *Bellevue-Yorkville district* 6–8, 10, 15
Bronx, Borough of 1, 3
Deaths and death rate 3, 38, 39, 41, 44–46, 50, 54, 60–62, 64, 65, 72–75
Diseases, Transmissible 1–12
East Harlem 6–10
Infant deaths and death rate 9
Nursing service 1
Serums (entire)
Vital statistics 12, Note

WOMEN'S BUREAU, POLICE DEPARTMENT

1. Cases investigated by type (warned; referred to other authorities; etc.) and arrests by disposition (fined; probation; etc.). Jan.–June, each year, 1928, 1929. p. 79–82. **146**

WOOD INDUSTRY

1. Wood industries in New York and its environs: (a) maps showing location of plants in the wood industries with 20 or more employees in New York and its environs, 1900, 1912, 1917, 1922; (b) plants and employees (by size of plant; by type of industry), Manhattan south of 59th Street, 1900, 1912, 1917, 1922; (c) plants and employees by zones, 1900, 1912, 1917, 1922; (d) distribution of plants by type of industry and land value, Manhattan south of 59th Street, Manhattan north of 59th Street, 1922. "The Wood Industries." p. 11–52. **257**

See also: *Employment* 1–3, 7, 8, 10
Manufactures 1, 3, 4, 11
Salaries and wages 1–6
Workmen's compensation (entire)

WORKMEN'S COMPENSATION

Source Number

1. Compensated accidents to minors, coming under the jurisdiction of the New York City District Compensation Office: (a) age of children (under 14; 14–15; 15–16; 16–17); (b) sex; (c) industry; (d) manner of occurrence, by industry; (e) location of injury; (f) extent of disability; (g) double compensation cases. Year ending June 30, 1924. p. 18–28. **195**

See also: *Clinics* 12
Courts 84, 91–93, 96, 97, 100, 105, 106, 108

LIST OF SOURCES OF INFORMATION

NOTE: In the following list, the material has been published by the organization under which it is listed, unless otherwise indicated.

***A later report has been published, prior to June 1, 1930.**

The following abbreviations have been used to indicate libraries:

M.R.L. Municipal Reference Library
N.Y.A.M.L. New York Academy of Medicine Library
N.Y.P.L. New York Public Library
R.S.F.L. Russell Sage Foundation Library
OFFICE has been used to indicate the office of the organization by which the material has been published

Each source of information which can be found at the Russell Sage Foundation Library is followed by the initials of that library. Each source not found there is followed by the indication of a library or other place at which it may be found. A library reference shows, therefore, one place at which the given material may be found, but does not mean that it may not be found elsewhere. For example, practically all public documents of the city and State are found at the Municipal Reference Library.

Source Number

1 **Amalgamated clothing workers of America. Research Department.** unpublished material. OFFICE
Compiled annually.

2 **American association for labor legislation.** Non-institutional aged poor; report on aged dependents cared for outside of institutions by private agencies in New York City; a study directed by Neva R. Deardorff and prepared under the direction of a committee representing the Welfare council of New York City and others. (in American labor legislation review. v. 19, p. 193–224, June 1929) R.S.F.L.

3 **American child health association.** Statistical report of infant mortality for 1928 in 729 cities of the United States. 27p. R.S.F.L.
Issued annually.

Source Number

4 **American heart association. Committee on schools.** Special report on cardiac classes. 1923. 41p. N.Y.P.L.
A survey made by the American heart association at the request of the superintendent of schools and presented in his report to the Board of education.

*5 **American Jewish year book** 5689, September 15, 1928, to October 5, 1929, edited by Harry Schneidermann for the American Jewish committee. Phila. Jewish publication society of America, 1928. 446p. R.S.F.L.

6 **Asserson, M. Alice.** Tuberculosis in infants. (in American review of tuberculosis. v. 16, p. 359–378, October 1927). N.Y.A.M.L.

7 **Association of day nurseries of New York City.** Report, 1928. 76p. R.S.F.L.

8 **Association of tuberculosis clinics of the City of New York.** Twentieth annual report, 1928. 32p. R.S.F.L.
Published by the New York tuberculosis and health association.

9 ——— Consolidated statement of tuberculosis clinic work, New York City. OFFICE
Compiled quarterly.

10 **Bellevue-Yorkville health demonstration.** Physical defects in school children, Bellevue-Yorkville district; a study of records of medical examinations of school children in the third grades in the public and parochial schools during the school year 1925–1926. 26p. zincographed. OFFICE

11 ——— Study of street accidents in the Bellevue-Yorkville district, by Godias J. Drolet and Laura W. Nathan. December 1927. 22p. mimeographed. R.S.F.L.

12 ——— Vital statistics of the Bellevue-Yorkville district, years 1925, 1926, and five-year period 1922 to 1926; a reference handbook on the principal causes of mortality during the predemonstration period. 47p. zincographed. R.S.F.L.

13 **Boys' club federation.** Boy delinquency survey, lower East side, Manhattan, New York City. July 1926. 27p. mimeographed. R.S.F.L.

14 **Bronx board of trade.** (The) Bronx, New York City's fastest growing borough, 1927. 48p. N.Y.P.L.
Published also 1921–1925.

*15 **Brooklyn Catholic school board.** Diocesan school report, 1927/28. (in the Tablet. v. 20, p. 1, 7, November 10, 1928) OFFICE
The Tablet is a weekly newspaper maintained by and in the interests of the Roman Catholic diocese of Brooklyn.

Source Number

16 **Brooklyn chamber of commerce.** "Brooklyn." M.R.L.
Monthly publication of the Brooklyn chamber of commerce.

*17 ——— Brooklyn register and buyers' guide, 1929. 532p. M.R.L.
Issued annually.

18 ——— New industrial map of Brooklyn. n.d. M.R.L.

19 **Brooklyn chamber of commerce** and **Medical society of the County of Kings. Joint committee on health council.** Report of sub-committee. [1926]. 9p. mimeographed. OFFICE

20 **Brooklyn daily eagle.** Brooklyn daily eagle almanac, 1929. Volume 44. 482p. R.S.F.L.

21 **Brunet, Walter M.** Venereal disease prevalence in the City of New York. 1. Richmond County (Staten Island) 2. Kings County (Brooklyn) 3. Bronx County 4. Queens County 5. New York County (Manhattan). (in Long Island medical journal. v. 23, p. 87–94, 158–172, 229–239, 296–306, February–May, July, 1929) N.Y.A.M.L.

22 **Bureau of Jewish social research.** Child care study, New York, 1922. 91+120p. mimeographed. N.Y.P.L.

23 ——— Personnel-pension study of the personnel employed in organizations affiliated with the Federation for the support of Jewish philanthropic societies of New York City. August 1927. 60p. mimeographed. R.S.F.L.

24 ——— Survey of the Jewish blind—Brooklyn, by Gertrude E. Viteles. May 1928. 44+p. mimeographed. R.S.F.L.

25 ——— *Jewish communal survey of greater New York.* Studies in the New York Jewish population. 1928. 45p. R.S.F.L.

26 ——— ——— *Child care section.* Institutions; a study of children in orphan and infant asylums. March 1928. 183p. mimeographed. R.S.F.L.

27 ——— ——— ——— Study of children in foster homes. April 1928. 215p. mimeographed. R.S.F.L.

28 ——— ——— ——— Summary and recommendations. March 1928. 49p. mimeographed. R.S.F.L.

29 ——— ——— *Family welfare section.* Care of the Jewish homeless men. 1928. 19p. mimeographed. R.S.F.L.

30 ——— ——— *Health section.* Chapter 1. General hospital facilities. 1928. 45p. mimeographed. R.S.F.L.

Source Number

Bureau of Jewish social research. *Jewish communal survey of greater New York. Health section. (continued)*

31 ——— ——— ——— Chapter 2. Out-patient service in the Jewish hospitals and its relation to the Jewish charitable agencies. 1928. 30p. mimeographed. R.S.F.L.

32 ——— ——— ——— Chapter 3. Hospitals and homes for the chronically sick. 1928. 46p. mimeographed. R.S.F.L.

33 ——— ——— ——— Chapter 4. Hospital social service. 1928. 19p. mimeographed. R.S.F.L.

34 ——— ——— ——— Chapter 5. Convalescent homes. 1928. 57p. mimeographed. R.S.F.L.

35 ——— ——— ——— Chapter 6. Hospital affiliations of Jewish doctors. 1928. 11p. mimeographed. R.S.F.L.

36 ——— ——— *Jewish education section.* Jewish education. 1928. 85p. mimeographed. R.S.F.L.

37 ——— ——— *Recreation section.* Summary. March 1929. 16p. mimeographed. R.S.F.L.

38 **Bureau of social hygiene.** Housing conditions of employed women in the borough of Manhattan, 1922; a study made by the Bureau with the co-operation of an advisory committee. 163p. R.S.F.L.

39 **Burke foundation. Sturgis research fund.** Provision for the care of convalescents in New York City, by E. H. Lewinski-Corwin. [1923]. 19p. R.S.F.L.

*40 **Catholic church. Archdiocese of New York. Catholic charities.** Report, 1928. 126p. R.S.F.L.
Issued annually.

41 **Chamber of commerce of the State of New York.** Annual report for the year ending June 30, 1926. 3pts. in 1 v. R.S.F.L.
Ceased publication.

*42 ——— (The) City of New York; a few briefly stated facts of an economic, historical and descriptive character about the City of New York. June 1928. 54p. M.R.L.

43 **Charity organization society. Committee on criminal courts.** (The) Adolescent offender; a study of the age-limit of the Children's court. 1923. 85p. R.S.F.L.

44 **Charity organization society** and **the Welfare council of New York City.** Directory of clinics and health stations. [1929]. 110p. R.S.F.L.
Preprint: Directory of social agencies. N. Y., 1929.

Source Number

45 **Children's welfare federation of New York City.** Facilities in New York City for tonsil and adenoid operations, 1920. 6p. typewritten. OFFICE

*46 ——— Statistics of capacity and actual number of cases taken by vacation homes and camps, 1928. 2p. mimeographed. R.S.F.L.
Compiled annually.

*47 ——— Statistics of organizations operating baby health stations in New York City, 1928. 1p. mimeographed. R.S.F.L.
Compiled annually.

*48 ——— Survey of pre-school children under care, 1928. 1p. mimeographed. R.S.F.L.
Compiled annually.

49 ——— **Committee on vocational guidance.** Vocational guidance and placement work for juniors in New York City, 1923; report of a survey made under the direction of the Committee. 55p. R.S.F.L.

50 **Cities census committee, inc.** Distribution by boroughs of Slavic people, with Russia as country of origin, in New York City in 1920. 7p. mimeographed. R.S.F.L.
Formerly New York City 1920 census committee, inc.

51 ——— Statistical sources for demographic studies of greater New York, 1920; Walter Laidlaw, editor. 844p. R.S.F.L.

52 **Citizens committee on teachers' salaries.** Teachers' salaries in New York City; final report of the Committee. . . . 1927. 256p. R.S.F.L.
Distributed by Teachers college, Columbia university.

53 **City committee on plan and survey.** Report, June 1928. 218p. R.S.F.L.

*54 **Committee of fourteen, New York City.** Annual report for 1927. 52p. R.S.F.L.

55 **Consumers league of New York.** Behind the scenes in candy factories. March 1928. 68p. R.S.F.L.

56 **Corwin, E. H. Lewinski-.** New York as a hospital center. (in Modern hospital. v. 19, p. 45, 46, July 1922) R.S.F.L.

57 ——— Study of occupation and disease based on hospital records. (in Nation's health. v. 9, p. 34–37, January 1927) R.S.F.L.

58 **Corwin, E. H. Lewinski- and Conover, A. Eleanor.** Incidence of disease among hospital patients with reference to occupation. (in Journal of industrial hygiene. v. 8, p. 270–279, June 1926) R.S.F.L.

Source Number

59 **Drolet, Godias J.** Tuberculosis in children; a review of the mortality during the past quarter-century in New York City. (in American review of tuberculosis. v. 11, p. 292–302, June 1925) N.Y.A.M.L. (reprint at R.S.F.L.)

60 **East Harlem health center.** Diphtheria in the East Harlem district; a study of diphtheria morbidity, 1921–1927, and diphtheria mortality. 1916–1927, East Harlem district, New York City. 13p. mimeographed. R.S.F.L.

61 ——— (The) Health white house of East Harlem. (in (The) Survey. v. 54, p. 224–226, May 15, 1925) R.S.F.L.

62 ——— Helping to demonstrate health examinations to a community of 100,000 people; a summary of services and findings of the health examination clinic conducted at the East Harlem health center by the N.Y.C. health department, 1921–1927. 11p. mimeographed. R.S.F.L.

63 **East Harlem health center and others.** Casting the life lines for East Harlem, by G. J. Drolet and Marguerite Potter. 1927. 31p. mimeographed. R.S.F.L.

64 ——— Vital statistics for the East Harlem area; a comparison of 1927 vital statistics for East Harlem with data for 1916–1920 pre-health center period and individual years 1921–1926 inclusive. 1929. 8p. mimeographed. R.S.F.L.

65 **East Harlem nursing and health demonstration.** Comparative study of generalized and specialized nursing and health services. October 1926. 40p. R.S.F.L.

66 ——— Maternity service report; a statistical report compiled from medical, nursing, and nutrition data collected in a five-year demonstration period. Final report, section 1. June 1928. 32p. R.S.F.L.

67 ——— Morbidity service report of the East Harlem nursing and health demonstration. Final report, section 2. October 1928. 28p. R.S.F.L.

68 **Editor and publisher.** Space-buyers' chart and market survey of the City of New York. v. 53, p. I-XXXVI, March 5, 1921. N.Y.P.L.

69 **Emerson, Haven.** Causes of the rapidly increasing fall of the tuberculosis death rate in the last five years. (in Journal of the outdoor life. v. 19, p. 247–255, August 1922) R.S.F.L.

Source Number

Emerson, Haven. *(continued)*

70 ——— (The Chronic disabled heart patient; extent of problem and cost of their institutional care in New York City. (in Nation's health. v. 5, p. 387–391, June 1923) R.S.F.L.

71 **Galdston, Iago.** Public health aspects of tuberculosis and heart disease. (in American journal of public health. v. 17, p. 1037–1041, October 1927) R.S.F.L.

72 ——— Ten years of measles in New York City. (in Medical review of reviews. v. 33, p. 318–322, July 1927) N.Y.A.M.L.

73 **Gebhart, John C.** Funeral costs; what they average; are they too high? Can they be reduced? N.Y. Putnam, 1928. 319p. R.S.F.L.

74 **Goldberg, Jacob A.** Distribution of medical agencies attended by East side families. (in Hospital social service. v. 11, p. 225–232, April 1925) R.S.F.L.

75 ——— Findings in 3331 examinations of children attending settlements. (in Hospital social service. v. 13, p. 491–494, May 1926) R.S.F.L.

76 **Hacker, Louis M.** Communal life of the Sephardic Jews in New York City. (in Jewish social service quarterly. v. 3, no. 2, p. 32–40, December 1926) R.S.F.L.

77 **Hamilton, James A.** Crime and the drug habit. (in New York medical journal. v. 114, p. 355–357, September 21, 1921) N.Y.A.M.L.

78 **Hexter, Maurice B.** (The) Business cycle. Part 2, analysis of number of desertion cases reported from New York City to the National desertion bureau. (in Jewish social service quarterly. v. 1, no. 2, p. 27–56, May 1924) R.S.F.L.

79 **Holmes, Norman A.** Sociological survey of the Negro population of Columbus Hill of New York City. October 1922. typewritten. OFFICE

80 **Jewish board of guardians.** Eighth annual report of the Jewish board of guardians and twenty-second annual report of its predecessor, the Jewish protectory and aid society, year ending December 31, 1928. 57p. R.S.F.L.

81 **Jewish education association.** Directory of Jewish religious schools in the City of New York. 1928. typewritten. OFFICE
Compiled annually.

Source Number

Jewish education association. *(continued)*

82 ——— Estimate of income and expenditures of Jewish religious schools in New York City, based upon study of financial reports of 76 schools. 1926/27. typewritten. OFFICE

•83 ——— Jewish population in the City of New York. 1928. typewritten. OFFICE
Estimated annually, except when Yom Kippur falls on a day on which school is not in session.

•84 ——— Salaries of teachers in Jewish religious schools in New York City. 1926. typewritten. OFFICE

•85 ——— Study of the increase and decrease in register of Jewish religious schools. 1928. typewritten. OFFICE
Compiled annually.

86 **Joint board of sanitary control in the cloak, suit and skirt, and dress industries.** Fifteenth anniversary report, 1926. 62+p. R.S.F.L.

87 **King, Mrs. Edith Statto** and **Frear, A. H.** Finances of New York's social work; a study . . . made by the Bureau of advice and information of the Charity organization society (in Better times. v. 6, p. 21–29, June 1, 1925) R.S.F.L.

88 **Kiwanis club of New York City.** Survey of New York City boys, by F. F. C. Rippon. 1926. 51p. R.S.F.L.

89 **Levine, Louis.** Women's garment workers; a history of the International ladies' garment workers union. N.Y. B. W. Huebsch, 1924. 608p. R.S.F.L.

90 **Medical society of the State of New York.** Report of the committee to make a study of heart disease in the State of New York. May 1928. 154p. OFFICE

91 **Merchants' association of New York.** "Greater New York." R.S.F.L.
Monthly publication of the Merchants' association of New York.

92 ——— **Industrial bureau.** Holiday practices of offices, stores and factories in New York City. February 1925. 21p. R.S.F.L.

93 ——— ——— Staten Island, New York City; its industrial resources and possibilities. 1922. 53p. R.S.F.L.

94 **Methodist Episcopal church. Board of temperance, prohibition and public morals.** Prohibition with half a chance in New York City. March 7, 1927. clip sheet. OFFICE

Source Number

95 **Metropolitan life insurance company.** Statistical bulletin. R.S.F.L.
Monthly.

96 ——— **Statistical bureau.** Mortality of early infancy, by Louis I. Dublin. 1923. 13p. (pamphlet no. 83) OFFICE

97 **Milbank memorial fund.** Quarterly bulletin. R.S.F.L.

*98 **Moderation league, inc.** National survey of conditions under prohibition, 1928. 10p. R.S.F.L.
Issued annually.

99 **Nathan, Laura W.** and **Drolet, Godias J.** Recorded causes in five hundred stillbirths in New York City. (in New York State journal of medicine. v. 28, p. 78–80, January 15, 1928) N.Y.A.M.L. (reprint at R.S.F.L.)

100 **National bureau of economic research.** Business cycles and unemployment; an investigation under the auspices of the Bureau made for a committee of the President's conference on unemployment. N.Y. McGraw-Hill, 1923. 405p. R.S.F.L.

101 **National committee for mental hygiene.** Report of a mental health survey of Staten Island made at the request of social agencies of Staten Island and directed by Edith R. Spaulding. 1925. 100p. R.S.F.L.

102 **National industrial conference board.** Cost of living in New York City, 1926. N.Y. The Board, 1926. 129p. (Studies in the cost of living) R.S.F.L.

103 ——— Cost of living in twelve industrial cities. N.Y. The Board, 1928. 76p. R.S.F.L.

104 ——— Cost of living in the United States, 1914–1927. N.Y. The Board, 1927. 201p. (Studies in the cost of living) R.S.F.L.

105 **National safety council.** Press release on children's accidents, 1927. OFFICE

106 **National urban league.** Study of the Negro population in Flushing, Long Island. 1922. typewritten. OFFICE

107 **Negro child study in New York City. Joint committee on, and others.** Study of delinquent and neglected Negro children before the New York City Children's court, 1925. 48p. R.S.F.L.

108 **New York (City). Ambulance service, Board of.** Annual report, 1926. 23p. N.Y.P.L.
The Board of ambulance service is now included in the Hospital department.

Source Number

New York (City). *(continued)*

109 ——— **Borough of the Bronx. President.** Annual report of the President of the borough of the Bronx, 1928. 31p. M.R.L.

110 ——— **Borough of Brooklyn. President.** Annual report of the President, 1928. 128p. M.R.L.

111 ——— **Borough of Manhattan. President.** Report of the business and transactions of the President for the year ending December 31, 1928. 140p. M.R.L.
Includes annual report of the Bureau of buildings.

*112 ——— **Borough of Queens. President.** Annual report of the President, 1927. 125p. M.R.L.

*113 ——— **Borough of Richmond. President.** Annual report, 1927. 119p. M.R.L.

114 ——— **Chief medical examiner.** Statistical report of the Chief medical examiner, January 1, 1928 to January 1, 1929; a report to the Mayor, by Charles Norris. 18p. R.S.F.L.

115 ——— **Child welfare, Board of.** Thirteenth annual report of the Board, 1928. 31p. R.S.F.L.

116 ——— **Children's court.** Annual report of the Children's court of the City of New York, 1928. 44p. R.S.F.L.

*117 ——— **City magistrates' courts.** Annual report, 1927. 147p. R.S.F.L.

*118 ——— ——— Annual report of Chief clerk, 1928. (in (The) City record. v. 57, p. 5220–5225, June 13, 1929) M.R.L.

119 ——— **College of the City of New York.** Table showing the population of the City of New York by boroughs from consolidation in 1898 to date, compiled from figures furnished by the Department of health. 1925. typewritten. R.S.F.L.

*120 ——— **Comptroller.** Report of the Comptroller of the City of New York for the fiscal year ended December 31, 1928. 399p. R.S.F.L.

121 ——— **Correction, Department of.** Report of the Department for the year 1928, by Richard C. Patterson, Jr., Commissioner. 110p. R.S.F.L.

122 ——— **Court of special sessions.** Annual report of the Court for the year ending December 31, 1928. 69p. R.S.F.L.

Source Number

New York (City). *(continued)*

123 ——— **Education, Board of.** Minutes of meetings. M.R.L.
Issued weekly. For statistics, see minutes of last meeting of each month of school year.

124 ——— ——— Thirtieth annual report of the Superintendent of schools for the year ending July 31, 1928. 785p. R.S.F.L.

125 ——— ——— **Bureau of attendance.** Unpublished material on the work of the Bureau. OFFICE

126 ——— ——— **Office of the superintendent of schools emeritus.** Report of Dr. William L. Ettinger, Supt. emeritus, on health education, June 27, 1928. 21p. mimeographed. M.R.L.

*127 ——— **Elections, Board of.** Annual report of the Board for the year 1928. 111p. M.R.L.

*128 ——— **Estimate and apportionment board.** Budget for 1929. 373p. M.R.L.

129 ——— ——— New York City employees' retirement system; sixth annual report of the Board, 1926. 109p. R.S.F.L.

130 ——— **Fire department.** Annual report, 1928. 103p. R.S.F.L.

131 ——— **Health, Department of.** Annual report, 1928. 205p. R.S.F.L.

132 ——— ——— Food and drug bulletin. R.S.F.L.
Monthly. Ceased publication in 1925.

133 ——— ——— Monthly bulletin. R.S.F.L.
Nos. 1–12 in 1927 published in one number and called "Monthly vital statistics for 1927." Discontinued with this number.

134 ——— ——— Tables compiled from official statistics of the Department of health showing the infantile death rate of the old City of New York . . . in the years preceding the opening of the Nathan Straus pasteurized milk depots, and the 33 years succeeding . . . compiled 1925. N.Y.P.L.

135 ——— ——— Vital statistics; condensed annual report, years 1898–1928. 4p. M.R.L.

136 ——— ——— Weekly bulletin. R.S.F.L.

137 ——— ——— **Bureau of public health education.** School health news. R.S.F.L.
Monthly except July and August. Ceased publication in 1925.

Source Number

New York (City). *(continued)*

138 —— **Housing, Mayor's committee on.** Report of the Committee. February 1924. 16p. R.S.F.L.

*139 —— **Hunter college teachers' retirement system.** Tenth annual report of the Retirement board, 1927. 30p. N.Y.P.L.

140 —— **Industrial aid bureau.** Report of the employment activities for the year 1922. typewritten. M.R.L.

The Industrial aid bureau was discontinued in February, 1926.

141 —— —— Unemployment in the City of New York. March 1, 1922. typewritten. M.R.L.

*142 —— **Licenses, Department of.** Report of the Department of licenses, 1927, William F. Quigley, Commissioner. 31p. R.S.F.L.

*143 —— **Parole commission.** Annual report of the Commission, 1927. 22p. R.S.F.L.

*144 —— **Police department.** Annual report for the year 1928, Grover A. Whalen, Police commissioner. 100p. R.S.F.L.

*145 —— —— Annual report of police pension fund for year 1928. (in (The) City record. v. 57, pt. 3, p. 1926–1936, March 7, 1929) M.R.L.

146 —— —— Semi-annual report for six months ended June 30, 1929, Grover A. Whalen, Police commissioner. 116p. M.R.L.

Supersedes quarterly report.

147 —— —— Unpublished material on highway accidents. OFFICE

Compiled monthly.

148 —— **Public welfare, Department of.** Annual report, 1926. 308p. R.S.F.L.

*149 —— **Street cleaning, Department of.** Annual report of the Department, 1927, by Alfred A. Taylor, Commissioner. 39p. R.S.F.L.

*150 —— **Taxes and assessments, Department of.** Report for the year ending March 31, 1928. 58p. R.S.F.L.

*151 —— **Teachers' retirement system.** Eleventh annual report of the Retirement board. 1927. 37p. R.S.F.L.

Source Number

New York (City). *(continued)*

152 ——— **Tenement house department.** Report of the Department, 1928. typewritten. OFFICE

153 **New York (County). Court of general sessions. Probation department.** (The) Need of a psychiatric clinic. April 1928. 35p. mimeographed. R.S.F.L.

154 ——— ——— ——— Unpublished material regarding work of the Probation department. OFFICE
Compiled currently.

*155 **New York (State). Banking department.** Statement of the condition of the saving banks of the State, January 1, 1929. N.Y.P.L.
Issued semi-annually.

*156 ——— **Blind, Commission for the.** Sixteenth annual report of the Commission for the year ending June 30, 1928. 48p. (Legislative document (1929) no. 23) R.S.F.L.

157 ——— **Charities, State board of.** Sixty-second annual report of the Board for the year ending June 30, 1928. 284p. (Legislative document (1929) no. 22) R.S.F.L.

158 ——— **Child welfare, Commission to examine laws relating to.** Second report of the Commission, April 30, 1923. Part I. 110p. (Legislative document (1923) no. 111) R.S.F.L.

159 ——— ——— Third annual report of the Commission, April 9, 1924. 130p. (Legislative document (1924) no. 88) R.S.F.L.

160 ——— **Cloak, suit and skirt industry in New York City, Governor's advisory commission on. Bureau of research.** Wages and wage scales, 1925, by Morris Kolchin. 63p. N.Y.P.L.

161 ——— **Correction, Department of. Division of probation.** Twenty-first annual report of the Division for the year 1927. 215p. R.S.F.L.
Formerly State probation commission.

162 ——— **Correction, State commission of.** Second annual report of the Commission for the year 1928. 592p. R.S.F.L.

163 ——— ——— Youth and crime. December 1928. 3p. mimeographed. R.S.F.L.

Source Number

New York (State). *(continued)*

*164 ——— **Craig colony.** Thirty-fifth annual report of the Board of visitors of the Colony to the Commissioner of mental hygiene for the fiscal year ending June 30, 1928. 46p. R.S.F.L.

*165 ——— **Crime commission.** Report of the Commission, 1928. 669p. (Legislative document (1928) no. 23) R.S.F.L.

166 ——— ——— **Sub-commission on causes and effects of crime.** From truancy to crime—a study of 251 adolescents. (in Report of the Crime commission, 1928. p. 437–575) R.S.F.L.

167 ——— ——— ——— Study of delinquency in a district of Kings County. 1927. (in Report of the Crime commission, 1927. p. 327–383) R.S.F.L.

168 ——— ——— **Sub-commission on causes and effects of crime.** Study of environmental factors in juvenile delinquency. (in Report of the Crime commission, 1928. p. 577–669) R.S.F.L.

169 ——— ——— ——— Study of 201 truants in the New York City schools. 1927. (in Report of the Crime commission, 1927. p. 277–302) R.S.F.L.

170 ——— ——— **Sub-commission on penal institutions.** Report of the Sub-commission. (in Report of the Crime commission, 1928. p. 177–249) R.S.F.L.

171 ——— ——— **Sub-commission on statistics.** Statistical analysis of the criminal cases in the courts of New York State. (in Report of the Crime commission, 1928. p. 37–142) R.S.F.L.

172 ——— ——— ——— Statistical analysis of criminal cases in the courts of the State of New York for the year 1925. (in Report of the Crime commission, 1927. p. 95–174) R.S.F.L.

173 ——— **Education department.** Twenty-fifth annual report of the Department for the school year ending July 31, 1928. Volume 1. 299p. R.S.F.L.

*174 ——— ——— Twenty-fourth annual report of the Department for the school year ending July 31, 1927. Volume 2. Statistics. 355p. R.S.F.L.

175 ——— **Governor.** Message from the Governor relative to transit conditions in New York City, with report of Commissioner John A. McAvoy appointed to investigate the management and affairs of the Transit commission, February 1925. 59p. (Legislative document (1925) no. 75) N.Y.P.L.

Source Number

New York (State). *(continued)*

*176 —— **Health, Department of.** Forty-seventh annual report of the Department for the year ending December 31, 1926. Volume 2. Division of vital statistics. 313p. (Legislative document (1927) no. 97) R.S.F.L.

*177 —— —— Forty-eighth annual report of the Department for the year ending December 31, 1927. Volume 1. 254p. (Legislative document (1928) no. 39) R.S.F.L.

178 —— —— Health officers' bulletin. R.S.F.L.
Monthly. Discontinued December 1923.

179 —— —— Monthly vital statistics review. R.S.F.L.

180 —— **Housing and regional planning commission.** Message from the Governor transmitting report of the Commission. March 1925. 70p. (Legislative document (1925) no. 91) R.S.F.L.

181 —— —— Report of the Commission to Governor Alfred E. Smith and to the legislature of the State of New York, on the present status of the housing emergency. March 22, 1923. 102p. (Legislative document (1924) no. 43) R.S.F.L.

182 —— —— Report of the Commission to Governor Alfred E. Smith and to the legislature of the State of New York, on tax exemption of new housing. March 14, 1924. 26p. (Legislative document (1924) no. 78) R.S.F.L.

183 —— —— Message from the Governor transmitting report of the Commission for permanent housing relief. 1926. 78p. (Legislative document (1926) no. 66) R.S.F.L.

184 —— **Housing, State board of.** Report of the Board to Governor Alfred E. Smith and to the legislature of the State of New York. March 9, 1927. 64p. (Legislative document (1927) no. 85) R.S.F.L.

185 —— —— Report of the Board relative to the housing emergency in New York City and Buffalo and extension of the rent laws. February 25, 1928. 74p. (Legislative document (1928) no. 85) R.S.F.L.

186 —— —— Report of the Board to Governor Franklin D. Roosevelt and to the legislature of the State of New York. March 1929. 96p. (Legislative document (1929) no. 95) R.S.F.L.

Source Number

New York (State). *(continued)*

*187 ——— **Labor, Department of.** Annual report of the industrial commissioner for the twelve months ended June 30, 1927. 454p. (Legislative document (1928) no. 14) R.S.F.L.

188 ——— ——— Industrial bulletin. R.S.F.L.
Issued monthly by the industrial commissioner.

189 ——— ——— Special bulletin no. 109, (The) Employment of women in 5 and 10 cent stores, prepared by the Division of women in industry. September 1921. 68p. R.S.F.L.

190 ——— ——— Special bulletin no. 110, Women who work, prepared by the Division of women in industry. April 1922. 40p. R.S.F.L.

191 ——— ——— Special bulletin no. 121, Hours and earnings of women in five industries (confectionery, paper box, shirts and collars, tobacco, mercantile), prepared by the Bureau of women in industry. November 1923. 116p. R.S.F.L.

192 ——— ——— Special bulletin no. 132, (The) Trend of child labor in New York State; supplementary report for 1923, prepared by the Bureau of women in industry. November 1924. 8p. R.S.F.L.

193 ——— ——— Special bulletin no. 134, (The) Health of the working child, prepared by the Bureau of women in industry. December 1924. 91p. R.S.F.L.

194 ——— ——— Special bulletin no. 143, Employment and earnings of men and women in New York State factories, 1923–1925, prepared by the Bureau of statistics and information. June 1926. 208p. R.S.F.L.

195 ——— ——— Special bulletin no. 144, Some recent figures on accidents to women and minors, prepared by the Bureau of women in industry. June 1926. 70p. R.S.F.L.

196 ——— ——— Special bulletin no. 147, Homework in the men's clothing industry in New York and Rochester, prepared by the Bureau of women in industry. August 1926. 69p. R.S.F.L.

197 ——— ——— Special bulletin no. 153, Hours and earnings of women employed in power laundries in New York State, prepared by the Bureau of women in industry. August 1927. 72p. R.S.F.L.

Source Number

New York (State). Labor, Department of. *(continued)*

198 ——— ——— Special bulletin no. 154, (The) Paper box industry in New York City, prepared by the Bureau of women in industry. January 1928. 90p. R.S.F.L.

199 ——— ——— **Bureau of industrial hygiene.** Industrial hygiene bulletin. R.S.F.L.
Monthly.

200 ——— **Mental hygiene, Department of.** Fortieth annual report of the Department, July 1, 1927 to June 30, 1928. 318p. (Legislative document (1929) no. 29) R.S.F.L.
On January 1, 1927 the Department superseded the State hospital commission and the State commission for mental defectives.

201 ——— **Prison department.** Annual report of the Superintendent of State prisons for the fiscal year ending June 30, 1926. 400p. R.S.F.L.

202 ——— **Prisons, Commission of.** Drug addiction; report of special committee of the State commission of prisons. 1924. 29p. R.S.F.L.

203 ——— ——— (The) Psychopathic delinquent; report of special committee of the State commission of prisons. December 1925. 32p. R.S.F.L.

*204 ——— **Reformatory for women, Bedford Hills.** Twenty-eighth annual report of the Reformatory for the year ending June 30, 1928. typewritten. N.Y.P.L.

205 ——— **Secretary of State.** Enumeration of inhabitants, 1925; report presented to the legislature January 15, 1926 by Florence E. Knapp, Secretary of State. 350p. (Legislative document (1926) no. 10) N.Y.P.L.

206 ——— ——— Supplementary report on the enumeration-tabulation of the inhabitants of the State as of June 1, 1925, prepared by Florence E. Knapp, Secretary of State. 40p. R.S.F.L.

*207 ——— **Supreme court.** Judicial statistics of the work of the Supreme court of the State of New York in the First judicial department for the year 1928. 42p. M.R.L.

*208 ——— **Tax commission.** Annual report of the State tax commission, 1927. 691p. (Legislative document (1928) no. 11) R.S.F.L.

Source Number

New York (State). *(continued)*

209 ——— **Taxation and retrenchment, Special joint committee on.** Tax exemption in New York State; a preliminary report by the Committee, February 15, 1927. 263p. (Legislative document (1927) no. 86) M.R.L.

*210 ——— **Transit commission.** Statement showing the number of railroad and ferry passengers in and out of New York City for the year 1928. 7p. press release. mimeographed. M.R.L.
Issued annually.

*211 ——— ——— Seventh annual report for the calendar year 1927. 510p. (Legislative document (1928) no. 41) R.S.F.L.

*212 ——— ——— Summary of annual report for the year ended December 31, 1928. 74p. M.R.L.

213 ——— ——— Summary of reports of street railway companies operating in the City of New York. M.R.L.
Issued quarterly.

214 ——— **University of the State of New York.** Survey of educational facilities for crippled children in New York State, by J. S. Orleans. 26p. (University of the State of New York bulletin no. 835. September 1, 1925) R.S.F.L.

*215 **New York academy of medicine. Committee on public health relations.** Report of activities for the year 1926. 25p. R.S.F.L.

216 ——— **Public health committee.** Hospital situation in greater New York; report of a survey of hospitals in New York City prepared by E. H. Lewinski-Corwin. N.Y. Putnam, 1924. 356p. R.S.F.L.
NOTE: The Hospital information bureau, of the United hospital fund, has unpublished material which attempts to keep up to date the statistics given in "The Hospital situation in greater New York."

217 **New York association for improving the condition of the poor.** Health work for mothers and children in a colored community; including a study of venereal diseases as a prenatal problem. 1924. 15p. (publication 131) R.S.F.L.

218 **New York Catholic school board.** Unpublished statistics of Catholic schools in the archdiocese of New York, September 1929. OFFICE
Annual report not issued since 1923.

Source Number

219 **New York committee on after care of infantile paralysis cases.** Survey of cripples in New York City, under the auspices of a special committee on survey of cripples, Henry C. Wright, Director. October 1920. 104p. R.S.F.L.

220 **New York evening journal.** (The) Largest market in the world; working sales manual of the New York market. September 1928. OFFICE

221 **New York herald.** (The) New York market, compiled by the Research department of the New York herald, c1922. 134p. M.R.L.

222 **New York municipal reference library.** High school registration for New York City, compiled by Edith Harrell. 1925. typewritten. M.R.L.

223 ——— Queens, Borough of. Parks, statistics, 1924. typewritten. M.R.L.

224 ——— Richmond, Borough of. Parks, statistics, 1924. typewritten. M.R.L.

225 **New York school of social work. Research department.** Central reporting of statistics of family service agencies. mimeographed. OFFICE
Compiled monthly.

226 **New York sun.** Facts about New York, with a complete index; fifth edition, 1927. 116p. M.R.L.
Reprinted from the Sun.

*227 ——— Valuable data for the space buyer on the world's greatest market. 1928 edition. OFFICE

228 **New York telegram.** Facts and figures. 1927. OFFICE

229 **New York theatre program corporation.** New York theatre market vs. the New York market. [1928]. 24p. OFFICE

230 **New York tuberculosis and health association.** Bulletin. R.S.F.L.
Published irregularly. Discontinued with March-October 1926 number.

231 ——— Prevalence of communicable diseases in New York City, 1927, by G. J. Drolet. 8p. mimeographed. R.S.F.L.

232 ——— Unpublished material on population of tuberculosis clinic districts. OFFICE
Compiled semi-annually.

Source Number

New York tuberculosis and health association. *(continued)*

233 ——— **Associated out-patient clinics committee. Committee on professional work of the Superintendents' section.** Clinic fees in New York City. December 1927. 5p. mimeographed. R.S.F.L.

234 ——— **Bronx committee.** Health conditions in the Bronx, New York City; a graphic summary of the vital statistics of the borough of the Bronx, by Godias J. Drolet. March, 1928. 34p. zincographed. R.S.F.L.

235 ——— **Committee on community dental service.** Dental clinic services in the City of New York. 1928. 40p. R.S.F.L.

236 ——— **Heart committee.** (The) Health of a thousand newsboys in New York City. [1926]. 41+p. mimeographed. R.S.F.L.

Study made in cooperation with the Board of education.

237 ——— ——— Statistics of mortality from heart diseases, New York City. [1926]. 13p. R.S.F.L.

238 ——— ——— **Committee on cardiac clinics.** Cardiac clinic statistics; a graphic summary of clinic statistics of forty-two member clinics reporting for the year 1928. 21p. mimeographed. R.S.F.L.

•239 ——— ——— ——— Summary of clinic reports for the year 1928. zincographed. OFFICE

Issued annually and quarterly.

240 **New York university. Bureau of business research.** Study of the New York market and its newspaper situation, made for the World and the Evening world. 1927. 37p. OFFICE

241 ——— ——— Survey of the New York market, compiled by the Bureau of business research for various newspapers. c1923–1924. separate maps and charts. N.Y.P.L.

242 **New York urban league.** Annual report, 1927. ("A Challenge to New York") 20p. R.S.F.L.

243 ——— Distribution of Negroes in Harlem, 1913, 1920, 1926. map. M.R.L.

•244 **New York world.** World almanac and book of facts, 1929. Forty-fourth year of issue. 928p. N.Y.P.L.

245 **(The) 100,000 group of American cities.** Study of all American markets, including all cities and towns of 1000 population or more in the United States. Chi. The Group, 1927. 606p. N.Y.C. OFFICE

Source Number

246 **Pearl, Raymond** and **Reed, L. J.** Predicted growth of population of New York and its environs. 42p. (Regional plan of New York and its environs, 1923) R.S.F.L.

*247 **Playground and recreation association of America.** Playground and community recreation statistics for 1928. (in Playground. v. 23, p. 92–121, May 1929) R.S.F.L.
Published annually.

248 **Pollock, H. M.** and **Nolan, W. J.** Mental diseases in cities, villages, and rural districts of New York, 1915–1920. (in State hospital quarterly (now Psychiatric quarterly). v. 7, p. 38–65, November, 1921) R.S.F.L.

249 **Prison association of New York.** Two reports on the reorganization and reconstruction of the New York City prison system, by Hastings H. Hart. March 1925. 53p. R.S.F.L.

250 **Public education association. Cardiac vocational guidance committee.** Annual report, 1925. 15p. R.S.F.L.
On January 1, 1927, this committee was merged with the New York tuberculosis and health association.

251 **Queensboro chamber of commerce.** "Queensborough." N.Y.P.L.
Monthly publication of the Queensboro chamber of commerce.

*252 **Real estate board of New York.** Diary and manual, thirty-third annual edition, 1929. 377p. N.Y.P.L.

253 ——— "Real estate magazine of New York." N.Y.P.L.
Monthly publication of the Real estate board of New York.

254 ——— *Law committee.* Some economic aspects of the recent emergency housing legislation in New York; memorandum report on a fact-finding inquiry prepared for the Law committee . . . under the direction of Samuel McCune Lindsay. February 1924 (revised edition). 137p. R.S.F.L.

255 **Reed, Ruth.** Negro illegitimacy in New York City. N.Y. Columbia, 1926. 136p. (Columbia university studies in history, economics, and public law no. 277) R.S.F.L.

256 **Regional plan of New York and its environs.** *Regional survey of New York and its environs.* Volume 1, Major economic factors in metropolitan growth and arrangement; a study of trends and tendencies in the economic activities within the region of New York and its environs, by R. M. Haig and R. C. McCrea. 1927. 111p. R.S.F.L.

257 ——— ——— Volume 1a, Chemical, metal, wood, tobacco and printing industries; present trends and probable future developments. 1928. v.p. R.S.F.L.

Source Number

Regional plan of New York and its environs. *Regional survey of New York and its environs. (continued)*

258 ——— ——— Volume 1b, Food, clothing and textile industries, wholesale markets, and retail shopping and financial districts; present trends and probable future developments. 1928. v.p. R.S.F.L.

259 ——— ——— Volume 2, Population, land values and government; studies of the growth and distribution of population and land values, and of problems of government, prepared by Thomas Adams and others. 1929. 320p. R.S.F.L.

260 ——— ——— Volume 3, Highway traffic, including a program by Nelson P. Lewis for a study of all communication facilities within the region of New York and its environs, by H. M. Lewis in consultation with E. P. Goodrich. 1927. 172p. R.S.F.L.

261 ——— ——— Volume 4, Transit and transportation, and a study of port and industrial areas and their relation to transportation, by H. M. Lewis; with supplementary reports by chiatric quarterly). v. 7, p. 624–628, August 1922) R.S.F.L.

262 ——— ——— Volume 5, Public recreation; a study of parks playgrounds and other outdoor recreation facilities, by L. F. Hanmer in collaboration with Thomas Adams and others. 1928. 256p. R.S.F.L.

263 **Salmon, Thomas W.** Study of the psychopathic hospital situation in New York City; memorandum submitted by Dr. Salmon to the Public health committee of the New York academy of medicine, May 1922. (in State hospital quarterly (now Psychiatric quarterly). v. 7, p. 624–628, August 1922) R.S.F.L.

264 **Smith, Adelaide Ross.** Silicosis among rock drillers, blasters, and excavators in New York City. (in Journal of industrial hygiene. v. 11, p. 39–69, February 1929) R.S.F.L.

265 **State bureau of municipal information of the New York State conference of mayors and other city officials.** Automobile accidents in New York State cities in 1923. 6p. Report no. 1007. mimeographed. M.R.L.

266 ——— Municipal hospitals. October 1926. 26p. Report no. 2196. mimeographed. M.R.L.

267 ——— Playground and community recreation statistics for 1925. 6p. Report no. 2200. mimeographed. M.R.L.

Source Number

268 **State probation commission.** New goals in probation, by Edwin J. Cooley. 1926. 71p. R.S.F.L.

The Commission was succeeded in 1927 by the Division of probation of the New York (State) Department of correction.

269 **Stearns, Maude E.** Correlation between lodgings of homeless men and employment in New York City. (in Papers and proceedings of the ninetieth annual meeting of the American statistical association, published as Supplement, March 1929, to the Journal of the American statistical association. p. 182–190) R.S.F.L.

270 **Truxal, Andrew G.** Outdoor recreation legislation and its effectiveness; a summary of American legislation for public outdoor recreation, 1915–1927, together with a study of the association between recreation and juvenile delinquency areas in Manhattan, 1920. 218p. (Columbia university studies in history, economics, and public law no. 311) R.S.F.L.

*271 **Tuberculosis sanatorium conference of metropolitan New York.** Reports of tuberculosis institutional work in the New York metropolitan area during the year 1928. 7p. mimeographed. R.S.F.L.

*272 **United hospital fund of New York.** Forty-ninth year book, including supplement. October 1928. 87p. R.S.F.L.

273 ——— **Committee on dispensary development.** Medical care for a million people; a report on clinics of New York City and of the six-years' work of the Committee, 1920–1926. March 1927. 90p. R.S.F.L.

274 ——— ——— New clinics for old; a study of clinics unattached to hospitals in New York City; the passing of the old dispensary and the rise of health centers and of other clinics rendering health services, by Michael M. Davis and Anna M. Richardson. February 1927. 90p. R.S.F.L.

275 ——— **Hospital information bureau. Convalescence service.** Urgent need of facilities for Negro convalescence. (in Hospital social service. v. 14, p. 105–110, August 1926) R.S.F.L.

276 **United real estate owners' association.** "(The) Citizen." M.R.L.

Monthly publication of the United real estate owners' association.

277 **United States. Agriculture, Department of. Bureau of agricultural economics** and **Port of New York authority.** Push cart markets in New York City; a preliminary report. April 1925. 67p. mimeographed. R.S.F.L.

Source Number

United States. *(continued)*

278 ——— **Census bureau.** Biennial census of manufactures, 1927. Statistics for cities. 86p. R.S.F.L.

***279** ——— ——— Birth, stillbirth, and infant mortality statistics for the birth registration area of the United States. 1926. Twelfth annual report. Part 1, Summary and rate tables and general tables. 253p. R.S.F.L.

280 ——— ——— Census of electrical industries, 1922; electric railways. 256p. R.S.F.L.

281 ——— ——— Children under institutional care, 1923; statistics of dependent, neglected, and delinquent children in institutions and under the supervision of other agencies for the care of children, with a section on adults in certain types of institutions. 381p. R.S.F.L.

282 ——— ——— Estimated mid-year population of New York City, 1920–1928. typewritten. WELFARE COUNCIL OFFICE

***283** ——— ——— Financial statistics of cities having a population of over 30,000, 1926. 505p. R.S.F.L.

284 ——— ——— *Fourteenth census of the United States taken in the year 1920.* Volume 1, Population, 1920; number and distribution of inhabitants. 695p. R.S.F.L.

285 ——— ——— ——— Volume 2, Population, 1920; general report and analytical tables. 1410p. R.S.F.L.

286 ——— ——— ——— Volume 4, Population, 1920; occupations. 1309p. R.S.F.L.

287 ——— ——— ——— Volume 9, Manufactures, 1919; reports for states, with statistics for principal cities. 1698p. R.S.F.L.

288 ——— ——— ——— State compendium, New York. Statistics of population, occupations, agriculture, manufactures, and mines and quarries for the state, counties, and cities. 1924. 268p. R.S.F.L.
Data for year 1919 or 1920.

289 ——— ——— Hospitals and dispensaries, 1923. 40p. R.S.F.L.

***290** ——— ——— Marriage and divorce, 1926; statistics of marriages, divorces, and annulments of marriage. 90p. R.S.F.L.

Source Number

United States. Census bureau. *(continued)*

291 ——— ——— Mortality from automobile accidents. mimeographed. LIBRARY OF THE NATIONAL BUREAU OF CASUALTY AND SAFETY UNDERWRITERS, N.Y.C.
Issued monthly.

*292 ——— ——— Mortality statistics, 1925. Part 2, Text and text tables. 169p. R.S.F.L.

*293 ——— ——— Mortality statistics, 1926, twenty-seventh annual report. Part 1, Summary and rate tables and general tables for the death registration area in continental United States, with supplemental statistics for Hawaii and Virgin Islands. 430p. R.S.F.L.

294 ——— ——— Patients in hospitals for mental disease, 1923. 257p. R.S.F.L.

295 ——— ——— United States abridged life tables, 1919–1920, prepared by Elbertie Foudray, expert special agent. 84p. R.S.F.L.

296 ——— ——— United States census of agriculture, 1925; reports for states, with statistics for counties and a summary for the United States. Part 1, (The) Northern states. 1318p. R.S.F.L.

297 ——— **Children's bureau.** Maternal mortality; the risk of death in childbirth and from all diseases caused by pregnancy and confinement, by Robert Morse Woodbury. 1926. 163p. Bureau publication no. 158. R.S.F.L.

*298 ——— ——— Sixteenth annual report of the Chief of the Children's bureau to the Secretary of labor, fiscal year ended June 30, 1928. 53p. R.S.F.L.

299 ——— **Commerce, Department of.** Weekly health index. multigraphed. N.Y.P.L.

300 ——— **Education bureau.** Bulletin, 1926, no. 14, Statistics of private commercial and business schools, 1924–1925. 29p. (Advance sheets from the Biennial survey of education in the United States, 1924–1926) R.S.F.L.

*301 ——— ——— Bulletin, 1927, no. 31, Statistics of private high schools and academies, 1925–1926. 40p. (Advance sheets from the Biennial survey of education in the United States, 1924–1926) R.S.F.L.

Source Number

United States. Education bureau. *(continued)*

302 ——— ——— Bulletin, 1928, no. 8, Schools for the deaf, 1926–1927. 17p. (Advance sheets from the Biennial survey of education in the United States, 1926–1928) R.S.F.L.

303 ——— ——— Bulletin, 1928, no. 9, Schools and classes for the blind, 1926–1927. 7p. (Advance sheets from the Biennial survey of education in the United States, 1926–1928) R.S.F.L.

304 ——— ——— Bulletin, 1928, no. 10, Industrial schools for delinquents, 1926–1927. 22p. (Advance sheets from the Biennial survey of education in the United States, 1926–1928) R.S.F.L.

*305 ——— **Internal revenue, Commissioner of.** Statistics of income from returns of net income for 1926, including statistics from estate tax returns. 437p. R.S.F.L.

306 ——— **Labor, Department of. Bureau of labor statistics.** Bulletin no. 300, Retail prices, 1913 to December 1920. May 1922. 217p. (Retail prices and cost of living series) R.S.F.L.

307 ——— ——— ——— Bulletin no. 398, Growth of legal aid work in the United States, by Reginald H. Smith and John S. Bradway. January 1926. 145p. (Miscellaneous series) R.S.F.L.

308 ——— ——— ——— Bulletin no. 435, Wages and hours of labor in the men's clothing industry, 1911 to 1926. 63p. (Wages and hours of labor series) R.S.F.L.

309 ——— ——— ——— Bulletin no. 439, Handbook of labor statistics, 1924–1926. 828p. (Miscellaneous series) R.S.F.L.

310 ——— ——— ——— Bulletin No. 462, Park recreation areas in the United States. May 1928. 95p. (Miscellaneous series) R.S.F.L.

311 ——— ——— ——— Bulletin no. 464, Retail prices, 1890 to 1927. 221p. (Retail prices and cost of living series) R.S.F.L.

312 ——— ——— ——— Bulletin no. 469, Building permits in the principal cities of the United States in 1927. 105p. (Miscellaneous series) R.S.F.L.

313 ——— ——— ——— Bulletin no. 482, Union scales of wages and hours of labor. May 15, 1928. 241p. (Wages and hours of labor series) R.S.F.L.

314 ——— ——— ——— Monthly labor review. R.S.F.L.

Source Number

United States. Labor, Department of. *(continued)*

315 ——— ——— **Naturalization service. New York office.** Unpublished material on naturalization. OFFICE
Compiled annually.

316 ——— ——— **United States employment service.** Monthly report of activities of state and municipal employment services co-operating with the United States employment service. R.S.F.L.

317 ——— **Public health service. Division of sanitary reports and statistics.** Public health reports. R.S.F.L.
Issued weekly.

318 **Vocational adjustment bureau for girls.** (An) Industrial calendar, by Katherine Treat. 1926. 54p. R.S.F.L.

319 **Vuillenmier, J. F.** Comparative study of New York City and country criminals. (in Journal of criminal law. v. 11, p. 528–550, February 1921) R.S.F.L.

320 **Welfare council of New York City.** Securing employment for the handicapped; a study of placement agencies for this group in New York City, by Mary La Dame. 1927. 133p. R.S.F.L.

321 ——— **Health administration and education section.** Health area map—New York City, compiled by Research service, New York tuberculosis and health association, in co-operation with the Bureau of records, New York City department of health. October 1928. (second edition) R.S.F.L.

322 ——— **Research bureau.** Central reporting of statistics of agencies caring for the homeless. mimeographed. OFFICE
Compiled monthly.

323 ——— ——— Central reporting of statistics of family service agencies. mimeographed. OFFICE
Compiled monthly.

324 ——— ——— Central reporting of statistics of homes for the aged. mimeographed. OFFICE
Compiled monthly.

325 ——— ——— Central reporting of statistics of non-profit-making employment bureaus. mimeographed. OFFICE
Compiled monthly.

326 ——— ——— Central reporting of statistics of room registries. mimeographed. OFFICE
Compiled monthly.

Source Number

Welfare council of New York City. Research bureau. *(continued)*

327 ——— ——— Central reporting of statistics of sheltered workshops. mimeographed. OFFICE
Compiled monthly.

328 ——— ——— (The) City's lodgers; memorandum on the use of the Municipal lodging house by residents and non-residents, January 1927 to January 1928, inclusive, by Annabel M. Stewart. typewritten. OFFICE

329 ——— ——— Health inventory of New York City; a study of the volume and distribution of health services in the five boroughs, by Michael M. Davis and Mary C. Jarrett. 1929. 367p. (Study no. 1 of the Research bureau of the Welfare council) R.S.F.L.

330 ——— ——— *Income and expenditure study of social welfare agencies in New York City, 1910–1926.* Report on financial trends of agencies engaged in giving outdoor relief in New York City, by Kate E. Huntley. September 1929. 73p. mimeographed. OFFICE

331 ——— ——— ——— Trends in organized legal aid in New York City, by Kate E. Huntley. April 1929. 11p. mimeographed. OFFICE

332 ——— ——— ——— Trends in settlements and neighborhood houses in New York City, by Kate E. Huntley. March 1929. 61p. mimeographed. OFFICE

333 ——— ——— *Settlements' study.* Boys' athletics in thirty-three settlements in the City of New York, by Anne E. Geddes. March 1929. 55p. mimeographed. OFFICE

334 ——— ——— ——— Health work in thirty settlements in the City of New York, by Louise P. Brown. April 1929. 52p. mimeographed. OFFICE

335 ——— ——— ——— Membership of eighteen settlements in the City of New York, by Kathryn Farra. May 1929. 40p. mimeographed. OFFICE

336 **Women's city club of New York.** Study of child and youthful marriages in New York County. 1929. 30p. R.S.F.L.

337 **Women's city club** and **City recreation committee.** Report of the Advisory dance hall committee, by Maria Ward Lambin. 1924. 39p. R.S.F.L.

Source Number

338 **Woofter, T. J., Jr.** Negro problems in cities; a study. N.Y. Doubleday, c1928. 284p. (Institute of social and religious research) R.S.F.L.

339 **World league against alcoholism.** New York City under prohibition; data compiled for the Committee on prohibition studies of the National temperance council of the United States of America. [1923]. 7p. M.R.L.

340 ——— Record of one hundred American cities; arrests for drunkenness and arrests for all causes before and after national prohibition. [1923]. 6p. N.Y.P.L.

341 ——— Ten-year record of arrests for all causes and arrests for intoxication in the principal cities of the United States of America; partial result of survey made by the League. December 1924. 13p. N.Y.P.L.

342 ——— **Research department.** Saloon survey, New York City; changes in saloon property after the first three years and after five years of prohibition, by Robert E. Corradini. [1925]. 31p. R.S.F.L.

343 **Worthington, George E.** and **Topping, Ruth.** Summary and comparative study of the special courts in Chicago, Philadelphia, Boston and New York. (in Journal of social hygiene. v. 9, p. 348–375, June 1923) R.S.F.L.

344 ——— (The) Women's day court of Manhattan and the Bronx, New York City. (in Journal of social hygiene. v. 8, p. 393–510, October 1922) R.S.F.L.

APPENDIX 1

DETAILED AND ABRIDGED INTERNATIONAL LISTS OF CAUSES OF DEATH

Taken from Manual of the International List of Causes of Death, 1920, issued by the United States Bureau of the Census.

Detailed International List of Causes of Death	**Abridged International List of Causes of Death** *(Title numbers of detailed list included as shown in parentheses).*
I. Epidemic, Endemic, and Infectious Diseases	
1. Typhoid and paratyphoid fever (a) Typhoid fever (b) Paratyphoid fever	1. Typhoid and paratyphoid fever (1)
2. Typhus fever	2. Typhus fever (2)
3. Relapsing fever (spirillum obermeieri)	
4. Malta fever	
5. Malaria (a) Malarial fever (b) Malarial cachexia	3. Malaria (5)
6. Small-pox	4. Small-pox (6)
7. Measles	5. Measles (7)
8. Scarlet fever	6. Scarlet fever (8)
9. Whooping-cough	7. Whooping-cough (9)
10. Diphtheria	8. Diphtheria (10)
11. Influenza (a) with pulmonary complications specified (b) without pulmonary complications specified	9. Influenza (11)
12. Miliary fever	
13. Mumps	
14. Asiatic cholera	10. Asiatic cholera (14)
15. Cholera nostras	11. Cholera nostras (15)
16. Dysentery (a) amebic (b) bacillary (c) unspecified or due to other causes	

Detailed International List of Causes of Death *(continued)*	**Abridged International List of Causes of Death *(continued)***
	(*Title numbers of detailed list included as shown in parentheses*).
I. EPIDEMIC, ENDEMIC, AND INFECTIOUS DISEASES (*continued*)	
17. Plague (a) bubonic (b) pneumonic (c) septicemic (d) unspecified	
18. Yellow fever	
19. Spirochetal hemorrhagic jaundice	
20. Leprosy	
21. Erysipelas	
22. Acute anterior poliomyelitis	
23. Lethargic encephalitis	
24. Meningococcus meningitis	
25. Other epidemic and endemic diseases (a) Chicken-pox (b) German measles (c) Others under this title	12. Other epidemic and endemic diseases (3, 4, 12, 13, 16, 17, 18, 19, 20, 21, 22, 23, 24, 25)
26. Glanders	
27. Anthrax	
28. Rabies	
29. Tetanus	
30. Mycoses	
31. Tuberculosis of the respiratory system	13. Tuberculosis of the respiratory system (31)
32. Tuberculosis of the meninges and central nervous system	14. Tuberculosis of the meninges and central nervous system (32)
33. Tuberculosis of the intestines and peritoneum 34. Tuberculosis of the vertebral column 35. Tuberculosis of the joints 36. Tuberculosis of other organs (a) Tuberculosis of the skin and subcutaneous cellular tissue (b) Tuberculosis of the bones (vertebral column excepted) (c) Tuberculosis of the lymphatic system (mesenteric and retroperitoneal glands excepted) (d) Tuberculosis of the genito-urinary system (e) Tuberculosis of organs other than the above 37. Disseminated tuberculosis (a) acute (b) chronic or unspecified	15. Other forms of tuberculosis (33, 34, 35, 36, 37)

Detailed International List of Causes of Death ***(continued)***

I. EPIDEMIC, ENDEMIC, AND INFECTIOUS DISEASES (*continued*)

38. Syphilis
39. Soft chancre
40. Gonococcus infection
41. Purulent infection, septicemia
42. Other infectious diseases

II. GENERAL DISEASES NOT INCLUDED IN CLASS I

43. Cancer and other malignant tumors of the buccal cavity
44. Cancer and other malignant tumors of the stomach, liver
45. Cancer and other malignant tumors of the peritoneum, intestines, rectum
46. Cancer and other malignant tumors of the female genital organs
47. Cancer and other malignant tumors of the breast
48. Cancer and other malignant tumors of the skin
49. Cancer and other malignant tumors of other or unspecified organs
50. Benign tumors and tumors not returned as malignant (tumors of the female genital organs excepted)
51. Acute rheumatic fever
52. Chronic rheumatism, osteoarthritis, gout
53. Scurvy
54. Pellagra
55. Beriberi
56. Rickets
57. Diabetes mellitus
58. Anemia, chlorosis
    (a) Pernicious anemia
    (b) Other anemias and chlorosis
59. Diseases of the pituitary gland
60. Diseases of the thyroid gland
    (a) Exophthalmic goiter
    (b) Other diseases of the thyroid gland

Abridged International List of Causes of Death ***(continued)***

(*Title numbers of detailed list included as shown in parentheses*).

16. Cancer and other malignant tumors (43, 44, 45, 46, 47, 48, 49)

Detailed International List of Causes of Death *(continued)*	Abridged International List of Causes of Death *(continued)*
	(Title numbers of detailed list included as shown in parentheses).
II. General Diseases Not Included in Class I *(continued)*	
61. Diseases of the parathyroid glands	
62. Diseases of the thymus gland	
63. Diseases of the adrenals (Addison's disease)	
64. Diseases of the spleen	
65. Leukemia and Hodgkin's disease (a) Leukemia (b) Hodgkin's disease	
66. Alcoholism (acute or chronic)	
67. Chronic poisoning by mineral substances (a) Chronic lead poisoning (b) Others under this title	
68. Chronic poisoning by organic substances	
69. Other general diseases	
III. Diseases of the Nervous System and of the Organs of Special Sense	
70. Encephalitis	
71. Meningitis (a) Simple meningitis (b) Nonepidemic cerebrospinal meningitis	17. Meningitis (71)
72. Tabes dorsalis (locomotor ataxia)	
73. Other diseases of the spinal cord	
74. Cerebral hemorrhage, apoplexy (a) Cerebral hemorrhage (b) Cerebral embolism and thrombosis	18. Cerebral hemorrhage and softening (74, 83)
75. Paralysis without specified cause (a) Hemiplegia (b) Others under this title	
76. General paralysis of the insane	
77. Other forms of mental alienation	
78. Epilepsy	
79. Convulsions (nonpuerperal; 5 years and over)	
80. Infantile convulsions (under 5 years of age)	
81. Chorea	
82. Neuralgia and neuritis	
83. Softening of the brain	
84. Other diseases of the nervous system	
85. Diseases of the eye and annexa	

Detailed International List of Causes of Death *(continued)*	**Abridged International List of Causes of Death *(continued)***
	(Title numbers of detailed list included as shown in parentheses).
III. DISEASES OF THE NERVOUS SYSTEM AND OF THE ORGANS OF SPECIAL SENSE (*continued*)	
86. Diseases of the ear and of the mastoid process (a) Diseases of the ear (b) Diseases of the mastoid process	
IV. DISEASES OF THE CIRCULATORY SYSTEM	
87. Pericarditis 88. Endocarditis and myocarditis (acute) 89. Angina pectoris 90. Other diseases of the heart	19. Diseases of the heart (87, 88, 89, 90)
91. Diseases of the arteries (a) Aneurysm (b) Arteriosclerosis (c) Other diseases of the arteries	
92. Embolism and thrombosis (not cerebral)	
93. Diseases of the veins (varices, hemorrhoids, phlebitis, etc.)	
94. Diseases of the lymphatic system (lymphangitis, etc.)	
95. Hemorrhage without specified cause	
96. Other diseases of the circulatory system	
V. DISEASES OF THE RESPIRATORY SYSTEM	
97. Diseases of the nasal fossae and their annexa (a) Diseases of the nasal fossae (b) Others under this title	
98. Diseases of the larynx	
99. Bronchitis (a) acute (b) chronic (c) unspecified (under 5 years of age) (d) unspecified (5 years and over)	20. Acute bronchitis (including unspecified under 5 years of age) (99a. 99c) 21. Chronic bronchitis (including unspecified 5 years and over) (99b, 99d)
100. Bronchopneumonia (a) Bronchopneumonia (b) Capillary bronchitis	
101. Pneumonia (a) lobar (b) unspecified	22. Pneumonia (101)

Detailed International List of Causes of Death *(continued)*	**Abridged International List of Causes of Death *(continued)***
	(Title numbers of detailed list included as shown in parentheses).
V. DISEASES OF THE RESPIRATORY SYSTEM (*continued*)	
102. Pleurisy	
103. Congestion and hemorrhagic infarct of the lung	
104. Gangrene of the lung	
105. Asthma	
106. Pulmonary emphysema	
107. Other diseases of the respiratory system (tuberculosis excepted) (a) Chronic interstitial pneumonia including occupational diseases of the respiratory system (b) Diseases of the mediastinum (c) Others under this title	23. Other diseases of the respiratory system (tuberculosis excepted) (97, 98, 100, 102, 103, 104, 105, 106, 107)
VI. DISEASES OF THE DIGESTIVE SYSTEM	
108. Diseases of the mouth and annexa	
109. Diseases of the pharynx and tonsils (including adenoid vegetations) (a) Adenoid vegetations (b) Others under this title	
110. Diseases of the esophagus	
111. Ulcer of the stomach and duodenum (a) Ulcer of the stomach (b) Ulcer of the duodenum 112. Other diseases of the stomach (cancer excepted)	24. Diseases of the stomach (cancer excepted) (111, 112)
113. Diarrhea and enteritis (under 2 years of age)	25a. Diarrhea and enteritis (under 2 years of age) (113)
114. Diarrhea and enteritis (2 years and over)	25b. Diarrhea and enteritis (2 years and over) (114)
115. Ancylostomiasis	
116. Diseases due to other intestinal parasites (a) Cestodes (hydatids of the liver excepted) (b) Trematodes (c) Nematodes (other than ancylostoma) (d) Coccidia (e) Other parasites specified (f) Parasites not specified	
117. Appendicitis and typhlitis	26. Appendicitis and typhlitis (117)

Detailed International List of Causes of Death *(continued)*	Abridged International List of Causes of Death *(continued)* *(Title numbers of detailed list included as shown in parentheses).*
VI. DISEASES OF THE DIGESTIVE SYSTEM (*continued*)	
118. Hernia, intestinal obstruction (a) Hernia (b) Intestinal obstruction	27. Hernia, intestinal obstruction (118)
119. Other diseases of the intestines	
120. Acute yellow atrophy of the liver	
121. Hydatid tumor of the liver	
122. Cirrhosis of the liver (a) specified as alcoholic (b) not specified as alcoholic	28. Cirrhosis of the liver (122)
123. Biliary calculi	
124. Other diseases of the liver	
125. Diseases of the pancreas	
126. Peritonitis without specified cause	
127. Other diseases of the digestive system (cancer and tuberculosis excepted)	
VII. NONVENEREAL DISEASES OF THE GENITOURINARY SYSTEM AND ANNEXA	
128. Acute nephritis (including unspecified under 10 years of age) 129. Chronic nephritis (including unspecified 10 years and over)	29. Acute and chronic nephritis (128, 129)
130. Chyluria	
131. Other diseases of the kidneys and annexa	
132. Calculi of the urinary passages	
133. Diseases of the bladder	
134. Diseases of the urethra, urinary abscess, etc. (a) Stricture of the urethra (b) Others under this title	
135. Diseases of the prostate	
136. Nonvenereal diseases of the male genital organs	
137. Cysts and other benign tumors of the ovary 138. Salpingitis and pelvic abscess (female) 139. Benign tumors of the uterus	30. Noncancerous tumors and other diseases of the female genital organs (137, 138, 139, 140, 141)

Detailed International List of Causes of Death *(continued)*	**Abridged International List of Causes of Death *(continued)***
	(Title numbers of detailed list included as shown in parentheses).
VII. NONVENEREAL DISEASES OF THE GENITOURINARY SYSTEM AND ANNEXA (*continued*)	
140. Nonpuerperal uterine hemorrhage 141. Other diseases of the female genital organs	30. Noncancerous tumors and other diseases of the female genital organs (137, 138, 139, 140, 141)
142. Nonpuerperal diseases of the breast (cancer excepted)	
VIII. THE PUERPERAL STATE	
143. Accidents of pregnancy (a) Abortion (b) Ectopic gestation (c) Others under this title	
144. Puerperal hemorrhage	
145. Other accidents of labor (a) Cesarean section (b) Other surgical operations and instrumental delivery (c) Others under this title	
146. Puerperal septicemia	31. Puerperal septicemia (146)
147. Puerperal phlegmasia alba dolens, embolus, sudden death	
148. Puerperal albuminuria and convulsions	
149. Following child-birth (not otherwise defined)	
150. Puerperal diseases of the breast	32. Other puerperal accidents of pregnancy and labor (143, 144, 145, 147, 148, 149, 150)
IX. DISEASES OF THE SKIN AND OF THE CELLULAR TISSUE	
151. Gangrene	
152. Furuncle	
153. Acute abscess	
154. Other diseases of the skin and annexa	
X. DISEASES OF THE BONES AND OF THE ORGANS OF LOCOMOTION	
155. Diseases of the bones (tuberculosis excepted)	
156. Diseases of the joints (tuberculosis and rheumatism excepted)	
157. Amputations	
158. Other diseases of the organs of locomotion	

Detailed International List of Causes of Death *(continued)*	Abridged International List of Causes of Death *(continued)*
	(Title numbers of detailed list included as shown in parentheses).
XI. MALFORMATIONS 159. Congenital malformations (still-births not included) (a) Congenital hydrocephalus (b) Congenital malformations of the heart (c) Others under this title XII. EARLY INFANCY 160. Congenital debility, icterus, and sclerema 161. Premature birth; Injury at birth (a) Premature birth (not still-born) (b) Injury at birth (not still-born)	33. Congenital debility and malformations (159, 160, 161)
162. Other diseases peculiar to early infancy 163. Lack of care	
XIII. OLD AGE 164. Senility	34. Senility (164)
XIV. EXTERNAL CAUSES 165. Suicide by solid or liquid poisons (corrosive substances excepted) 166. Suicide by corrosive substances 167. Suicide by poisonous gas 168. Suicide by hanging or strangulation 169. Suicide by drowning 170. Suicide by firearms 171. Suicide by cutting or piercing instruments 172. Suicide by jumping from high places 173. Suicide by crushing 174. Other suicides	36. Suicide (165, 166, 167, 168, 169, 170, 171, 172, 173, 174)
175. Poisoning by food 176. Poisoning by venomous animals 177. Other acute accidental poisonings (gas excepted) 178. Conflagration 179. Accidental burns (conflagration excepted) 180. Accidental mechanical suffocation	35. Violent deaths (suicide excepted) (175, 176, 177, 178, 179, 180, 181, 182, 183, 184, 185, 186, 187, 188, 189, 190, 191, 192, 193, 194, 195, 196, 197, 198, 199, 200, 201, 202, 203)

Detailed International List of Causes of Death *(continued)*	Abridged International List of Causes of Death *(continued)* (*Title numbers of detailed list included as shown in parentheses*).
XIV. EXTERNAL CAUSES (*continued*)	
181. Accidental absorption of irrespirable, irritating, or poisonous gas 182. Accidental drowning 183. Accidental traumatism by firearms (wounds of war excepted) 184. Accidental traumatism by cutting or piercing instruments 185. Accidental traumatism by fall 186. Accidental traumatism in mines and quarries (a) Mines (b) Quarries 187. Accidental traumatism by machines 188. Accidental traumatism by other crushing (vehicles, railways, landslides, etc.) (a) Railroad accidents (b) Street-car accidents (c) Automobile accidents (d) Aeroplane and balloon accidents (e) Motorcycle accidents (f) Injuries by other vehicles (g) Landslide, other crushing 189. Injuries by animals (not poisoning) 190. Wounds of war 191. Execution of civilians by belligerent armies 192. Starvation (deprivation of food or water) 193. Excessive cold 194. Excessive heat 195. Lightning 196. Other accidental electric shocks 197. Homicide by firearms 198. Homicide by cutting or piercing instruments 199. Homicide by other means 200. Infanticide (murder of infants less than 1 year of age) 201. Fracture (cause not specified) 202. Other external violence 203. Violent deaths of unknown causation	35. Violent deaths (suicide excepted) (175, 176, 177, 178, 179, 180, 181, 182, 183, 184, 185, 186, 187, 188, 189, 190, 191, 192, 193, 194, 195, 196, 197, 198, 199, 200, 201, 202, 203)

Detailed International List of Causes of Death *(continued)*	Abridged International List of Causes of Death *(continued)*
	(Title numbers of detailed list included as shown in parentheses).
XIV. External Causes *(continued)*	37. Other diseases (26, 27, 28, 29, 30, 38, 39, 40, 41, 42, 50, 51, 52, 53, 54, 55, 56, 57, 58, 59, 60, 61, 62, 63, 64, 65, 66, 67, 68, 69, 70, 72, 73, 75, 76, 77, 78, 79, 80, 81, 82, 84, 85, 86, 91, 92, 93, 94, 95, 96, 108, 109, 110, 115, 116, 119, 120, 121, 123, 124, 125, 126, 127, 130, 131, 132, 133, 134, 135, 136, 142, 151, 152, 153, 154, 155, 156, 157, 158, 162, 163)
XV. Ill-Defined Diseases	
204. Sudden death 205. Cause of death not specified or ill-defined (a) Ill-defined (b) Not specified or unknown	38. Unknown or ill-defined diseases (204, 205)

www.ingramcontent.com/pod-product-compliance
Lightning Source LLC
LaVergne TN
LVHW020214110826
845151LV00003B/706